"Spain, Greece, and Cyprus were the three EU countries with the worst employment crisis in recent years. Gregoris Ioannou's book is the first to examine them together and in detail, with a clear analytical approach that digs into the causes and consequences of the crisis, challenging the mainstream institutional explanations and proposing alternative prospects for Southern Europe's labour markets."

**Prof. Guglielmo Meardi,** *Sociology of Economic Labour Processes, Scuola Normale Superiore Florence, Editor of the European Industrial Relations Journal*

"This book offers an indispensable review of recent changes in the fields of employment, trade union activity, political representation, social security, gender, and composition of the working class in Southern Europe. The study covers the impact of neoliberalism, the Global Financial Crisis, and COVID-19. Drawing upon the best literatures in the social sciences, law, and economic policy, the book examines how economic practices and social relations were (re-)regulated under neoliberalism and its crises. A valuable resource for our understanding of the dynamics of labour in contemporary Europe."

**Prof. Alfredo Saad Filho,** *Political Economy & International Development, King's College London*

"Employment, Trade Unionism, and Class: The Labour Market in Southern Europe since the Crisis is a crucial contribution to the literature on how the implementation of economic reforms contribute to labour flexibility and economic precariousness. Gregoris Ioannou has strong command of the political economy of Southern Europe in exploring the transformation of trade unionism and its impact on class composition in Spain, Greece, and Cyprus in the aftermath of the Great Financial Crisis. This book is a crucial contribution to the labour and political economy in Europe."

**Prof. Immanuel Ness,** *Political Science, City University of New York*

"Gregoris Ioannou provides a detailed and insightful assessment of the changes in industrial relations systems in Southern Europe since the emergence of the 2007-2008 economic crisis. In charting effectively, the economic, social, and political dynamics in which industrial relations systems and labour regulation are embedded in, the analysis offers valuable lessons about the impact of these developments in the European periphery and beyond."

**Aristea Koukiadaki,** *Senior Lecturer in Labour Law, University of Manchester*

# Employment, Trade Unionism, and Class

The economic crisis has brought about a watershed in institutional, political, and social relations, reshaping the labour market and the class structure in southern Europe. This book provides a critical comparative assessment of the dynamics of change in the employment field, focusing on Spain, Greece, and Cyprus.

The book assesses how the liberalisation and deregulation processes and the promotion of market-enhancing reforms progressed in three different national settings, identifying the forces, agents, contexts, and mechanisms shaping the employment and industrial relations systems. The comparative perspective used deciphers the interplay of external and internal dynamics in the restructuring of the labour field in Southern Europe, examining austerity and its contestation in connection with prevailing societal ideologies and class shifts. The first part of the book sets the theoretical and historical context, the second is comprised of three empirical national case studies, and the third discusses comparatively the handling of the crisis, its impact, and its legacy from the standpoint of a decade later. The book presents differences in industrial relations systems, trade union forms, and class composition dynamics, accounting for the development of the crisis and the reshaping of the employment field after one decade of crisis.

It will be of value to researchers, academics, professionals, and students working on issues of employment and industrial relations, labour market and labour law, political economy and class structure, as well as those interested in the contemporary society and economy of southern Europe in general, and Spain, Greece, and Cyprus in particular.

**Gregoris Ioannou** is a political sociologist and research fellow at the Law School of the University of Glasgow, UK.

## Routledge Research in Employment Relations

Series editors: Rick Delbridge and Edmund Heery
*Cardiff Business School, UK*

Aspects of the employment relationship are central to numerous courses at both undergraduate and postgraduate level.
Drawing from insights from industrial relations, human resource management and industrial sociology, this series provides an alternative source of research-based materials and texts, reviewing key developments in employment research.
Books published in this series are works of high academic merit, drawn from a wide range of academic studies in the social sciences.

**Workplace Attachment**
Managing Beneath the Surface
*James Grady, Victoria Grady, Patrick McCreesh, and Ian Noakes*

**Posted Work in the European Union**
The Political Economy of Free Movement
*Edited by Jens Arnholtz and Nathan Lillie*

**The Professionalization of Human Resource Management**
Personnel, Development, and the Royal Charter
*Ruth Elizabeth Slater*

**Contemporary Work and the Future of Employment in Developed Countries**
*Edited by Peter Holland and Chris Brewster*

**Work and Labor Relations in the Construction Industry**
*Edited by Dale Belman, Janet Druker and Geoffrey White*

**Employment, Trade Unionism, and Class**
The Labour Market in Southern Europe since the Crisis
*Gregoris Ioannou*

# Employment, Trade Unionism, and Class

## The Labour Market in Southern Europe since the Crisis

Gregoris Ioannou

Routledge
Taylor & Francis Group
NEW YORK AND LONDON

First published 2022
by Routledge
605 Third Avenue, New York, NY 10158

and by Routledge
2 Park Square, Milton Park, Abingdon, Oxon, OX14 4RN

*Routledge is an imprint of the Taylor & Francis Group, an informa business*



*Library of Congress Cataloging-in-Publication Data*
Names: Ioannou, Gregoris, author.
Title: Employment, trade unionism and class : the labour market in Southern Europe since the crisis / Gregoris Ioannou.
Description: 1 Edition. | New York : Routledge, 2021. |
Series: Routledge research in employment relations | Includes bibliographical references and index.
Identifiers: LCCN 2021002608 (print) | LCCN 2021002609 (ebook) | ISBN 9780367142889 (hardback) | ISBN 9780429031168 (ebook)
Subjects: LCSH: Labor market--Europe, Southern. | Labor unions--Europe, Southern. |
Industrial relations--Europe, Southern. |
Social classes--Europe, Southern. | Europe, Southern--Economic conditions--21st century. | Global Financial Crisis, 2008-2009.
Classification: LCC HD5811.84.A6 I63 2021 (print) |
LCC HD5811.84.A6 (ebook) | DDC 331.12094--dc23
LC record available at https://lccn.loc.gov/2021002608
LC ebook record available at https://lccn.loc.gov/2021002609

ISBN: 978-0-367-14288-9 (hbk)
ISBN: 978-1-032-03963-3 (pbk)
ISBN: 978-0-429-03116-8 (ebk)

Typeset in Sabon
by MPS Limited, Dehradun

To Evgenia and Ilektra

# Contents

# Tables

# Acknowledgements

Many people have contributed in various ways, direct and indirect, in the writing of this book. I would like to thank all those with whom I have conversed in the last years and especially those that I interviewed during 2019–2020. Also, Stephanie Ioannou, Katerina Sergidou, and Marina Demetriadou who helped me in the conduct of fieldwork.

I would also like to thank my academic colleagues Ruth Dukes and Giorgos Charalambous who reviewed an earlier draft of the manuscript giving me valuable feedback. Additionally, I would like to thank colleagues who reviewed parts of the manuscript and with whom I have discussed some of the topics dealt with by the book; Vera Pavlou and Antonio Garcia-Munoz Alhambra as well as my colleagues in the 'Work on Demand' project[1] team Eleanor Kirk, Alessio Bertolini, and Ou Lin.

Finally, I want to thank Evgenia Nikiforou and Ilektra Ioannou for supporting me in this journey.

Gregoris Ioannou
Glasgow, December 2020

## Note

1 The project leading to this publication is funded by the European Research Council (ERC) under the European Union's Horizon 2020 research and innovation programme (grant agreement No 757395).

# Preface: The Book and its Parts

This book offers an account of the main social and political developments during the Great Recession in Southern Europe and examines the impact of the economic crisis and its management on the field of employment. The analytic frame oscillates between the general and the specific identifying the forces, the agents, and the mechanisms producing change in the labour markets and industrial relations systems of South European countries. Reforms in employment law and the institutional context of collective bargaining and the upheaval and contentious politics sparked by the adoption of austerity are assessed in relation to trade unionism and class relations in three different national settings. The comparative perspective adopted is instrumental in deciphering the interplay of external and internal dynamics and discussing how and to what extent the crisis has transformed and restructured the world of labour in Southern Europe since the crisis.

Part One illustrates the dynamics of change in Southern Europe's labour market providing an overview of the development and aftermath of the economic crisis. It identifies the main issues and trends, sets the context, and outlines the key facts of recent developments at a general level, opening the way for a more detailed and specific examination through the three country-case studies in Part Two. Spain, Greece, and Cyprus are examined in more detail separately in the three chapters comprising Part Two identifying the national particularities and contextual settings as well as the different political temporalities and developments. Part Three brings the case studies together discussing convergences and divergences in how the crisis was handled in the three countries and what its legacy has been from the standpoint of a decade later. It also offers a brief and preliminary examination of the impact of the Covid-19 pandemic in 2020 and its management on the Southern European economies and societies and concludes bringing the insights from the whole volume together.

# Abbreviations

| | | |
|---|---|---|
| 15M | 15th Mayo | 15th May |
| AKEL | Ανορθωτικό Κόμμα Εργαζομένου Λαού | Party for the Uplifting of Working People |
| ASDYK | Ανεξάρτητη Συντεχνία Δημοσίων Υπαλλήλων | Independent Union Civil Servants (Cyprus) |
| CGIL | Confederazione Generale Italiana del Lavoro | Italian General Confederation of Labour |
| CGTP | Confederação Geral dos Trabalhadores Portugueses | General Confederation of the Portuguese Workers |
| CIG | Confederación Intersindical Galega | Galician Unions Confederacy |
| CISL | Confederazione Italiana Sindacati Lavoratori | Italian Confederation of Trade Unions |
| CCOO | Commissiones Obreras | Worker Commissions |
| COLA | Αυτόματη Τιμαριθμική Αναπροσαρμογή | Cost of Living Adjustment (Cyprus) |
| DEOK | Δημοκρατική Εργατική Ομοσπονδία Κύπρου | Democratic Labour Federation of Cyprus |
| DIKO | Δημοκρατικό Κόμμα | Democratic Party |
| DIMAR | Δημοκρατική Αριστερά | Democratic Left |
| DISY | Δημοκρατικός Συναγερμός | Democratic Rally |
| EC | | European Commission |
| ECB | | European Central Bank |
| ELA | Euskal Langileen Alkartasuna | Basque Workers Solidarity |
| ERTE | Expediente de Regulación Temporal de Empleo | Temporary Employment Leave Regulation |
| ESM | | European Stability Mechanism |
| ETYK | Ένωση Τραπεζικών Υπαλλήλων Κύπρου | Union of Bank Employees of Cyprus |
| EU | | European Union |
| GMI | | Guaranteed Minimum Income |

| | | |
|---|---|---|
| GDP | | Gross Domestic Product |
| GSEE | Γενική Συνομοσπονδία Εργατών Ελλάδας | General Workers Confederation of Greece |
| IMF | | International Monetary Fund |
| KKE | Κομμουνιστικό Κόμμα Ελλάδας | Communist Party of Greece |
| LAB | Langile Abertzaleen Batzordeak | Nationalist/Patriotic Workers' Committees |
| LAOS | Λαϊκός Ορθόδοξος Συναγερμός | Popular Orthodox Rally |
| MoU | | Memorandum of Understanding |
| ND | Νέα Δημοκρατία | New Democracy |
| PAME | Πανεργατικό Αγωνιστικό Μέτωπο | All workers Militant Front |
| PASIKY | Παγκύπρια Συντεχνία Κυβερνητικών Ιατρών | Pancyprian Union of Public Doctors |
| PASOK | Πανελλήνιο Σοσιαλιστικό Κίνημα | Panhellenic Socialist Movement |
| PASYDY | Παγκύπρια Συντεχνία Δημοσίων Υπαλλήλων | Pancyprian Union of Civil Servants |
| PASYNO | Παγκύπρια Συντεχνία Νοσηλευτών | Pancyprian Union of Nurses |
| PEO | Παγκύπρια Εργατική Ομοσπονδία | Pancyprian Federation of Labour |
| PIGS | | Portugal Italy Greece Spain |
| POED | Παγκύπρια Οργάνωση Ελλήνων Δασκάλων | Pancyprian Organisation of Greek Teachers |
| PP | Partido Popular | People's Party |
| PSOE | Partido Socialista Obrero Español | Spanish Socialist Workers Party |
| SEK | Συνομοσπονδία Εργαζομένων Κύπρου | Cyprus' Employees Confederation |
| SYRIZA | Συνασπισμός Ριζοσπαστικής Αριστεράς | Coalition of Radical Left |
| TINA | | There Is No Alternative |
| UGT | Unión General de Trabajadores | Workers' General Union |
| UK | | United Kingdom |
| VAT | | Value Added Tax |
| WWII | | Second World War |

# Part I

# Southern Europe: The Labour Market and the Crisis

# 1 The Themes, the Concepts, and the Field

This introductory chapter outlines the theoretical and conceptual framework, articulates the research questions that will be addressed in the following chapters, and provides the necessary background against which historical change has occurred. In doing so it draws insights not only from industrial relations and sociology of work literatures but also from relevant adjacent disciplines and subdisciplines such as political economy and political sociology. It adopts a historical standpoint and provides an overview of the employment field as it has evolved in the last decades of the 20th Century accounting for the institutional setting and the main dynamics in operation. The analytic frame is international and identifies the main themes that are of relevance in this book, such as the institutional context of the labour market and the politics and operation of trade unionism.

The scholarly literature on employment and its regulation and on the role and function of trade unions is reviewed with a view to examining in parallel both the evolution of the world of work and the research about it. The debates on flexibility and precariousness and on worker interests and their representation in the corporatist and post-corporatist neoliberal contexts are briefly presented along with the main features of the Mediterranean industrial relations systems in order to map out the contours of the analysis that will follow. Subsequently the notion of the economic crisis is defined and an overview of its appearance, management, and social and political consequences in Southern Europe is provided.

The chapter ends with a note on the method and the logic of the analytic approach adopted and finally by introducing the content of the remainder of the book in a brief, chapter by chapter summary. It includes a reflection on the process of the writing of this book, the context in which it appears, and an explanation of the choices made in terms of the focus and structure as well as definitional matters and specified analytic aims. This chapter thus accounts for the rationale and the scope of the book and provides the necessary backdrop for the answering of the main question of the book, namely how the crisis in Southern Europe played out in different countries.

Serving as the introduction, this chapter constitutes a general overview of the key notions that structure the book, how they are approached, understood, and operationalised in the analysis of a specified domain and a specified spatio-temporal context. The labour market is conceptualised as a field shaped by dynamics operative in employment relations and determined by a changing correlation of class forces. The institutional order, understood as the result of the constellation of power relations and the framework that bounds interaction and conflict at the workplace and the labour market, is also influenced by economic conditions, social customs, ideological orientations, political expediency. Hence, all these dimensions are brought into the analysis in order to explain the shifts produced by and during the economic crisis in Southern Europe. In addition to the thematic presentation and the theoretical outline, this chapter sketches the basic factual content of the crisis so as to serve as a backdrop for the more detailed empirical accounts that follow in the subsequent chapters.

## Employment in Transition: Flexibility and Precariousness

In the last decades of the 20th Century a series of significant changes took place at a global level producing shifts in the economic and political domains. The establishment of the European Economic Community, its consolidation and expansion in the 1970s and its evolution into the European Union, the downturn of the Soviet Union and its implosion and collapse created a new universe based on altered political dynamics in the labour field. On the ideological plane the steady ascendancy of neoliberalism which became a dominant policy framework by the early 1990s exerted further pressures on trade unionism, social partnership politics and the institutional framework of the labour market in general (Hall 2017 [2011]). Decline in trade union density, accelerated deregulation of the labour market, the increasing fragmentation of the labour force, the return of high unemployment and the rise of atypical employment and precariousness were the new contours of the labour field (Streeck 2014). Trade unions found themselves increasingly unable to influence policy at both the national and the EU levels in the last decades of the 20th Century and were weaker than ever before in terms of their basic collective bargaining function (Waddington et al. 2019).

The depth of the transformation of the employment field in Europe under way in the last decades of the 20th Century was fully revealed only in the recent economic crisis (Baccaro and Howell 2017). When it became clear that what had been lost in terms of social and employment rights was irreversible and that the road ahead seemed even bleaker. The end of the Keynesian era brought with it the end of social democracy as a distinct political position and by the 1990s the premises of neoliberalism had become hegemonic even within the centre left, constituting a sort of new 'common sense' (Seymour 2014). Flexibility became the new buzz word in the labour market, national competitiveness became the absolute law of survival in the new globalised economy, and privatisations the new political norm. Irregular employment grew at the expense of regular employment, industrial production shrank significantly as manufacturing units moved to low labour cost destinations further east and the service sectors emerged as the dominant ones in the European economies.

At the level of society, social inequalities increased, and the welfare state in all its variants (Esping-Andersen 1990) came under pressure to different extents and in different ways and already by the turn of the Century in several countries. European economies continued to grow but an increasing proportion of their populations was excluded and marginalised. From the mid-1980s to the mid-2000s all developed countries with the single exception of Greece in different magnitudes and time periods experienced an increase in income inequality (Therborn 2013). Beyond the traditionally vulnerable groups in the labour market, where women, youth, and migrants were over-represented, other social groups were facing increasing difficulties to be included in the world of standard, permanent, well-paid employment. It was not just the industrial workers who were laid off in the de-industrialisation decades – it was more importantly their children who was the first for centuries to find themselves worse off than their parents' generation.

Beyond the traditional industrial working class, other white collar strata with higher educational attainments and even higher expectations also found themselves in some cases trapped in low paid service jobs with limited prospects and in others led into professional self-employment, working intermittently, most experiencing much more enhanced employment and income insecurity (Burchell 2002). For some flexibility worked out, either because their middle-class backgrounds helped them to avoid being stuck too long in jobs without prospects, or because their networks connected at the right time with the right people or because they possessed or were able to develop some particular skill or attribute valued within specialised niches. But for most workers, the flexibilisation of the labour market meant more time and effort investment, less real income, and more insecurity.

Subcontracting and informal labour emerged as overtly significant dimensions in shaping the work environment and the experience of increasing sections of the working class and thus structuring the dialectic of exploitation and resistance in the new globalised economy (Schierup 2007; Slavnic 2007; Wills 2009). Subcontracting is part of the broader questioning of the 'normal labour relation' which promotes the conception of the worker as a business person of her own labour power, assuming part of the risk and part of the cost of production (Paleologos 2006: 201–215). It usually involves piecework, therefore directly linking not just reward to productivity, but remuneration to output. This in conjunction with the neglect or downplay of health and safety measures which are deemed costly and for which responsibility is also passed to workers, exacerbating the intensification of work, a process taken to the extreme in the gig economy.

In the last decades subcontracting or outsourcing has expanded resulting in the increase of the incidence of temporary agency work. Beyond allowing employers to avoid and evade employer responsibility and tax burdens, subcontracting and outsourcing exacerbates the fragmentation of the labour force and workplace divisions between the workers who are directly employed and those who are in-directly employed who typically are in a disadvantaged position (Bertolini 2020). It has also developed in parallel and connected to self-employment which has also risen substantially in recent decades and which includes a large proportion of bogus self-employment. This 'dependent self-employment' has become a serious issue of concern and the topic of a small but burgeoning literature (Williams and Lapeyre 2020).

Flexibility is ultimately a very open notion whose theoretical definition, the extent of its empirical identification and most importantly its practical interpretation for the purposes of policies and politics has been long debated and remains still disputed. The boundary between its positive and its normative dimension has always been fluid and shifting while its scope, focus and meaning, let alone purpose and implication, have been matters of some controversy.[1] At a considerable level of generality the concept of flexibility refers to a new organising principle of production (Piore and Sabel 1984) and a new accumulation regime (Harvey 1989) or even a new spirit of capitalism (Boltanski and Chiapello 2005) that is seen as a paradigm shift away from Fordist rigidities into post-Fordist fluidities (Vallas 1999; Neilson and Rossiter 2008).

Flexibility has multiple dimensions affecting both the employment relation and the work act (Beck 1992 [1986]) – determining both the numerical composition of the workforce, the total working time, and its distribution, as well as issues of task assignment and remuneration. Its implication is seen as the segmentation of the labour market both externally and internally into a core and a periphery, increasing the distance between skilled and unskilled work, well paid and badly paid jobs, permanent and casual employment (Beck 2000; Vallas and Prener 2012). More importantly flexibility is not only, or not yet a general condition but also and primarily a general tendency (Gallie et al. 1998; Felstead and Jewson 1999; Kalleberg 2011). Therefore, it is more suitable to refer to flexibilisation as a dynamic situation, in the process of which managerial policy and labour organisation is undergoing change (Doellgast et al. 2018).

Flexible work arrangements are generally taken to be both a condition and a choice for women, sometimes originating from employers' preferences but sometimes also from women employee needs. The over-representation of women in less regulated service sectors, and the relatively higher proportion of women engaged in part-time work were used at the same time as an empirical fact of a connection of labour market flexibility with the employment of women and its normative justificiation. Research focusing on the subjective experience of women, especially immigrants, reveals however that what is at work is a specifically gendered dimension of insecurity in employment and work, compounding precarious work with more general gender inequalities existing in contemporary societies (Purcel 2000; Anthias 2000; Parreñas 2001; Cranford et al. 2003).

By the late 1990s the notion of flexibility had become established and included as part of the general neoliberal consensus with national and EU governments and business circles attempting to realise the strategy of the 'flexible labour market' through processes of deregulation (Standing 1999; Kouzis 2001; Barbieri 2009) and re-regulation (Rubery and Grimshaw 2003; Davies and Freedland 2007). However, the fear of the implications of the promotion of flexibility in labour on workers' security, actual as well as potential, was evident from the beginning. Richard Sennet (1998) argued that the short-termist character of contemporary employment brings illegibility and loss of coherent biographical narrative, superficiality of involvements and erosion of trust, leading to the corrosion of character. Among radical academics and activists, the concept of 'precarity' as a life condition or a new norm of work life re-emerged with a double edge – theoretical as well as political – in an attempt to both understand as well as subvert the flexibility discourse (Foti 2004; Frassanito network 2005; Mitropoulos 2006; Tsianos et al. 2008; Foti 2017). The attempt to reclaim flexibility from capital and address workers' need for security led some scholars and activists to put forward the idea of 'guaranteed basic income' (Fumagalli 2005) which subsequently opened up a new thread of debate, significantly boosted by the work of Guy Standing (Standing 2011).[2]

The idea of using social policy as an instrument with which to address the worse effects of the on-going liberalisation process, control the vicissitudes of flexibility in the labour market and protect the workers was also brewing in establishment quarters who were in search of a means to consolidate the legitimacy of the idea of the flexibility. By 2007 the EU formally endorsed the idea of "flexicurity" a notion deriving from northern countries such as Denmark and the Netherlands (European Commission 2007). The idea of flexicurity was developed along the lines of state intervention to improve the efficiency of labour mobility, adjusting labour force skills to economic needs and facilitating the smooth transition from one occupation to the other (Wilthagen 1998; Wilthagen and Tross 2004). Both Denmark and the Netherlands were hailed as successful examples of balancing flexibility needed for the economy and security needed by society and flexicurity became a buzz word in the debates prevailing on the eve of the economic crisis. The Danish model was commended for combining generous welfare with high labour mobility and replacing job security with employment and income security promoting active labour market policy and life-long learning. The Dutch model was commended for offering employment, welfare, and education and training rights to non-standard workers (Viebrock and Klasen 2009).

The focus on labour flexibility and precarity in the research and politics agendas at the turn of the Century came along with a new interest in gender and its role in the structuring of the work and employment relation. This took many forms such as the focus on the interplay of emotion and sexuality at work (Adkins 1995; Taylor and Tyler 2000), the re-examination of more traditional themes such as male breadwinning ideologies (Charles and James 2003) and the lower cost of female labour (Rubery 2006) as well as the childcare needs and identity projects of women (Casey and Alach 2004). The form and the functionality of flexibility and its interaction with gender divisions and dynamics varies and cannot be deduced theoretically and *a priori*, remaining ultimately an empirical question that needs to be analysed in concrete examples.

The field of employment and the workplace have always been terrains determined by power dynamics. Beneath the increasing complexity of organisational forms in the modern era and the utilisation of new technologies and digitalisation, the issue of power and control over the labour process in general and particularly the relations within the workplace remain central. At the same time, today managerial power is not merely an outcome of the separation of conception from execution of the work task (Braverman 1974) nor can it be fully analysed by means of the typology of simple, technical, and bureaucratic control (Edwards 1979). While employment and work rules are today more developed and elaborate than in the past, they are not sufficient to explain how workers' consent is produced and how hegemony is built at the workplace (Burawoy 1979). In the current post-industrial conditions of decentralisation and informality and increased socialisation, hierarchy and conflict are also instituted and substantiated on other dimensions such as communicative and social skills, group dynamics and networking not only within but also outside the workplace.

One need not adopt the exaggerations of the theories of transformation about the network society (Castells 2000) or the dominance of immaterial labour (Hardt and Negri 2000) to recognise that relations in employment and work have undergone significant change. The general servicisation of the economy and the subsequent replacement of the 'mass worker' by the 'social worker' has neither eradicated the factory logic nor has it abolished the antagonism that is inherent in it (Negri 1988). Class remains a central category in sociological analysis as class divisions based on employment and derived from the positionality in production determine social structures (Crompton 2010). Arguably servicisation has not even challenged the fundamentals of Taylorism such as overtly scripted and routinised acts and interactions, rehearsed time and time again (Ritzer 2004 [1996]). Yet at the same time the increased interpenetration of production imperatives by consumption logics, preferences, and actors beyond the mere size of demand, has however altered the contours of the dialectical conflict between labour autonomy and capitalist control.

The expansion of the service sectors and the increase of service jobs has enhanced the role of emotional labour, the manipulation that is of emotion in the process of capital accumulation which leads to a disjuncture between what one feels and what one is required to display (Hochschild 2003 [1983]). The idea of a 'customer oriented bureaucracy' linking both workers' empowerment and capitalist rationalisation (Korczynski 2002) or the notion of the 'triadic work relation' (Lucas 2004; Arrowsmith 2010) emerged precisely as attempts to expand the scope of analysis, to take into account the new service logic (and customer presence), into the labour process. This becomes even more important in more recent years with the emergence of the gig economy (Prassl 2018) and the transposition of the logic of algorithmic management in several industries (Wood 2020).

In the debate on flexibility in the labour market and labour relations and more recently on precarity or precariousness there have also been scholars standing as they say against the 'new common sense'. Using strict definitions of employment statuses and available statistics going back to the 1970s the claim is made that the prevalence of non-standard employment is in fact exaggerated, that flexibility has always existed and that there are limits to how much it is feasible or even desirable as an employer strategy and that precarity is in no way the new norm in the labour market (Doogan 2009; Choonara 2019). While these perspectives emphasise the continuities in the labour field rejecting the grand claims of the transformation of employment relations, they overlook the significance of the broader changes occurring in the institutional order, political sphere and societal relations and how these impact the world of work. The weakening of trade unionism for example, the diffusion of neoliberal ideology, the financialisation process, the individualisation of labour law have all resulted in increasing volatility and precariousness in working life.

## Trade Unionism and Class Composition

Just as employment relations do not operate in an institutional vacuum but within a definite socio-cultural context shaped by political and ideological values and views, legal rules, and norms, so do trade unions and industrial relations systems (Hyman 1989). Often trade unions have a significant role in the construction of industrial relations systems and an even more important one in their reproduction. Industrial relations systems may vary both in terms of their rationale of operation and in terms of the means that are employed to achieve the generally accepted outcomes – economic prosperity and social peace. However, no typology can do justice to the description and analysis of industrial relations systems as elements from one inter-penetrate the other and in real life there exists no 'pure' form beyond the theoretical models. Nevertheless, as far as the procedures and practices of labour macro management are concerned, liberalised or market-oriented systems are typically distinguished from more coordinated or statist systems differing from each other with respect to the degree and form of involvement by national law and state practice in the labour affairs (Burawoy 1985).

On the one hand, is the voluntarist system whereby labour relations are regulated by 'free collective bargaining' with the state restricting itself to a supporting and mediating role, offering the institutional framework and political facilitation but abstaining from acts of legislative intervention and political arbitration except in extreme cases. This system is the traditional British industrial relations model of the 20th Century also described as 'collective laissez faire', a term initially coined by Kahn-Freund to emphasise that negotiation was both collective and autonomous from the state (Dukes 2009). Employers and unions are the protagonists, and their field of action and interaction occupies the space 'between market and class' as the schema of Hyman (2001) posists.

For the voluntarist system to function effectively, strong trade unions are needed that are able to both organise the workforce and represent its economic interests vis-à-vis capital, achieving both recognition and a place at the negotiating table through their de facto power (Howell 2005). Voluntarism is based on the idea of the balance of forces between labour and capital that make the self-restraint and the mutual understanding amongst employers' organisations and trade unions possible, desirable, and achievable. Whether at national or regional, sectoral, or local workplace level, the voluntarist system has collective bargaining and collective agreement as its fundamental characteristic, primary regulatory mechanism as well as its dominant ideological framework which can accommodate both conflict and consent.

The continental systems on the other hand, in opposition to the system of voluntarism, have state intervention and legislation as the primary regulatory means and are inevitably more prone to the politicisation of industrial conflict. France is the more extreme example of statism and the forces of organised labour and the Left in France have no hesitation to use the law as an instrument of struggle in order to secure rights and benefits and ensure the enforcement of collective agreements (Goetschy and Jobert 2004: 186). The state thus becomes an active agent in labour affairs, beyond the mere provision of a legal-institutional framework, in two ways – both as a site of political struggle about and as an agent of policy in the shaping of national industrial relations.

The German model on the other hand, while attributing a significant role to the state, this role is more procedural rather than substantive compared to the French system of industrial relations. This is because it both recognises the autonomy of the labour market and the labour process while simultaneously it integrates their regulation within the state form. The state does assume its responsibility for the welfare of society like in the French model, but this must be facilitated through the market which plays a central role like in the voluntarist system. The 'social market' philosophy as an over-arching framework, bigger than industrial relations and encompassing public policy and the whole management of the economy, seeks to integrate employers and workers and curb the overt politicisation of industrial relations. The diffusion of Works Councils and the 'co-determination' procedures through which workers 'participate' in management promote the principle of a consensual industrial democracy as an ideal (Keller 2004). The industrial relations system which German trade unions have shaped and to which they remained oriented occupies the space 'between society and the market' in Hyman's (2001) schema.

The German model, based on the idea of social partnership, has heavily influenced the emergence of an EU labour relations discourse in the 1970s, the heyday of corporatism. However, as early as the 1980s, the rise of neoliberalism and globalisation eroded the idea of social partnership, and when elements of it were adopted as guiding principles in the EU institutional framework, and more so in the EU narrative in 1990s they were essentially hollowed out (Streeck 2019). The trend of the juridification of labour affairs an ongoing process throughout Europe is also a fundamental attribute of the German industrial relations system whose logic has been transposed at the EU level as well.

The different systems and traditions in place have reacted in different ways to the increasing economic volatility and the changed political dynamics in the last decades of the 20th Century (Frege 2007). Whereas the Scandinavian systems were able to maintain high trade union density and high collective bargaining coverage amidst growing liberalisation and flexibilisation, voluntarist and continental systems were less able to do so, resulting in deteriorating conditions (Thelen 2014). Nevertheless, the two 'extreme' Scandinavian and Anglo-Saxon models seem to converge in terms of allowing a transition from precarious into regular employment setting them apart from Continental and especially South European systems whereby atypical workers are used as a substitute for standardly employed ones as a cost cutting strategy leading to the entrapment of workers in precariousness (Bertolini 2020).

The organisational structure of trade unionism again differs from country to country and from one historical era to the other (Offe 1985). Trade unionism emerged in the 19th Century as a response to the proletarianisation process that characterised the passage of society into modernity. It was a primarily skilled workers' movement initially organised on a craft basis.[3] Industrial organisation, however, which was consolidated in the maturation stage of trade unionism, was unable to resolve the tensions emanating from narrow conceptions of economic interests, sectoral parochialism, and the inability to articulate a unified and systematic class viewpoint regarding socio-economic policy in general and labour issues in particular continued to trouble the socialists of the 20th Century. Moreover the 2nd international split of the labour movement after the Bolshevik revolution[4] and the appearance and strengthening of centrist and conservative trade unions (liberal, nationalist, and/or Christian) segmented ideologically and politically as well the structure and practice of trade unionism.

Nevertheless, trade unionism in Europe, remained broadly speaking social democratic in values and orientation irrespective of party-political affiliation, stronger or weaker, and was able to constitute a significant socio-political force by mid-20th Century. Despite the diversity as a result of the different national contexts and state traditions which inevitably affected both the historical development of trade unionism and the industrial relations systems, a convergence into corporatism, of one sort or another became the norm by the 1970s, before the process of decline begun (Crouch 1993; Visser and Ebbinghaus 2000). This was characterised by developed systems of individual and collective labour law, recognition of trade unionism as a legitimate form of organised interest representation and collective bargaining at various levels: national, sectoral, as well as at enterprise level.

Collective bargaining is central in all industrial relations systems, although the level at which this happens, the form it takes, the scope it has, the procedural and legal frameworks in which it occurs differs again from country to country and from era to era. Some even claim that collective bargaining processes are 'the regulation of labour' and subsume and structure trade unionism itself and that they should be at the centre of the attempt to theorise trade unionism (Clegg 1976). Sisson (1987) takes up this route and examines how collective bargaining is managed in practice to explain the decentralisation process that occurred in Britain and the shift form multi-employer to single-employer bargaining in several industries. His comparative study points out both the essentially voluntary form of collective bargaining institutions and the contingency of employers' preferences of the bargaining level and the degree of centralisation in the process. Yet, although collective bargaining is central in industrial relations, it is neither the only form of labour process regulation nor the only realm of trade union action.

Kelly's (1998) focus on workers' mobilisation and collective action as the central dimension of industrial relations links the concepts of struggle and organisation and addresses the theoretical and political question of class conflict. The notion of 'justice' is suggested as the central theme determining militancy and the issue of leadership is addressed from below and at the micro-level as well. Activists, especially left-wingers, have been and remain the key factor in workers' mobilisations by pointing out injustice and the need for action, contributing to the formation of group identity and defending the legitimacy of collective action (Kelly 1998: 35, 44–51). Within the trade union structures and the various workplace committees of different sorts, militant communists, whether characterised as working-class heroes or trouble-makers according to one's perspective, were more or less seen as the local leaders and agitators, stirring up industrial unrest and coding politically workers' discontent and grievances.

Often these militants, whether inside the official communist movement or in the last decades outside of it, constituted *a priori* targets for employers' authoritarianism and repression (Franzosi 2006 [1995]: 220) in the more or less conservative, anti-communist climate of the Cold War era and its post-Cold War continuation and diffusion. In the UK the shop stewards appeared in the front scene as the disruptive force behind the wildcat strikes that signalled the 'exhaustion of consent' (Hall et al. 1978) while in Spain at the same time the belief of workplace leaders in the democratic state after four decades of authoritarian rule was instrumental in the smooth transition to democratic rule (Fishman 1990). In either case the agency of the local working-class leaders remains the key with respect to social contention and mobilisation and to the directions of socio-political change.

The power of capital can only be challenged systematically and substantially by organised and political class struggle which raises the working class beyond its objective position and orientation, a class in itself 'as against capital', to the level of consciousness, becoming a class 'for itself' (Lukacs 1968 [1920]: 76). Organisation and politicisation can theoretically and potentially achieve unification at two levels – both overcoming the socio-cultural divisions (mental from manual labour, gender and ethnicity etc) and transcending the socio-economic hierarchies (based on occupational position) within the working class. Effective class unity, especially if it manages to neutralise the special role assigned by capital to the managerial and technical stratum, may lead to the achievement of class autonomy, breaking in other words the reproduction of capital which is based on the subordination of the collective labourer through the integration of labour regulation within the production process and the multi-segmentation of the labour force (Clarke 1991: 191).

Nevertheless, organised and political class struggle which produces working class unity and breaks the hegemony, and subsequently the power of capital, is neither a clear-cut nor a frequently occurring phenomenon. Whereas workplace conflict is ever-present in tacit as well as open forms it is often unorganised and non-politicised. A significant proportion of strike activity is not organised and not officially sanctioned, let alone instigated or led from the outside or from above, but only approved and supported by trade union leaders as it develops. Often the dichotomy between a union-led and a non-union-led strike is not as stark as it seems. Wildcat strikes, unmediated in form and existential in character with their anti-authoritarian implications, have always been an integral part of the labour movement and have often evolved into generalised struggles. Yet, at the same they have often been ineffective due to the lack of strategy and planning.

At the micro, workplace level, workers' resistance is not always collective and need not always reach the threshold of industrial action. It might also take indirect and subversive forms that are of a more elemental nature. Just as at the macro level of sectoral and national collective bargaining, strike action or non-cooperation can be also used as a threat, or in more subtle ways as an insinuated potentiality. Grievances concerning the time, the pace or the conditions of work might be satisfied or repressed immediately and locally before being fully and systematically articulated and taken up to the trade union or the firm's management. It is probably futile to try to estimate the threshold at which discontent leads to industrial action or construct models in order to explain the incidence and measure the intensity of class struggle (Franzosi 2006 [1995]) while models of long waves of mobilisation (Kelly 1998) can be useful theoretical exercises but carry the danger of determinism and historicism, missing the inherent historicity and empirical specificity of class struggle.

Conflict at work, just as in society, takes different forms and neither its occurrence nor its implications can be explained at the level of theory. Class, and the class struggle which shapes it, remain at the end of the day historical phenomena that cannot be grasped adequately with sociological nets and which require a study of the historical contexts in which they are embedded (Thompson 1991 [1963]). What theory can offer to the analysis of instances of class struggle is insights concerning the correlation of forces in concrete historical moments and settings. Tarrow's (1994) schema for example of the five dimensions shaping the political opportunity structure for successful mobilisation contributes in this direction. More broadly social movement theory and social movement tactics can enrich the power resources approach of trade unionism and assist trade union revitalisation (Ioannou 2020b).

Class relations are essentially relations of power that although rooted in the division of labour and structured in the realm of production, extend beyond the economy and shape the institutional order, influence societal ideologies and constitute the political domain (Umney 2018). Hence, whereas labour sociology and political economy remain indispensable to the analysis of social class and class dynamics in contemporary societies, they need to be complemented by political sociology which is more suitable to provide nuanced analysis of institutional change, ideological shifts and contentious politics as they are played out not only in the workplace, the labour market and the economy but society and the public sphere broadly defined. Trade unions, like other social actors such as political parties and social movements take account of the environment while they act assessing not only their own power resources but also those of their opponents (Kriesi 2006).

Contrary to the view that neoliberalism involves the retreat of the state from the economy, like with a series of other domains, in fact the state has an enhanced role to play in industrial relations. The state operates as an active agent in promoting marketisation and liberalisation, regulating and re-regulating work, employment, and class relations (Howell 2016). In fact, in recent decades, the decline of trade unionism and collective bargaining has created more space for law in the regulation of employment. Even in the UK, operating in the tradition of voluntarism, the scope and depth of legislation has expanded with key employment standards now set by the government through statute law (Colling 2010). However, statute law cannot really substitute for social regulation and the mere existence of dense nets of employment law does not ensure protection of workers' rights. Law reflects social beliefs but in the longer-term it also nurtures values and norms. In the UK for example an anti-collectivist culture was fostered, and partnership came to mean between employers and employees, not employers and unions, with non-unionism supported by law (Dickens and Hall 2009).

The state is thus a material force that intervenes with legal and policy instruments shaping the field of employment but also the equally important field of available welfare which is inter-related with the world of work. The state oversees both class conflict and class compromise not only by establishing the framework of collective bargaining but also through narrowing its scope by taking over issues such as pensions and health insurance and assists in the decommodification of class relations through redistribution policies (Meardi et al. 2016). At the same time, the state is both a site for and engaged in symbolic and cultural struggles about the meaning and the appropriate forms of social solidarity (Vallas 2018).

The increasing difficulty of European trade unions in the neoliberal age to achieve universal progressive outcomes for the social majority it directly and indirectly represents, resulted in a sort of permanent crisis of trade unionism as its social influence shrank provoking a process of soul-searching. Trade unions turned to recruitment campaigns especially in low paid service sectors as the key instrument to revitalisation (Ibsen and Tapia 2017). Yet success in that field has been modest for various external reasons as well as their reluctance to invest valuable and limited resources for uncertain outcomes (Gumbrell-McCormick and Hyman 2013). Underlying this reserved stance was the ambivalence as to whether they should adapt to the changing environment and cling on their existing power resources, primarily of the institutional type, or whether they should aim to transform their operational context and themselves along the way (Serrano 2014).

The de-institutionalising neoliberal dynamics unsettled the traditional relationship between trade unions and social democratic parties posing the dilemma for trade unions on whether to pursue an accommodation strategy or whether to adopt more confrontational stances (Taylor, Mathers, and Upchurch 2011). The resolution to this dilemma by many trade unions has increasingly been in recent decades the opening up to civil society organisations and social movements, with all the difficulties that this entails deriving from their different histories, orientations, functions, and organisational logics. Social alliances were seen by trade unions as an unavoidable step in the effort to avoid marginalisation (Della Porta 2006; Hyman 2015; Hyman and Gumbrell-McCormick 2017). In addition, a new minority trend of 'radical political unionism' appeared at the fringe of centre left parties, or as splinters from large, mainstream trade unions or through autonomous establishment and organisation. Beyond its engagement in social movement activity, this re-establishes an emphasis on class struggle and adopts politicised strategies aligned to new left-wing formations that present themselves as outsiders from establishment politics (Upchurch et al. 2009; Upchurch and Mathers 2011).

## Mediterranean Industrial Relations Systems and the Labour Market in Spain, Greece, and Cyprus

It has been established in the political economy and employment relations literatures that the Mediterranean countries constitute a so-called third variety of capitalism (Hall and Soskice, 2001), distinct both from the Liberal Market Economies with the UK being the model, and the Coordinated Market Economies with Germany being the model in Europe. In schematic terms the 'Mediterranean model' has the market as the dominant regulatory force but the state also maintains a key role in industrial relations and social protection, there are weaker education and training schemes in place resulting in less capacity for industrial strategies geared to value-added production and the banks dominate corporate financing (Lallement 2011). It is also plagued by a higher degree of clientelism (Becker 2009: 60). Being in the periphery of the European economy and with much weaker industrial base compared to the European north, Mediterranean countries have lower GDP per capita income, lower median and minimum wages, and usually also less comprehensive welfare systems (Sapelli 1995).

The industrialisation and urbanisation processes occurred many decades later in Mediterranean countries compared to the European north and agriculture remained an important economic sector until the mid-20th Century (Crouch 1993). Furthermore, this process was very uneven resulting in major regional differentiation in the bigger countries such as Spain and more so Italy which remains substantially divided economically between its northern and southern regions (Van der Meer 2000). Industrialisation and technological development, except in northern Italy and Catalonia, never progressed in Southern Europe to the extent and the intensity with which it happened in Northern Europe and often a direct leap occurred from agriculture to services. Urbanisation also occurred at a later stage peaking in the decades of the mid-20th Century and its magnitude, concentration, and rapidity provoked social dislocations. The specific industrialisation and urbanisation patterns had consequences not only with respect to the structure of South European economies where the small and even the micro firm form prevailed, but also with respect to the political order, the welfare state and institutional development more generally. Sapelli argues that these processes resulted in the continued influence of systems of power and cultural values based on status as opposed to contracts, of political capitalism rather than rational capitalism in the Weberian sense (Sapelli 1995: 13, 15, 93).

The strength of the institution of the family both in terms of its influence on the realms of the economy and the labour market and in terms of providing the basic safety net and the main site of social reproduction is another attribute that characterises South European societies in general. This is obviously a result of a complex set of historical and cultural factors related to the pace, the form and the type of the modernisation process southern Europe underwent during the whole 20th Century. One need not adopt a linear conception of modernisation or an evolutionary understanding of social development to observe that several processes that characterised continental Europe occurred later in southern European countries. Nor was the survival and significance of kinship networks a result of the patterns of economic development. The delay in the establishment of advanced and elaborate systems of social welfare which only approached continental levels towards the end of the 20th Century, when the latter were already under significant pressures from the onslaught of neoliberalism, served to reinforce familial and informal social reproduction systems.

The long historical experience of political authoritarianism in the 20th Century is another characteristic shared by most South European countries and it has undeniably had an impact on the development of their political systems, state-society relations, and institutional contexts. Dictatorial regimes survived until the mid-1970s in Portugal, Spain, and Greece while extreme right-wing forces, although not in power were active in the politically unstable post WWII Italy and shaping the post-colonial transition in Cyprus. Trade unionism has always been an overtly political matter in southern Europe and the political polarisation and the Left and Right cleavages in the social and political milieu left their marks both within trade unionism and between trade unionism as a whole and the state (Hamann 2011; Visser 2000; Kouzis 2007; Ioannou 2016b; Ioannou and Charalambous 2020). Not only has it been impossible to establish umbrella organisations and concerted trade unions at the national level, but even cooperation and coordination with respect to limited common goals has proved especially difficult. The incorporation of trade unionism within the state and the development of corporatist forms, already under way since the inter-war years and dominant in northern Europe after WWII could not really progress until the late 1970s in most south European countries. The corporatist structures instituted by the Franco regime in Spain were based on suppression rather than incorporation and as such were largely a sham, far from corporatism as a historical phenomenon (Crouch 1993: 329).

The rapid development and overt expansion of the tourist industry in the Mediterranean countries that took off in the 1970s and continues unabetted until today has also shaped not only the economies and the labour force structures but also more specifically the employment fields and the industrial relations systems. Mass tourism, made possible as a result of the golden era of capitalism in the first three decades after WWII, was seen by the Mediterranean countries as the easy road to economic development. Exploiting nature and climate, and requiring only limited infrastructural investment, the sun and sea mass tourism model allowed South European countries to attract foreign exchange, create jobs and expand their economies. The hospitality industry that developed in Southern Europe became by the 1990s the motor of economic growth and in fact at the time of the Great Crisis two decades later, it was the only industry that remained standing in economic terms.

The corporatist industrial relations systems of South European countries established in the 1970s were characterised by the protection of employment and strong collective bargaining procedures primarily at sectoral level. However, the internationalisation processes, of which the development of the tourism industry was one part of, gradually expanded the role of market forces as the regulation mechanism, enhanced the chasm between institutional forms and mechanisms and the reality on the ground and did not substantially impact on the already comparatively large informal economy. Undeclared work, a complex phenomenon existing in a variety of forms, and embedded in different institutional and cultural contexts (Pfau-Effinger 2009), did not decrease notably with the modernisation processes under way in the decades before the crisis. Flexibility in the labour market was already growing de facto before it began to be legislated for, from the 1990s onwards. Yet the fall in trade union density and the decentralisation of collective bargaining were moderate trends even in the 2000s before the crisis arrived. National political traditions and national politics contexts constitute a significant determining factor for trade union reach and influence and can account for the survival of corporatism up until the eve of the crisis (Schmitt and Mitukiewicz 2012).

Collective bargaining coverage remained high, in some cases as high as 80% as a result of erga omnes clauses, binding establishments independent of membership (Köhler and Calleja Jiménez 2017; Kouzis 2007; Katsaroumpas and Koukiadaki 2019) or in the absence of that, through the sheer weight of tradition and political climate as expressed in conventions and case law (Leonardi 2017; Ioannou and Sonan 2019). Despite their declining power resources in structural and organisational terms, trade unions retained some of their political influence and through social dialogue and political pressures were able to thwart the full onslaught of the neoliberal deregulation process that was spreading from north to south by the turn of the 21st Century. Behind the surface of their real and apparent ability to maintain the balance amidst industrial relations systems that were being eroded, however, they were increasingly becoming more vulnerable. Their growing reliance more on the institutional realm, social dialogue procedures, law, and policy to protect their members and the workers in general from deteriorating conditions meant that when that institutional context was overturned during the crisis, they had nothing to hold on to.

Trade unions in Southern Europe have always been more political than their counterparts in northern countries. In Spain, Portugal, Cyprus, and Italy there are separate federations and confederations on the basis of ideology and party-political affiliation whereas in Greece although at confederation level there is unity, coming under great strain in the last years, ideological and political divisions exist within the confederation structure at all levels through the trade union factions and fronts that compete internally. The stronger ideological orientation within South European trade unionism was and remains social democracy, although particular historical trajectories in countries such as Italy and Cyprus where formal social democratic parties were weak, it was the communist or reformed communist parties that became the dominant players in the left of centre political spectrum and therefore in the trade union landscape as well.

South European economies, especially since the 1990s came to depend more and more on their service sectors and primarily those associated with tourism. This was facilitated after the globalisation pressures, such as the unrestricted trade of textile imports, and the collapse of the Eastern European bloc led to the dismantling of their limited manufacturing in the form of light industries with clothing and footwear being the most significant ones (Crouch 2013). The fact that the small firm and often the micro family business was the dominant characteristic in the structure of South European economies also played a role in the persistence and even growth of the informal section of their labour markets. The broader trends towards declining trade union density and decentralisation of collective bargaining in addition to the particular characteristics of Southern Europe as an economically weaker EU periphery resulted in the expansion of precarious work affecting primarily the younger generation and the immigrants who took up the increasing number of jobs created in the service sectors.

Although economic growth continued and the general living standard continued to improve, structural imbalances and dependence on particular sectors rendered southern European economies especially vulnerable. The construction and the banking industries were expanding beyond proportions and borrowing funded a real estate bubble that burst in the initial stage of the global financial crisis. This was more enhanced in Spain and Cyprus and the particular path of the crisis there although as a trend it concerned all southern Europe. Greece had also more specific issues with respect to public debt and fiscal imbalances – but the banking system and the collusion of bankers with the political system remained the key issue (Tombazos 2018).

## The Onset, Development, and Aftermath of the Crisis

Economic crisis is ultimately endemic in capitalism, and a historically recurring phenomenon. As capitalism is an all-encompassing socio-economic system not restricted to the economic realm, so are its crises (Marx 1976; Marx 1981). Although the notion of 'crisis' is an elusive one, as well as potentially misleading and prone to be overtly exaggerated or diffused across historical time and social space, it is impossible to discuss the developments of the last fifteen years without reference to it. There is disagreement among scholars and analysts as to whether the West, where the economic crisis was more pronounced, has truly overcome it or not, what were its exact causes and the most significant of its consequences, and of course with respect to how it was managed and how it should have been and should be managed. There is less disagreement about the 2008 crisis being of historical significance, analogous to if not more severe than the 1929 crisis.

For the purposes of this book, the crisis will be defined somewhat narrowly as a sudden economic downturn producing a series of consequences in the social, political, and cultural domains. This is because in this analysis, the crisis is approached as a sort of independent variable upon which a discussion of change in the labour market in Southern Europe and more specifically employment, trade unionism and class structure can be grounded. Although theoretical insights will be utilised and observations about historical and conceptual themes will be made as they arise out of the empirical data, no grand theorisations about the deeper causes and the core essences of the crisis per se or detailed projections and suggestions about the future will be provided.[5] In any case the accelerating on-going environmental crisis and the new economic crisis provoked by the attempts to manage the Covid-19 pandemic during 2020 raised new issues, widened further the questions and put new viewpoints on the table. The crisis for the purposes of this book is treated above all as historical context, a chain of events, a backdrop against which agents acted, institutions adapted, and structures were altered.

Notwithstanding the above clarification, I still need to briefly outline the basic theoretical contours in which I understand the crisis to lie and in which I propose that it be approached. This crisis is a capitalist crisis, or in stronger terms it is a crisis of the capitalist system, and as such it has historical causes that go back to at least the 1970s (Harman 2009; Tombazos 2019). The crisis originated from the financial sector, whose expansion and colonisation of the economy, society, and political systems of the West has been unprecedented in the last four decades (Calhoun 2011). It is a crisis of neoliberalism, as a distinct phase of capitalist development that has facilitated the privatisation of several domains previously thought of as being public goods, the commodification of things previously operating on a non-market logic and the increase of social inequality. However, financialisation and neoliberalism are the forms in which capitalism has evolved into after the 1970s crisis of the Keynesian form (Saad Filho 2010). This means that examining the crisis within these two distinct, yet parallel forms is necessary but not sufficient, and it might even be constraining and distorting. Financialisation underpins neoliberalism but neoliberalism is not reducible to financialisation. Both are historical phenomena and institutionalised contexts of the production process and to understand their emergence as well as their operation at the societal level one must examine deeper structures, modalities and forces – at the level of the state, social ideology, and class dynamics (Seymour 2014; Fine and Saad Filho 2017).

The 2008 crisis began in the US and was soon diffused globally, hitting Europe and especially the weaker economies of the Eurozone with great severity. The limited productive investment in the preceding decades combined with the falling real wages in the US as well as major European countries produced a corporate savings glut. The accumulated cash was lent out to consumers as well as governments keeping the global economy growing at the cost of rising private and public debt. Financialisation and neoliberalism which were the solutions to the exhaustion of the Keynesian model of the golden postwar era expanded the volatility of the capitalist system, as a whole (Harman 2009). The crisis originated in the banking sector as the recklessness and short-termism that had guided banking investment resulted in a huge real estate bubble and a mass of mortgages that could not be serviced.

Bankers postponed the bursting of the bubble as much as they could, making huge profits in the process through the invention of ever more sophisticated tactics of spreading the risks through securities and then their derivatives. There was a limit however to how much this system of alchemy and tricks and creative accounting could last as the guaranteeing by banks of each other's credit against default strengthened their connections and increased both the possibility and the magnitude of the imminent collapse (Calhoun 2011). The collapse of the huge US investment bank, Lehman Brothers set a sort of domino process in motion spreading the crisis to the global financial system and to the global economy.

The extension and diffusion of the financial crisis across space and domains meant that immediate political measures were needed to contain it. These measures initially took the form of governments supplying credit and bailing out banks, considered 'too big to fail' and subsequently initiating a series of austerity measures in order to adapt to the financial meltdown, and maintain fiscal balances. In the Eurozone, where governments had no control of monetary policy mechanisms, and since the financial crisis was threatening the faulty architecture of the 'euro' itself, this role was undertaken by the European Union itself. Greece was the first country to experience the new institution of the Troika, (the combined mechanism set in place that is comprising of the European Commission (EC), the European Central Bank (ECB) and the International Monetary Fund (IMF) which was invited to contribute both in its financial capacity and in its capacity as a technocratic body which had conducted and overseen analogous operations in third world countries in the last decades of the 20th Century.

In Europe, the crisis developed rapidly from a financial to an economic and a sovereign debt crisis hitting particularly hard Southern Europe and Ireland. The Troika effectively took over control of Greece, Ireland, Portugal, and Cyprus where the states were in imminent danger to default payments bailing them out and imposing a series of structural and institutional reforms. In Spain and Italy, this happened sort of informally without these two big countries having to undergo the procedure of the Support Mechanism and all its potentially politically destabilising and somewhat humiliating aspects of having teams of foreign technocrats entering Ministries, processing records and dictating policy on a trimonthly basis for several years. The famous secret or confidential letters of the European Central Bank Governor to the Spanish and Italian Prime Ministers were sufficient in precipitating a series of changes in economic, social and employment policy in neoliberal directions (Moreno 2014). In fact, the external force was so overwhelming that surprised even domestic forces of neoliberalism that desired many such policies but deemed them to be impossible. Meardi (2014) shows for example that with respect to employment relations, employers were able to gain reforms that prior to the crisis could only dream of.

In the countries rescued by formal bail-out programmes, sometimes including bail-in schemes as well, the process of instituting socio-economic and employment reforms was overseen very directly by the Troika itself which managed and supervised closely the whole affair. The treatment of the South European crisis-stricken countries however should not be seen as something exceptional or unique. It was a moment in a broader process of development of the EU which in its attempt to deal with the crisis instituted a series of mechanisms which became known as the 'new economic governance' extending to all member states. These involved a shift from the previous soft governance approach involving various consultation procedures and social dialogue to more top-down approaches which moved decision making power upwards and increasingly imposing these decisions through 'conditionality' practices (Karakioulafi 2018). This 'conditionality' strategy extensively used by the IMF in the context of structural adjustment programmes in the third world in the 1980s and 1990s was also used by the EU in the context of its eastward enlargement at the turn of the Century but was significantly extended with the onset of the economic crisis.

Although there were diverging factors and causal mechanisms in the crises of different South European countries, the treatment they all received by the Troika was strikingly similar. Cut-back management in terms of public expenses, privatisation and marketisation in the public services, shrinking and re-organisation of social policy, wage cuts and increased tax contributions and deregulation of the labour market. Despite the variations with respect to the timing of each intervention and the particularities of each state as well as the prevailing political dynamics, there was an over-arching framework that was common guiding the Troika operations and this involved both the principles and the substance as well as the modalities and the mechanisms.

Behind the seemingly technocratic and politically neutral accounting spirit and the quantification rationale guiding the 'support programmes', which were to be sure real enough, there was overt ideology and politics. Doctrinaire both in terms of positive ideas as to 'how the economy works' as well as normative ones as to 'how the economy should work'. And the Troika interventions were political in another sense – they were fully conscious of the power dynamics in each case, of the risks and the stakes at play and quite pragmatic in some cases at the same time as ruthless in others.

The role of the media in the management of the South European crisis by the EU and national elites cannot be over-emphasised. The mainstream media were indispensable tools in hands of governments in their efforts to manipulate public opinion, present austerity policies as beneficial in the long term and as inevitable in the immediate term. It was the international media that set the tune and constructed the pillars of the narrative of the inefficient economies of the European periphery, their wasteful public sectors and populations who 'spent more than they produced'. It was the adaptation and adoption of that rhetoric however at the national level by the national media that was more effective in generating sufficient support for welfare cuts and market-enhancing reforms. The narrative constructed in defence of austerity was able to make inroads across the political spectrum and win over segments from many political spaces as it tied in with pre-existing dominant discourses about the need for modernisation and development and in which northern Europe was a model.

To be sure, austerity remained largely unpopular, its necessity doubted, and its implementation contested. The media might not have been successful in manufacturing consent for the policies themselves, but they were sufficiently successful in propagating the selected facts and values with which the crisis was understood, and its management framed (Herman and Chomsky, 1988). As such the media assisted the national elites to make damage control, partially neutralising societal mobilisations and preventing popular reactions from surpassing the threshold that could threaten the established order. Using classic divide and rule tactics such as pitting one social group against the other, pounding out neoliberal policy suggestions as self-evident truths and painting the image of protests as irrational, irrelevant or futile the mainstream media's assistance to the European and national elites was invaluable.

The economic crisis in Southern Europe and especially its management provoked significant political upheavals in most South European countries. The biggest political restructuring as a direct implication of the economic crisis and its handling took place in Greece, the country where the crisis developed into a humanitarian disaster and where the Troika intervention was at its most brutal. The first significant development was the rise of technocratic governments in Greece and in Italy, headed by Loucas Papademos and Mario Monti respectively,[6] to oversee the first bunch of austerity measures imposed before handing power back to politicians (Verney and Bosco 2013). In Italy, the populist Five Star Movement emerged as the new player and was soon able through an alliance with the right and the far right to rise to executive power. In Greece it was the left in the form of SYRIZA that was able to capitalise on the anti-austerity protests, oust the Panhellenic Socialist Movement

(PASOK) from the centre-left space of the political spectrum and in 2015 assume executive power as well, but proved ultimately unable to change the country's fortunes.

In Portugal, a centre-left coalition came to power after the end of the Memorandum of Understanding and modestly yet persistently attempted to reverse some of the worse impacts of the crisis and austerity era. In Spain, the most significant change was the rise of the PODEMOS who had been however unable to rise to executive power as the Spanish Socialist Workers Party (PSOE), despite the damage it suffered, did not have the fortune of PASOK. In 2019 PODEMOS, after uniting with the bulk of the Left was forced to also collaborate with PSOE entering as a junior partner the PSOE led coalition government. In Cyprus, although the political system also lost support and legitimacy it proved relatively resilient as no new force was able to rise to prominence (Ioannou and Charalambous 2017). The left wing AKEL which headed the government when the crisis hit the country lost many votes and two presidential elections since but remained the 2nd strongest party and supporting more strongly an anti-austerity stance once it moved into opposition.

## A Note on the Method, Analytic Approach, and Historicity of this Book

This book was written during the last three years but the programme of research on which it is based began almost a decade back, following in real time the developments which it discusses. At the time of the completion of my PhD thesis, which focused on employment relations in Cyprus, in 2011, the economic crisis was already in full sway in Southern Europe sinking societies into austerity and restructuring labour markets across the board. I initially focused on Greece, as on the one hand, it was where the crisis was deepest and its management most dramatic, and on the other hand its geographical, cultural, and political proximity to Cyprus as well as the tight connection of Greek and Cypriot banking systems made the crisis' repercussions more directly impactful on the society I lived in. The crisis in Spain was also evolving and encompassing the political sphere, but it still felt somewhat remote. In early 2013 when the crisis peaked in Cyprus and the bail-in instrument surfaced in the public sphere, I read in the media about reactions in Spain, fearing that a Cypriot bail-in could set a precedent.

It was clear, at least since 2012, that what was going on was a Eurozone crisis and that developments in the countries of Eurozone's periphery were directly related. To adequately understand the impact of the crisis in one South European country one needed to not only examine the 'vertical' axis linking the EU level and the national level, but also to assess 'horizontally' multiple national levels and compare their different experience of the same crisis. Different national settings can both converge as well as diverge while faced with the same phenomenon as different actors may be mobilised, different coalitions can be formed in each case and ultimately the terms of conflict can be framed and fought differently (Thelen 2018). The comparative method adopted in the analysis which makes up this book aims to understand institutional change, including both political and legal change, occurring in Southern Europe during the 2010s as a consequence of the global 2008 financial crisis and its subsequent transposition in the Eurozone. It is essentially an exercise in international political economy and in comparative institutional analysis with a focus on the employment and social policy domains. The main research question addressed by the book is how the liberalisation and deregulation process, intended by the EU and facilitated by the Troika administered bail-outs, progressed in three different countries and what was the effect of the measures adopted in each case.

Yet, it differs from other international political economy and comparative institutional analysis accounts in two significant ways. Firstly, the discussion is not restricted to the institutional order but also examines the ideological context in which political and legal change was framed, promoted, and challenged including how the media transmitted, expressed, and moulded societal ideology. Secondly, it heightens the significance of agency in the process of change, focusing on how actors, in particular social movements, and political parties, but also trade unions and employers, mobilised and demobilised, contested and acquiesced, exploited and were obstructed by, the on-going institutional reforms. As a result, the book synthesises multiple insights and provides a comprehensive account of the crisis decade experience in Southern Europe.

In addition to the review of the main secondary literature, published about the impact of the crisis on employment relations and social policy in Southern Europe in the 2010s, and especially on Spain, Greece, and Cyprus, empirically it draws on fieldwork conducted intermittently in the last five years and is also based on diverse sources examined such as press articles, reports, collective agreements and statements by industrial relations' actors and other grey literature. Additionally, a series of interviews were conducted in Spain, Greece, and Cyprus in 2019 and 2020, twelve of which are also cited. These expert interviews with trade union leaders and researchers and policy advisors cover gaps in the literature and were useful in documenting motivations and understandings of actors and connecting analytically knowledge and experience of the crisis impact from different perspectives enhancing overall the explanatory account.

At a time when a new crisis provoked by the Covid-19 pandemic is gaining pace, a crisis that is centred on the disruption of the labour process and the labour market, a discussion of the legacy of the previous crisis on the world of labour becomes highly topical. Departing from the political economy of capitalism, zooming in to examine the political economy of employment and work, and adjusting the analytic frame to the institutional level, the book illuminates the connections between different spheres: labour law and industrial relations systems, class and ideological structures and economic, social, and political dynamics. Oscillating between the macro, the micro, and the meso levels and analysing phenomena at different levels of abstraction allows a more complete understanding of the process of historical change.

Labour law frames and is at the same time framed by the industrial relations system for which it serves as a regulatory context and an institutional background. Class relations and ideological dispositions with which they are entangled, understood with and acted upon, both underpin social and political change and are at the same time shaped by it. By counterposing these inter-connected spheres and analysing them simultaneously, the book constructs a comprehensive and synthetic account of the condition of the labour market in Southern Europe since the crisis. The structuring and restructuring of the field of employment is explained by examining how political elites, representatives of capital, and trade unions perceived the changing economic environment and how far their responses directed the path of that change.

The conceptualisation of employment in this book draws from the definition developed by Ruth Dukes of the contract for work as simultaneously an instance of economic, social, and legal behaviour that requires to be analysed in its specific economic, social, and legal context. Being a member of the 'Work On Demand' research project team at the University of Glasgow during the last two years has further enhanced the multi-disciplinary character of my analytic perspective inducing me to focus on the frontier between social science and labour law. I conceptualise class relations in Marxian terms and like trade unionism I approach them as being at the same time structure and agency, basis and component of the institutional order but not reduced to its confines and potentially able not only to modify but also to rupture it.

Law, like policy, lies in the intersection between politics and social ideology. Labour law systems and social policy attempt to order economic practices and regulate social relations. They are also shaped by existing material conditions and the norms that prevail in society. Only by examining both ends of this relationship can institutional change be adequately understood (Dukes and Streeck 2020a). Labour market reforms and austerity policies need to be set in their context, both with respect to the moment of their adoption and with respect to the moment of their implementation. Institutional change cannot be fully explained unless the political and ideological dynamics prevailing are also brought within the analytic lens. Thus, the intended and actual institutional and legal reforms are discussed taking account of history and traditions, structures, and norms, and ultimately the shifts in politics and class relations (Streeck 2010). This is done both at the general EU and Southern Europe level, but also separately within the three different national settings.

At this point a clarification is in order. The book talks about Southern Europe in its title but focuses on three South European countries, namely Spain, Greece, and Cyprus. This decision was based on an intension to balance the general and the specific, the breadth and the depth of the analysis and the ability to have a rigorous comparative analysis yet at the same time maintaining the focus on the broader region and the historical trend. Many of the developments described and explained also occurred in identical or analogous ways in other South European countries, especially Portugal and Italy, the other two states of the 'PIGS' category.[7] However, for practical reasons of space availability and the theoretical goal of maintaining the narrative coherence and not overburden the book structure with the analysis of two or even more additional national contexts with their unique elements, nuances and specificities, references to other South European countries were kept to the minimum. In this way, it was possible to present more comprehensively the experience of the crisis in the three main national settings selected. Spain, Greece, and Cyprus, as three countries varying in size, industrial relations systems, institutional orders, and political traditions, yet sharing common elements in their historical trajectories, the structure of their economies and the temporality and magnitude of the crisis that hit them constitute a fruitful matrix for this exercise in comparative political economy.

## The Focus and Structure of the Book

Whereas this chapter introduced the conceptual framework and the general thematic area, the next narrows the focus to account in more detail for the specifics of employment relations in southern Europe. Neoliberal globalisation, migrant labour and gender are examined in terms of how they reshaped the labour force, social production, and class restructuring. The EU policy framework on employment is discussed and its role in the deregulation and re-regulation processes already underway before the onset of the crisis. The industrial relations systems in Southern Europe are then outlined identifying the key characteristics of employers and trade unions and the labour force structure. Chapter Two then traces the development of the economic crisis, its management, and the major changes it brought about in institutional, political, and social relations, transforming the labour market and class relations in southern Europe. It also discusses the consequences of the austerity politics, the deterioration of employment terms and living standards, the rise of poverty and social inequality and the political upheaval provoked.

Chapter Three examines the Spanish experience of the crisis. The collapse of the real estate market which was the motor of economic growth since the 1990s effectively destroyed the construction industry and the banking sector with which it was associated. With sky-rocketing unemployment and bankruptcies, the Spanish state begun bailing out banks and cutting its central and regional budgets while as the crisis deepened the European Central Bank had to come to its rescue. Due to its size, Spain, like Italy, was treated differently to Greece, Portugal, and Cyprus. The financial aid given was not accompanied by a formal political monitoring of the programme of structural reform and the implementation of austerity policies. The social and the political system crises that accompanied the economic crisis were in some respects more profound than other countries leading to the emergence and relative success of various social movements. Social mobilisation brought new players into the political system which was destabilised while the pre-existing industrial relations system was also partly restructured. As the economy contracted, the overall standard of living dropped while fiscal austerity and social policy cuts in conjunction with declining wages and weakening of trade unionism resulted in deteriorating labour market conditions especially for young people, increasing poverty and emigration.

Chapter Four focuses on Greece, which faced the most severe crisis of the south European countries and after a decade of austerity still resembles a war destroyed territory. Unemployment and underemployment were already relatively high before the crisis and soon after the austerity policies begun, they climbed further up as the country sank into a recessionary spiral. In parallel to cuts in public spending, increases in taxation and fiscal reforms in general, a series of political and legal measures were undertaken that overhauled the Greek labour relations system. Collective bargaining was severely weakened, and low wages were institutionalised in both the public and private sectors. These highly contested policies of the 'Memoranda' provoked mass protests and subsequently a comprehensive restructuring of the political system. The main aim of this chapter is to identify the drivers of the restructuring process and to assess the agency and role of different external and internal forces in producing the shift in both the employment and the social and political domains.

The Cyprus case is the subject of Chapter Five. The employment relations field in Cyprus was fragmented and facing considerable pressures prior to the crisis. Despite the high growth rates and the relatively low unemployment, the deregulation of employment relations, the erosion of collective bargaining and the weakening of trade unionism set a changing context in the labour market and the class structure. The recession exacerbated all these processes as the shrinking of the economy during the crisis and its management through austerity tilted further the balance of power in favour of capital. Precariousness became more widespread as the recession led to increasing unemployment, underemployment, emigration and drop in wages. In addition to accounting for the above the main research question posed by this chapter concerns the retreat and resilience of trade unionism in the new 'post crisis' context and the dynamics that escorted it and which shape this altered or in some respects 'new' employment field.

Chapter Six brings together the three preceding country case study chapters and subjects them to a comparison at different aspects and dimensions. It identifies the convergences and divergences in terms of the forms taken by the crisis, its management, and its consequences. Although the causes and the character of the crisis in the three countries differed, in Greece being primarily a debt crisis while in Spain and more so in Cyprus being essentially a banking crisis, the recipes suggested by the Troika were in some respects identical and in others analogous. Also, although pre-crisis socioeconomic conditions in the three countries were different and remained different after the crisis, the impact of the austerity measures was in all cases severe. Finally, despite operating in different national institutional frameworks, and varying in structure and operation, trade unionism in the three countries has proven similarly incapable of resisting the rapid deterioration in employment relations and protecting its members and the wider society from the worse consequences of the crisis. The main research aim of this chapter is the comparative assessment of the crisis management and implications in order to illustrate variations in terms of institutional reordering, public discourse and political dynamics as well as identify the forms of class resistance, the impact of social movement activism and the limits of change. This can be used to discuss the variations in the general as well as the group specific impact on employment and society of the austerity decade in the three countries.

Chapter Seven offers a preliminary examination of the new and ongoing economic crisis provoked by the management of the Covid-19 pandemic. As growth had returned in the second half of the 2010 decade, the gradual expansion of the economy and the drop in unemployment along with the moderate but steady increase in wages brought optimism in Southern Europe that the recovery of what was lost was during the crisis was within sight. The rapid spread of the pandemic however with Italy and Spain being among the most severely hit countries in Europe and the lock-down policies enforced provoked a shock to the economy in early 2020 and raised again the specter of an economic collapse. This chapter discusses the temporary relief measures adopted and their logic and tentatively assesses the expected impact on employment and class relations as a result of the prolonged decline in economic activity of key sectors such as tourism, the shrinking of consumption and the rising public debt as well as the political tensions surfacing at national and EU levels.

The concluding Chapter Eight utilises the preceding historical and comparative analysis to explicate the internal and external dynamics of change in South European employment relations and induce some more general insights about ideology, class struggle and contentious politics. At the same time, it sets the crisis decade in a historical frame, summing up the findings also highlighting the limits of change and the elements of continuity. Finally, some modest projections are made concerning the future trends of employment relations and the prospects and potentialities of trade unionism and the politics of class in contemporary times.

## Notes

1 A comprehensive review of this literature is beyond the aim and scope of this book, and I will restrict the analysis to a brief introduction to map out its main contours.
2 Although the debate on precarity and even the notion of the 'precariat' predates Standing's famous book in 2011, he was the one who framed the division between the precarious workers and the rest in such absolute and stark terms opening thus the way for both mainstreaming and popularisation of the term 'precariat'. I consider Standing's formulation about the emergence of a new, distinct social class, as too schematic and exaggerated, and the notion of higher or lower labour market attachment as a defining characteristic theoretically insufficient and empirically unfounded. At the same time, irrespective of the diverging view of many labour studies and industrial relations scholars, Standing's work managed to significantly influence stratification analysis and policy debate in the 2010s.
3 Although craft unionism has its roots in pre-modern or early modern artisan forms and guild organisational rationales, it is an essentially modern phenomenon because of the capitalist socio-economic context in which it appeared and operated (industrialisation, labour market, wage form etc.) and because of the mass movement and representational roles it assumed. From the beginning, however, broader, and more inclusive organisational forms were needed, propagated, and instituted. Industrial unionism, bringing together all the workers of each industry, both skilled and unskilled, was a superior structure, more progressive and just, and more effective at both the economic and the political fronts. By the early decades of the 20th century the logic of industrial organisation had prevailed.
4 The first political split of the labour movement was that between social-democrats and anarcho-syndicalists in the 1870s while the second one was between socialists and communists in the 1920s.
5 For that exercise one may read the thought provoking articles of Silver and Arrighi (2011), Wallerstein (2011), and Frazer (2011).
6 These interim, unelected governments were appointed after the escalating crisis led to the resignations of Papantreou's and Berlusconi's governments and had a temporary cross-party support in the Greek and Italian parliaments.
7 PIGS was coined as an acronym for Portugal, Italy, Greece, and Spain, the first four EU states that went into financial trouble and required assistance from the EU. The clear, negative connotation of the cheeky acronym is illustrative of the arrogance prevailing among the EU elites with respect to the European periphery.

# 2 Employment Relations and Crisis Management

This chapter examines the main parameters of the employment and class structure in Southern Europe focusing on the state of the labour market at the time of the crisis. The reshaping of the labour force through the processes of neoliberal globalisation and the influx of migrant labour and the full entry of women into the labour market is discussed along with the EU legal and policy framework. The development of the crisis and how it was managed is outlined in terms of the broader Europeanisation process shedding light on what was central and what was peripheral, what was cause and what was effect in the changing institutional order. Subsequently, the key characteristics of employers and trade unions, industrial relations systems and labour force composition in south European countries are mapped out, briefly sketching the political context and the class power correlation upon the arrival of the crisis.

The content of the Troika support programmes is examined only in so far as and to the extent that the policy and legal reforms adopted had a direct or indirect impact on employment and social policy effecting changes on the labour market and social welfare. The more general impact of austerity on south European societies is also analysed to complete the picture of deteriorating economic conditions at the societal level and shifts in class relations. Finally, the declining living standard and the increasing poverty is discussed in relation to social mobilisation and political upheavals examining the causes and consequences of changing political dynamics.

The aim of the chapter is to provide an overview of the field of employment and its regulation and the change occurring in the last two decades. A second aim is to outline the unfolding crisis and how European Union policy adapted to it, forcing national states, which were essentially unable to refinance their debts, to introduce or intensify market-enhancing reforms. This is set against an evolving contestation landscape, the main contours of which are sketched to foreground the analysis which will follow in the subsequent single country case studies. Austerity has not been just a set of policies – it has been an overarching political framework sustained for a decade with some of its key features fortified by politics, ideology, and law. The austerity milieu has not just resulted in exacerbated poverty and inequality. It has also shaken political systems, precisely because contesting austerity meant going against a dominant modality, against a comprehensive worldview backed by brute economic force.

This chapter then serves as the historical contextualisation for the book. Coming after the thematic and theoretical introduction offered in Chapter One, Chapter Two presents the evolution of the labour field in Southern Europe as this has been shaped by the European and national policy frameworks, how these frameworks functioned and how they were reformed during the crisis years. It identifies the broader policy trends and assesses how these emerged through the interaction of supranational and national forces in the temporality of the economic crisis. The fiscal and monetary constraints imposed on Spain, Greece, and Cyprus due to their European Union and Eurozone membership are discussed in relation to both the causes and the consequences of the crisis.

## Neoliberal Globalisation, Migrant Labour, Gender and Class in Southern Europe

By the turn of the Century, South European countries were experiencing both the positive and the negative results of their increasing integration in the dynamics of the international economy. Whereas globalisation processes increased the competitive pressure on manufacturing and agriculture necessitating diversification in the case of the former and EU subsidies in the case of the latter to slow down its shrinking, the service sectors expanded further. The substantial development of digital technology and communications in the last decades of the 20th Century boosted the further servicisation of the economy increased professional, managerial and administrative work positions in both the public and the private sectors expanding the labour aristocracy or new middle-class stratum of better off employees. As economic growth resulted in increasing living and educational standards of the local labour force, labour shortages were created in manual and unskilled work which were covered by yet further internal migration from the countryside to the urban centres and international migration from poorer regions such as the Balkans, the Middle East and North and Central Africa but also South East and Central Asia and in the case of Spain and Portugal also Latin America.

Beyond the substantial increase in the proportion of women entering the labour market in the last decades of the 20th Century, the influx of migrant labour further transformed the composition of the labour force. Combined with the changes in the character of work, facilitated by technological and organisational factors and economic restructurings, this resulted in shifts in the processes of social production and social reproduction. New dynamics were developed with respect to the labour process and class relations but also family and welfare. The sharp increase of female formal education and the Europeanisation process which contributed to the promotion of female participation in the formal labour market, especially in professional and technical professions, resulted in the female employment rate rising sharply since the early 1980s and approaching the male employment rate by the late 2000s (Karamesini 2012). The rate of childbirth decreased, and its timing was delayed, while more generally old familistic structures were eroded as couples' informal cohabitation and out-of-wedlock births, divorce, and single parenthood all increased. However, the family remains more important as an institution of social care and material support in Southern Europe compared to Northern Europe, taken for granted by governments that exploit the strong household micro-solidarity and intra-family pooling of resources reinforcing a social policy model of over-exploitation of family resources primarily provided by women (Salido and Moreno 2012).

The mass entry of women into the labour market was a decisive moment in the struggle for gender equality in Southern Europe. Nevertheless, the increased economic independence achieved by women did not fully extend to the private / home context and did not liberate them from unpaid housework and reproductive work which disproportionally continues to burden them. It is important to note that the key driver for many women's entry into formal employment was the inadequacy of the male wage to support the family in the changed circumstances from the mid-1970s onwards. Furthermore, in the labour market, women came to occupy disproportionally temporary, part-time, and low paid positions and were concentrated in feminised occupations such as cleaners, salespersons, clerical workers, nurses, kindergarten teachers, and child-carers.

The women belonging to the new, middle-class stratum of better off employees which expanded substantially by the turn of the Century, in the context of the rise of office-based work, were however able to also free themselves from some of the household care responsibilities by employing migrant care workers. Beginning in the 1990s, such workers, primarily south east Asian women, arrived in increasing numbers in western as well as south European countries fulfilling a new function, that of the 'servants of globalization' as Parreñas (2001) aptly termed it. The combination of an ageing population, highly gendered notions that care is women's work and thus men contributing little to it, and the absence of state infrastructure in southern Europe on the one hand produced the demand, while global inequality and the development of global transportation on the other hand facilitated the supply of these workers. Typically, they work in exploitative conditions deriving not only from their class position but also because of their gender and ethnicity (Panayiotopoulos 2005). Although the combination of immigration regime, gender and employment status renders domestic care workers vulnerable, differences in the national regulatory frameworks shape in diverging ways their working conditions and rights (Pavlou 2016).

Migrant workers in South European countries are generally concentrated in low-paid jobs in labour-intensive industries. Beyond domestic work, they populate the labour force in agriculture and construction and are often found as general unskilled workers working back of house in warehouses, industrial kitchens, and buildings cleaning. Whereas there is some variation in the trajectories of migration and the predominant ethnic composition of the migrant labour force in different South European countries, it is accurate to say that the integration of migrants into the host countries remains at best partial if not limited. Besides being over-represented in low paid and precarious jobs, migrants are more likely to work informally and are less likely to be trade union members compared to natives. This is essentially a global phenomenon connected to the fact that immigration laws tend to impose various formal restrictions on migrant workers' right to lawful stay (Anderson 2010). Migrant workers are typically granted temporary work visas which are difficult to renew even in industries where they cover permanent labour shortages as states try to avoid giving them residency and subsequently citizenship rights.

While many migrants also view their stay as temporary and leave after the expiry of their visa, some return, while others stay under a regime of informality or semi-informality. Occasional attempts to regularise the migrant workers in the interest of combating informal employment often collide with immigration policy which aims to prevent the growth of permanent migrant residents and the consequent rights deriving thereof. In Greece SYRIZA government's attempt to regularise atypical migrant work resulted in the institution of a new regime of 'para-legality' whereby work was made legal while residence remained illegal, resulting in the further erosion of labour law (Kapsalis 2018).

Trade unions gradually reversed their initial opposition to migrant workers to a friendlier stance of incorporation. However, the shift from a policy of exclusion and marginalisation of migrant workers to one of inclusion and recruitment was neither comprehensive nor complete. There were numerous cases in the 2000s when trade unions ignored migrant workers and tolerated violations of their rights even in unionised workplaces. Sometimes the recruitment of migrant workers to the trade unions was formal rather than substantive and was restricted to individualised support and trade union services rather than full representation and collective bargaining coverage sustaining thus the existing fragmentation of the labour force (Ioannou 2015). In industries with weak unionisation, migrant workers were fully neglected and often did not even get to find out anything about trade unions, even what a trade union is.

From the perspective of migrant workers, there is also an ambivalence towards trade unions and hesitation to join. Especially in the early phase of their employment, reluctance to join is a consequence of fear of their employer's possible reaction operating in addition to doubts as to whether the trade union could and would stand up for them. Gradually, however, migrant workers in unionised workplaces would come to see their joining of a trade union as a means of better integration within the firm and the host country. Yet, often, they remain passive and instrumentalist in their relations with trade unions (Danaj et al. 2018). Overall, although there is substantial variation, if a generalisation can be made is that the integration of migrants in their host societies remains in the best case incomplete. Southern Europe, unlike Northern Europe, has only become a place with a mass influx of migrant workers in recent decades, a process slowed down by the economic crisis. This coincided with the broader European trend of the rise of xenophobic ideas, diffused prejudice, and the resurgence of racial stereotyping. In such contexts, ethnic networks among migrant workers also fulfilled the function of communal solidarity and protection and were strengthened further enhancing at the same further the cleavages and the fragmentation of the labour force.

## The Labour Market and EU Policy on Employment Relations

The EU refrained from developing a comprehensive agenda on employment relations. Core issues of domestic labour law systems such as wage regulation, freedom of association, and the right to strike have always been excluded from the legislative competencies of the Union (Deakin and Koukiadaki 2013). EU policy was restricted to more peripheral issues such as the combat of discrimination, work-life balance measures, the promotion of labour market activation policies and procedural rights such as information and consultation on employment and redundancies. The Working Time Directive is perhaps the most substantive regulatory intervention at the EU level – yet its very loose framing, its ambivalence and lack of clarity, the possibility of derogations as well as its lax interpretation by courts in the last two decades render it much weaker as a regulatory instrument than intended and hoped for (Nowak 2018).

With respect to non-standard employment, the EU policy priority has been to combat discrimination and to normalise these employment statuses as equally legitimate and carrying analogous rights and protections. Hence the directives on fixed-term and part-time work and more recently the temporary agency work directive. Despite the equal treatment legislation, however, many part-time workers, like fixed term and temporary workers, continued to enjoy fewer employment rights and social protections (Eurofound 2020a). More importantly the inherent difficulty to pursue labour rights in courts, especially non-core ones and by vulnerable, often non-unionised workers who are the ones needing these rights most, renders the EU legal order in labour affairs largely irrelevant or to say the least inadequate.

At the same time, the impact of the EU on national industrial relations systems, employment practices and consequently class relations, has been significant and largely negative. Through its constitution, at both the microeconomic and the macroeconomic levels, the EU architecture prioritised the smooth operation of markets and competition within and across national borders while the social dimension was treated as secondary and as emanating from and within the bounds of the economic (Tsitsiou 2020). Improved working conditions and living standards were hailed as a goal, fundamental social rights were celebrated in the dominant discourse but little of substance in terms of policy or law was ever instituted to directly promote these. These were expected to follow somewhat automatically, through well-functioning free markets to which the emphasis shifted, not only by policy-making bodies but also by the Court of Justice of the European Union. While collective bargaining and social dialogue were recognised as key pillars of the employment and social policy fields, and were nominally supported, at the substantive level, the priority has steadily and unquestionably been the promotion of flexibility in the labour market.

Employment protection legislation was seen to be imposing rigidities in the labour market preventing firms from adapting to the ever-changing economic environment and non-standard employment was seen to be not only benefiting firms but also society through the lowering of unemployment. This was a gradual process beginning in the last decades of the 20th Century and accelerating by the first decade of the 21st Century. Although there was some recognition of the increased insecurity inherently associated with flexible labour markets, little was done to address this. By the mid-2000s, the idea of enhancing social protection to compensate for the decreasing of employment protection which was the raison d'être of flexible labour markets gained ground at EU level decision-making bodies (European Commission 2007). This idea, derived from the Scandinavian experience and made concrete via the flexicurity paradigm of Denmark, postulated that increased mobility in the labour market was desirable and that the state should promote it also by offering support in the form of welfare and re-training during the period that people found themselves between jobs.

However, this presupposed moderating the neoliberal rationale governing employment and social policy more broadly and strengthening the welfare state for which political commitment was lacking. In any case by the end of the 2000s, the financial crisis speeded up the liberalisation process of both employment protection and welfare systems already under way (Becker 2009). Budget questions set the tone of all policy-making, and in this context, fiscal discipline was overtly presented as a technical rather than a political decision (Supiot 2013). The uncertainty, intensified through the destabilising influence of European policy on national welfare states, labour market flexibilisation and collective bargaining destabilisation strengthened the hand of the 'real' neoliberals and the idea of flexicurity was blown off course (Crouch 2013). In Southern Europe concrete security measures were never adopted and as cost containment became the ultimate priority during the crisis years, it was labour market flexibility not labour market flexicurity that set the policy tone (Ladi and Graziano 2014).

The attempt to unify the European labour markets continued but this proved even more difficult in the crisis years. The differences in the local labour market conditions and minimum wage levels provoked increasing institutional difficulties to attempts to set a common wage policy. Attempts to monitor the effects of wage-setting systems and amend, abolish, or weaken indexation mechanisms were also not successful before the crisis allowed the EU to fortify these attempts with conditionality clauses. Overall, the effort to unify the European labour markets often went in parallel with attempts to deregulate labour law, as the prevailing idea was that the rigidity of labour law was blocking the flexible operation of the labour market. The crisis was thus used as a pretext to carry out reforms designed to boost business flexibility and reduce the alleged complexity and strictness of labour law (Wallusch and Wozniak-Jechorek 2015).

The Europeanisation process aiming to integrate the old and the new member states was in theory a shared goal but difficult to achieve and, in some aspects, contested. For example, a common wage policy was questionable as there was a diverging reaction of unemployment to changes in real wages: negative for new states, positive for the old ones (Wallusch and Wozniak-Jechorek 2015). The crisis increased the pressure, served to overcome objections and hesitations, and speeded up the process of Europeanisation, akin to putting Europeanisation on the fast-forward mode (Ladi and Graziano 2014). The rising bond market tensions and capital flights from countries such as Spain and Italy forced the national governments to embark on significant labour market reforms. The goal of increasing national competitiveness in some cases could suffice in the new crisis conditions to induce governments to liberalisation reforms. In other cases, it was the conditionality clauses in the support programmes and the fiscal compact policy provisions adopted at EU level that allowed what was in 1990s and 2000s mere recommendations for flexibilisation to become enshrined in domestic legal and policy frameworks.

Overall, there was little difference in the substance and philosophy of the messages of the European Commission to South European states before and during the crisis. However, the prevailing emergency conditions made the EU more forceful, its recommendations for policy reform more specific and detailed, and with a much tighter timing for their implementation. More crucially the ability of the EU to push through its agenda through the formal procedures was complemented and strengthened not only through the new conditionality instruments but also by means of backroom diplomacy (Pavolini et al. 2015). This can also be seen in the processes of economic governance instituted during the crisis and made universal. The fiscal compact, the Six-pack, the Two-pack, and other tools instituted in the early 2010s became essentially integral parts of the EU's socio-economic constitution, subsuming both employment and social policy within the now prioritised fiscal, monetary, and immigration policy (Streeck 2019). The European Semester process with its Country Specific Recommendations lies at the heart of this and is indicative not only of the prevailing neoliberal philosophy but of the ambiguities and contradictions that constitute it too.

The management of the economic crisis not only put pressure on the socio-economic order of the national states eroding the stability and legitimacy of existing institutional arrangements. It also put pressure on the ideological order, at both national and EU levels threatening the basic political consensus upon which the European project was founded (Heyes 2011). German Ordoliberalism remained the key agenda setter and retained its veto power over alternative economic thinking (Young 2015), but in these conditions it was also more openly contested than ever before. The most important line of division and confrontation became that between defenders of national welfare states and Europeanist 'reformers' aligned with the supranational European institutions which continue with even greater stealth the pre-crisis market – building project (Streeck 2019).

Beyond the rifts opening-up between groupings of states at the level of the European Council on several issues during the crisis period, there were also more quasi-permanent tensions within the EU apparatus. For example, the tacit competition between the DG Finance and DG Employment in the Commission can account to some extent for the contradictions that characterised the European Semester process documents, between 'regressive' and 'progressive' Country Specific Recommendations. The conflict at policy level between diverging goals of balanced budgets and social inclusion, flexible labour markets and labour rights is ultimately what constitutes the bigger picture within the EU apparatus. This conflict had a winner during the crisis, reflected in the fact that the Six-Pack ensures that only some of the Country Specific Recommendations carry penalties if not enforced; and these are the regressive ones (Erne 2015). In this context, the Commission's attempt to involve the trade unions in the Semester process, a framework whose philosophy goes in contrast with the most basic trade union concerns and over which their input could only ever have been limited, concerning peripheral issues, was more symbolic than substantive (Eurofound 2016, 2017a). Beyond the employers' structural advantage given their better mobilisation capacity and better knowledge of how the two-level game of European governance is played, 'the argument of force is always stronger than the force of argument' (Erne 2015: 356).

## The Economic Crisis and its Management via the Troika Rescue Operations

As mentioned in Chapter One, the roots of the 2008 economic crisis stretch back to the late 1970s: the exhaustion of the Keynesian model and the rise of neoliberalism. The deregulation of the financial system since the 1980s and the increasing mobility of capital in conjunction with the lowering of taxation rates and the increased capacity of corporations to evade taxation progressively over the last decades rendered states more dependent on international money markets. The Maastricht Treaty of 1991 which opened the road for the creation of the Eurozone sealed the neoliberal framework and strengthened further the prioritisation of the freedom of finance, centralising monetary policy by removing power from the national Central Banks and transferring it to the European Central Bank, from its inception established as a supranational institution, yet modelled on the German Central Bank (Heisenberg and Richmond 2002). The key policy instruments were declared to be interest rate controls and the key goal was the restraining of inflation. At the fiscal level, restrictions were put in place in terms of permissible budget deficits and national debt, but no fiscal union was attempted along the lines of the monetary union under the expectation that economic convergence was to follow the monetary union.

The Eurozone project not only did not lead to economic convergence and integration through monetary union during the 2000s, but in contrast exacerbated divergences between more and less technologically advanced states with different productivity levels and different positioning in the regional and global division of labour. Development and value flows were unequal enhancing the centrifugal forces within the Eurozone which could only be addressed through political decisions of resource transfers. That would presuppose a sort of federal EU political structure and a fully centralised economic policy that would treat national states as districts of an essentially European state. Something which was and remains until today politically unfeasible.

When the global recession set in, hitting the European periphery especially hard, there was neither the willingness on behalf of the northern core EU countries nor the mechanism in place within the

Eurozone institutional order to embark on a broader restructuring involving redistributing resources and redirecting the patterns of growth. Effectively, as the option of reversing the path with all that would entail was precluded, there was little that could be done in the existing framework. For the export-driven development of the north and the debt-driven development of Southern Europe to continue, internal devaluation was needed in the European periphery.

As the banking crisis was converted into a sovereign debt crisis, the EU set up the European Financial Stability Facility and the European Financial Stabilisation Mechanism in 2010 and invited the IMF in to assist it both financially and technocratically with the bail-out programmes needed by its member states. As the possibility of default remained open, especially for, but not exclusively to, Greece and as the threat to the Eurozone system continued, the more specialised European Stability Mechanism (ESM) was established in 2012 to act as the permanent firewall for the Eurozone. The ESM, set up via international treaty and operating as an inter-governmental organisation, effectively replaced the two previous mechanisms and became the emergency assistance mechanism for EU member states that came on the brink of bankruptcy. By offering low-interest loans to states that were practically ousted from the international money markets, the states were allowed to refinance their national debt, prevent the collapse of their financial sectors and manage the contraction of their economies in an organised way. These loans were attached to stringent conditions with respect to fiscal policy aimed at reducing public spending to levels that would allow the states to get back on track so that in a few years they could return to the international money markets.

Essentially it was a process of internal devaluation imposed on states in exchange for loans and that entailed a series of restrictions on social security benefits, cuts to education and health spending, reduction of the public sector payroll, sale of public assets and promotion of flexibility in the labour market. In Spain there was also the removal of legal support to sectoral collective bargaining and the promotion of temporary and fixed term work through changes in employment protection legislation while in Greece this was additionally compounded with substantial minimum wage reductions and extensions to the working week (Deakin and Koukiadaki 2013). In Greece, the attack on collective labour rights has been monumental, despite the fact, or precisely because it was a jurisdiction where collective labour rights were strongly constitutionalised. This was a combined result of an external, offensive constitutionalisation of capital rights and a defensive articulation of labour rights both domestically and transnationally (Katsaroumpas 2018).

Typically, these policies were unpopular and were initially contested by national governments who felt the pressure from their electorate already suffering from the deepening recession. However, the pressure from the money markets was felt to be bigger, as the credit rating agencies devalued South European economies further and further until their state bonds were denoted as being 'trash' and with default becoming imminent. As a Eurozone state could not default on its payments without posing a threat to the whole Eurozone system, the stakes were raised both for the EU and for the national states. Against the prospect of state bankruptcy and exit from the Eurozone, technocrats, and politicians in one after the other South European state consented to the terms imposed by the Troika. The elites were more than determined to pursue the politics of good behaviour that their international creditors expected (Polanyi 1944).

Although the terms of the bail-out programmes were negotiated with the national governments, signed by them and approved by the parliament of the state receiving the loan, and subsequently ratified by all other EU states, this was more of a formal than substantive process. The scope available for negotiation was severely restricted not only because 'the numbers had to add up' but also because the Troika had very specific preferences as to 'how the numbers were to add up'. Fiscal balance for example had to be achieved primarily through the reduction of public expenses and less through an increase of tax revenue; tax revenue had to come more from indirect rather than direct taxation, the reduction of public expenses needed to include the payroll cost but needn't affect military spending and so on. The bail-out programmes intensified the recession in the short run and increased the public debt in the medium run. Yet, as state bankruptcies were averted and internal devaluation achieved, they had served their purposes and were successful according to their own criteria. Even in the case of Greece, where two bail-out programmes were required before the country was able to borrow from the international money markets again, and a third one in 2015 to stabilise at the new low level reached.

Having said that it is important to also point out again that despite the severe pain inflicted on South European societies in the beginning of the 2010s, the South European economies remained weak at the end of decade with none of their structural problems resolved. The narratives propagated by the international as well as the national media invoking images of the 'lazy South Europeans' versus the 'hard-working North Europeans' and of the Troika 'putting South Europe in order' were instrumental in facilitating the crisis management process but one should not read too much into them. It was the correlation of political force backed by the global economic power structure that determined the path taken – not any victory of austerity management at the level of ideas. In northern European societies the Troika mechanism was seen as a technical tool with which to ensure that the loans would be repaid. From the standpoint of south European societies, however, the Troika was also seen as an external force dictating policy terms and violating national and popular sovereignty.

In Greece where the depth and duration of the subsumption of the country under the Troika support programmes was biggest, contesting the 'Memoranda' was also framed in terms of national dignity. There was a relative fusion of the demand for popular democratic control of the economy, or at least not being at all costs subjected to the rules of the money markets with more nationalist-oriented calls for sovereignty. However, the discourse which ultimately prevailed and escorted the contestation to Troika led by SYRIZA which rose to power in 2015 was that of 'a new deal for Europe', a Europe-wide shift to an alternative neo-Keynesian policy. Despite the resonance of this call to the left-wing and progressive forces throughout Europe bringing about solidarity expressions which culminated by the eve of the 2015 referendum, this was not enough to shift the correlation of force at the EU level and SYRIZA remained trapped within the deadlock of its own strategy leading it to capitulation.

The management of the economic crisis through the Troika mechanism resulted in the strengthening of Euroscepticism, of both right-wing and left-wing persuasion. The image of the EU was tarnished and the possibility of transforming the EU towards a progressive direction was revealed to be limited as neoliberalism proved too entrenched and rooted in its architecture. The means with which austerity policies were implemented, largely seen as a ruthless imposition converting the national institutional orders into a sham, reinforced the already existing disaffection with the European integration project and the calls for a return to national sovereignty. Whereas these views became widespread at the level of European societies, northern as well as southern, they never managed to become hegemonic. Very few elite actors at the level of the political system adopted Eurosceptic positions and even those that did voiced only mild, mostly rhetorical criticisms without any concrete alternative proposals. The neoliberal mantra of 'There Is No Alternative' (TINA), demonstrated in its most pure form in Greece in 2015, included Europhilia as one of its main constituents (Table 2.1).

## Employers, Trade Unions and Labour Force Structure in Southern Europe

Although the neoliberal framework was dominant by the 21st Century, industrial relations institutions built in previous times, under different conditions and with a different philosophy, remained largely in place in South European countries. Despite the more general trends of liberalisation, the rise of individual labour law at the expense of collective labour law, the decentralisation of collective bargaining and the erosion of trade union influence already under way, employment remained largely

*Table 2.1* Total population, Economically active population, Main trade union confederations, 2019

| | *Total population 2019* | *Economically active population (15–64) 2019* | *Main trade unions confederations* |
|---|---|---|---|
| Spain | 46 634 000 | 22 803 000 | CCOO and UGT |
| Portugal | 10 277 000 | 4 987 000 | CGTP and UGT |
| Italy | 60 360 000 | 25 254 000 | CGIL, CISL and UIL |
| Greece | 10 725 000 | 4 634 000 | GSEE (and PAME as separate but within it) |
| Cyprus | 876 000 | 435 000 | PEO (formally a federation but treated as a confederation for comparative purposes) and SEK |

Source: Eurostat.

regulated. Employer associations and trade union confederations continued to engage in negotiations and in social dialogue processes at the level of the state and collective bargaining, despite its shrinking scope and depth and increasing difficulty to be universally enforced, remained the central regulation mechanism in the labour market. The crisis shook this arrangement everywhere. In the extreme case of Greece, it dismantled the foundation of the system itself.

Employer associations generally welcomed the changes which resulted in the reduction of labour costs, while trade unions generally opposed it as it posed a direct threat both to their members as well as to themselves as organisations. However, neither of the two was a protagonist in this process. Both policymaking and its contestation were led by other actors; it was the European and national technocrats that exerted the primary influence on governments and legislatures not the social partners. And it was social movements and networks of citizen activists that were in the front line of the anti-austerity protests. In all countries, the main employer associations and the major trade union federations and confederations were generally reluctant to take the offensive and assume leading roles. They followed the developments, issued statements, and adapted to the changing market circumstances and state policy context. This was largely a result of path dependency and the sheer weight of tradition and custom pushing the social partners to act during the crisis as they had acted before the crisis. Nevertheless, the crisis was reshaping the field by further fragmenting the economy, the labour process and the labour force.

In Spain collectivism remained strong amidst the labour market restructuring occurring in the decades before the crisis. Trade union membership, although relatively low since the 1980s, was recomposed and even modestly increased on the eve of the crisis (Köhler and Calleja Jiménez 2012). Trade unions remained present in many workplaces and this enhanced collectivism, building incentives for action in inclusive systems of industrial relations while individualistic orientations and instrumental motives were largely marginalised (Jódar, Vidal and Alós 2011). In any case, trade union membership is not the determining factor in collective bargaining coverage in Spain. At enterprise level, in workplaces with more than 50 employees, it is the Works Council that bargains for the whole firm irrespective of how many workers are union members and to which union they belong, while at the sectoral level the erga omnes clauses ensure a much wider collective bargaining coverage than merely trade union members. Although trade unions suffered increasing challenges during the crisis with respect to their legitimacy and representation capacity, with a more aggressive centre-right in the political system, a less supportive legal framework and less fruitful political exchanges with the government, overall, the industrial relations system survived and collective bargaining remained fairly well regulated (Fernandez Rodriguez et al. 2019).

In Greece, the damage to the industrial relations system and to trade unionism from the crisis was much more severe. The combined impact of the depression and austerity policy in the early phase of the crisis undercut the ability of trade unions to function effectively. An already internally divided and weakened trade union confederation in an increasingly fragmented labour market was unable to withstand the onslaught of an essentially bankrupt economy. The legislative reforms of 2012 which removed the legal fortification of collective bargaining led to a rapid collapse of the collective bargaining structure and drove internal devaluation, that is wage compression (Ioannou 2019). Trade unions survived – at the early stage of the crisis they retained, and in some industries even increased their membership, as collective bargaining coverage became restricted to firms where both employers and workers were organised incentivising membership. However, they were quickly marginalised in most industries as the economic situation deteriorated and they lost the legal tools with which they had become so accustomed, such as the erga omnes clauses, the favourability principle, and the right of unilateral resort to arbitration.

In Cyprus although trade union density was steadily falling since its peak in the 1980s, membership continued to increase until the eve of the crisis. During the crisis years collective bargaining coverage shrank as a result of decentralisation and increasing precarious employment but there was no collapse as neither was it dependent on legal frameworks, nor was there a sustained attempt to politically marginalise it (Ioannou and Sonan 2019). Trade unions accepted wages and benefits cuts but where they could, negotiated and succeeded to get the employers to sign that these were to be temporary. This strategy of sacrificing the content to save the form, accepting worse terms of employment but maintaining the collective bargaining structure, prevented a collapse of the system. To be sure, the balance of power had shifted, and some losses at the organisational and institutional level were permanent. Both density and collective bargaining coverage decreased, yet overall trade union retreat remained manageable.

Contrary to the prevailing hegemonic discourse, and contrary to the Troika stated goals and some shared expectations, the 'structural reforms' imposed did not lead to any substantial structural changes in the economies of Southern Europe. Neither was productivity or national competitiveness enhanced, nor did the liberalisation produce any efficiency gains, nor was growth, when and where it did return, built on any more solid basis compared to the pre-crisis period. Clientelism, corruption and tax evasion continued to plague Greece despite the change of government and the draconian measures imposed – and the mild economic recovery which followed was based primarily on the further expansion of tourism. In Cyprus, recovery was at least partly based on the 'citizenship via investment scheme' (Rakopoulos 2021) which initiated and sustained a new real estate bubble from 2016–2017 onwards. Overall, the austerity period destabilised industrial relations and suppressed incomes, provoked shifts in the economic landscape and increased social inequality but did not lead to substantial alterations in the economic models prevailing in Southern Europe.

When economic growth returned, emigration rates slowed down, and immigration rates increased again. Although at the macro level, the division of labour and the class structure did not change in fundamental ways, the crisis transformed the lives of many millions throughout Southern Europe. While for the majority the change was a moderate deterioration in the standard of living through the decrease of disposable income, for a substantial minority the experience was one of fast downward social mobility. The losers of the crisis were numerous and included not only the working class but also sections from the middle strata (Spyridakis 2018). Besides the highly paid and free-lance professionals who experienced negatively and some dramatically so the collapse of demand, on the capital side many small businesses went bankrupt, and assets were destroyed or devalued during the financial restructuring. Some came out as winners as they were better positioned and able to benefit from the new space created by the bankruptcy of others and the generalised process of capital concentration (Marx 1978: 431; Marx 1981: 349). Political connections and elite networks generally protected businessmen from grave losses but in the business world too, there was differentiated distribution of crisis cost and crisis benefit (Table 2.2).

*Table 2.2* GDP per Capita in Purchasing Power Standards (PPS), Employment rate, Median income in €, % of persons at risk poverty and social exclusion, 2018

| | *GDP per Capita in Purchasing Power Standards (PPS)* | *Employment rate %* | *Median income in €* | *% of persons at risk of poverty and social exclusion* |
|---|---|---|---|---|
| EU [27] | 100 | 72.4 | 16 839 | 21.6 |
| Eurozone [19] | 107 | 72 | 19 245 | 21.6 |
| Spain | 91 | 67 | 14 785 | 26.1 |
| Portugal | 77 | 75.4 | 9 346 | 21.6 |
| Italy | 97 | 63 | 16 844 | 27.3 |
| Greece | 69 | 59.5 | 7 863 | 31.8 |
| Cyprus | 90 | 73.9 | 15 336 | 23.9 |

Source: Eurostat.

## Societies in Austerity, Poverty, and Political Upheaval

Everywhere, austerity policies effectively hit the most vulnerable worst. Despite the fact that in some cases some cuts were instituted in a progressive manner, and despite the increased relief spending for people facing extreme material deprivation, overall, at the peak of the crisis in each country the trend has involved more people becoming poor and the poor becoming poorer. Already from the early phase of the crisis whereas the population at risk of poverty increased in Western Europe by 6.6% from 2007 to 2011, in Italy the increase was 11% and in Spain 23.2% (Pavolini et al. 2015). Cyprus experienced the full brunt of the crisis a few years later and in its peak in 2014, youth unemployment and the proportion of people at risk of poverty were among the highest in the EU. Greece was however by far the worst hit with record negative scores in almost all the social indicators. It was also the country were recovery came later and has only been partial with low wages and relatively high unemployment becoming a permanent feature of its economy.

The economic crisis, the policies of its management and its societal impact provoked significant political upheaval. Anti-austerity movements emerged in the early stages of the crisis and a series of mass mobilisations took place throughout Southern Europe. Although the initiators of this were usually networks of activists able to tap into growing social discontent, organise local protests and engage in the new social movements which emerged, there were also many people, especially young who entered in activism for the first time in their lives (Campos Lima and Artiles 2013). The biggest protest waves were the square movements in the spring of 2011 in Spain (15M) and subsequently Greece, also inspired by the then on-going protests in Middle Eastern and North African countries, the so-called 'Arab spring'.

These occupations of the public squares in the major cities coming a few months after the global Occupy movement, sparked by the 'Occupy the Wall Street' movement in the United States constituted a resurgence of activism and a protest peak, analogous to the Global Justice movements a decade ago. There were elements of both continuity and change with respect to the orientation and priorities of these social movements, their strategy and tactics as well as impact (Della Porta 2015). Whereas the directly political dimension was more enhanced in the early 2010s compared to the early 2000s and while this can explain the smoother translation of some of their grievances into institutional politics a couple of years later, there were also some differences in the social profiles of these movements reflecting not just ideological but also class shifts occurring in early 21st Century.

The austerity times initiated with the 2008 global crisis came after more than two decades of slow yet steadily increasing precariousness in the labour market affecting an ever-growing proportion of the population. Although the old and new expanding middle class of highly educated professionals fared relatively well in the pre-crisis decades, there were already signs of difficulty in its social reproduction which were severely exacerbated during the crisis years. More and more young university graduates found it hard to find graduate, well-paid jobs in the 21st Century and were trapped in between successive temporary and short term, often badly paid jobs, and unemployment. The depression extended and accelerated this trend making more young people more dependent on their, often better-off, parents (Ioannou and Sonan 2016; Lobato 2018). At the same time many small firms went bankrupt and many jobs were lost during the crisis years, while the disposable income of middle strata was also depressed (Ioannou and Charalambous 2017; Siani-Davies 2017). Overall, most jobs created during the 2010s were on the high-paid and low-paid ends of the spectrum resulting in the shrinking of the middle-income earners and increasing social polarisation (Eurofound 2020a).

The anti-austerity movements of the early 2010s had thus their roots in changes in the class structure under way. As social inequality increased and class polarisation deepened, material questions came to the fore. Even much of what was conceived in the 1990s as post-materialist values and identity politics was remolded and transformed to resonate with the realities of the day. As more and more young people found it increasingly difficult to sustain the living standard promised by the consumerist culture, consumerist culture itself was seen more and more as inadequate. As in-work poverty expanded, educational credentials deflated, successful trajectories in the labour market became rarer, the expectations of more and more people were frustrated (Bartolini et al. 2017). By the early 2010s, various things that were considered distant in earlier times were felt to be much nearer to south European societies. Extended material deprivation was no longer only a third world issue. Climate change provoked by environmental destruction was not merely a future threat. Migration was no longer just about the others.

The rise of populism both on the right and the left of the political spectrum and the further erosion of the legitimacy of the already discredited political system were connected to broader societal shifts (Charalambous and Ioannou, 2020a). The increasing coercion in the workplace, deteriorating terms and conditions for workers, the shrinking welfare state, the distancing of the governance centres from the governed diffused disaffection and alienation to wide sections of society. System legitimacy and stability was reduced as precariousness spread among the popular strata and as also the middle strata faced increased pressure. Neoliberal economic governance remained the dominant policy framework but was no longer ideologically hegemonic in the way it was in earlier decades. As neoliberalism came to depend more and more on the political force of state and supra-state institutions, the demand for the democratic control of the economy became stronger (Streeck 2014).

The imposition of austerity was not restricted to Southern Europe even though that was the place where it took its most extreme form. There as elsewhere it was a contested process. The early 2010s was a time of popular mobilisation and contestation of the neoliberal framework both politically and at the level of public discourse. Although neoliberalism survived the challenge and no paradigm shift occurred by the end of the decade, the challenge it faced was wide in scope and multi-faceted. Beyond social movements composed of, and attracting, newly politicised masses of young people, the demand for policies designed to serve the welfare of people rather than business interests was able to permeate the political systems of Europe. Even in the United Kingdom, the heartland of neoliberalism, austerity was challenged with mass protests prefiguring the rise of Jeremy Corbyn (Bailey 2020). In the United States, just like Momentum in the United Kingdom which brought and sustained Corbyn at the leadership of the Labour Party until the end of 2019, an analogous assemblage of left-wing activists brought Bernie Sanders close to winning the Democratic Party presidential candidate nomination contest in 2016 (Worth 2020) and this was repeated four years later, effectively 'decriminalizing' the word 'socialism' and establishing it as a legitimate position in US politics.

It was in such climate that major trade union federations and confederations saw popular mobilisation as an instrument with which to exert pressure on policymakers, a means to break the impasse of stalled social dialogue as well as an opportunity for improving their image. Even a weak and bureaucratic institution such as the ETUC toyed with the idea of popular mobilisations as a pressure tool and as a method of revitalisation (Degryse and Tilly 2013). As mentioned above, however, despite participating in anti-austerity protests and discourse, trade unions were ultimately neither the protagonist force nor lured by the resurgence of populism (Ioannou and Charalambous 2020).

# Part II

# The Changing Context of Employment Relations in Spain, Greece, and Cyprus

# 3 Spain. Compression and Upheaval

Because of the country's size, the economic crisis in Spain provoked considerable alarm to the European Union. In Spain as in Italy, the bail-out procedure and crisis management proceeded in a different manner in comparison to Ireland and other smaller countries in Southern Europe. Although the pattern was the same at the substantive level – financial aid in exchange for austerity policy measures and market-enhancing structural reforms, this was not formally enshrined in a Memorandum of Understanding and did not include the strict monitoring that accompanied this in Greece, Portugal, and Cyprus. There was also perhaps a higher degree of ownership of the austerity programme and the labour market liberalisation measures by national elites, especially after the more aggressive Spanish Right came to power in 2012.

The crisis in Spain also had some special characteristics, or rather some elements of it were more enhanced compared to other cases. Firstly, the collapse of the real estate bubble was big and swift and brought not only the construction industry but also banking to its knees pleading into mass foreclosures. The social and the political system crises that developed alongside the economic crisis were also in some respects more profound than other countries with social movements being active longer and some of them, such as the initiatives against evictions, being quite effective. The instability of the political system also lasted longer although at no point did this extend to a questioning of Spain's positioning in the Eurozone.

As in the rest of Southern Europe the economy contracted, unemployment soared, the pre-existing industrial relations system was weakened, and the overall standard of living dropped. Fiscal austerity and social policy cuts in conjunction with declining wages and the weakening of trade unionism resulted in increasing poverty, magnified difficulties in the labour market and provoked youth emigration. Yet despite the significant changes in individual and collective labour law which relaxed protections and gave more scope for employer unilateralism, trade unionism retained its role and collective bargaining proved more resilient than initially expected. By the end of the 2010s, as growth returned, the labour movement was able to recoup some of its losses and be in a position to hope for more as a progressively reformed centre-left coalition returned to executive power.

This is the first empirical chapter of the book and serves the purpose of examining in considerable detail the play out of the economic crisis in a major national setting. While institutional liberalisation and employment deregulation were promoted swiftly and via the national elites acting in concertation with European elites, this did not keep social contention levels low. In fact, the compression of social and employment rights and the frontal attack on the capacity of trade unions to regulate the labour market was materialised in a context of social and political upheaval, marking the end of an epoch for Spain and the partial reshaping of its political system. At the same time, for all the monumental changes occurring at the level of politics and the legal order, the institutional order of the labour market manifested commendable stability with the forces of labour overcoming the initial shock by drawing on industrial relations traditions adapting to enterprise bargaining and shifting the field of struggle from the workplace to the protest and electoral fields.

## Banking Crisis and State Finance Crisis

Spain has traditionally been a country with a high per capita home ownership and high household debt. As in other Mediterranean countries, home ownership was both a sort of personal investment and a cultural norm. In a time of neoliberal financialisation at the turn of the 20th Century this social practice became associated with increasing financial debt whose servicing depended on economic stability, continuous employment and a constant and adequate flow of income, processes which were being gradually eroded in the 2000s and wholly disrupted by the early 2010s. In addition, the expansion of tourism and especially the holiday home buying from abroad resulted in a rapidly over-blown construction sector, financed by the banks which were insufficiently regulated hiding their risks, their losses and the volatility of the whole nexus that was developed. The Spanish economy became highly dependent on external funding, which dried up with the collapse of international financial markets provoking more damage than in other neighbouring economies (Ferreiro et al. 2016).

Between 1994 and 2007 around one third of the new jobs created were concentrated in the sectors of construction, real estate and business services (Banyuls and Recio 2012). Real estate operated as a speculative investment but although seen as such, it was left to grow because it was also an engine of economic growth, creating jobs and revenue for the state (Int. 3, 2020; Int. 4, 2020). The expansion of real estate and tourism in the last decades also became more significant in economic terms as it balanced out the de-industrialisation process already under way since the 1980s (Int. 2, 2020). The jobs created were low value-added and labour intensive, with low levels of technological sophistication and poor employment quality. Overall, the Spanish economy was weak as growth was concentrated in a few sectors related to construction and tourism, its manufacturing had limited international penetration and its more advanced tertiary services were few (Banyuls and Recio 2015). Furthermore, the pursuit of a procyclical expansionary fiscal policy on the eve of the crisis combining expenditure increases and direct tax cuts resulted in a sudden public deficit of 4.5% in 2008 restricting further the management scope of the state (Ferreiro et al. 2016).

Demand fell with the onset of the global economic recession, and as was to be expected, the real estate bubble burst, with the construction industry's accumulated debts being absorbed by the banks which declared heavy losses (Banyuls and Recio 2012). Loans were rolled ahead, and the banks needed to be bailed out by the state which became more and more strained. Private debt was exceptionally high standing at 886% of GDP in 2007 with liabilities of households standing at 89%, those of non-financial corporations at 386% and those of financial corporations at 411% respectively. Deleveraging and bail-out lowered private debt at the expense of public debt which rose during the time that GDP was shrinking, resulting in a public debt to GDP ratio of 132% by 2013 (Ferreiro et al. 2016). Unemployment soared to 20% and youth unemployment to 50%. The precariousness prevailing in the labour market was exacerbated and the weak welfare state was not in a position to absorb the economic shock.

The banking crisis was converted into a sovereign debt crisis while the absence of any mechanisms in the Eurozone to deal with the systemic risks by transferring resources left Spain, like other peripheral states, vulnerable. Because of the property led boom of the previous years, Spain was already an economy characterised by structural weakness and volatility. As public finance deteriorated and austerity measures began to be adopted as a way out of the crisis, the recession in the real economy deepened and intensified provoking political and social crises. Budget cuts and increased taxation formed the initial austerity measures which escalated as the crisis deepened (Banyuls and Recio 2012). Although employment relations had nothing to do with the economic crisis, by 2012 they became the key field of political intervention (Molina 2014).

## Employment Relations and Trade Unionism, Labour Law and Collective Bargaining

The industrial relations system in Spain has traditionally been based on extensive collective bargaining coverage under a complex system operating at various levels (Hamann and Martinez Lucio 2007). Although trade union density was relatively low, consistently below 20%, the erga omnes effect of the collective agreements allowed them to apply to everyone within their scope of application lifting overall coverage rates to more than 80%. The erga omnes effect reducing the relevance of affiliation to the signatory parties decoupled to some extent trade unionism from collective bargaining and operated as a disincentive for workers to join trade unions (Fernandez Rodriguez et al. 2019). Trade unionism is politicised in Spain with the two main trade union confederations, UGT and CCOO dominating collective bargaining oriented to the social democratic and communist/left wing parties respectively. Although these links to the political parties are not as strong as they once were, they are still active especially at the ideological level and a factor in the trade union landscape (Int. 4, 2020). Since the late 1980s however the competition between the two for members and the occasional divergence in ideological and political matters is never allowed to degenerate into antagonism, as cooperation between UGT and CCOO and unity of action in practice is solid.

As in most Western countries, the trade union movement in Spain had been weakened already by the turn of the 20th Century. Its main source of power had become institutional, relying that is on its recognition by the employers and the state as a partner, participating in social dialogue processes and making agreements and pacts (Campos Lima and Artiles 2011; De Rio Loira and Fenger 2019). This was facilitated by the boom years 1997–2007, when there was a relative decrease in unemployment. In the same period, the processes of marketisation involving creeping privatisation and financialisation in the context of financial deregulation advanced considerably. At the level of the labour market flexible working arrangements grew alongside undeclared work and were largely tolerated de facto by the trade unions as they involved the periphery rather than the core of the labour force (Int. 1, 2020). At the same time although trade union membership levels were maintained and even moderately increased in the years immediately before the crisis, trade union membership among workers in low-paid and precarious service jobs which proliferated remained low (Int. 3, 2020). Fixed-term employment rose to affect as much as 30% of the labour force (Las Heras and Ribera-Almandoz 2017).

As the economic crisis developed so did talk in the public sphere about the 'rigidities of the labour market' (Fernandez Rodriguez and Martinez Lucio 2013). While this was a standard position of employers, there did not seem to be any especially sustained or active agency on their part with regards to legal change (Int. 1, 2020). In fact, after long negotiations, employers had just signed a Pact with the trade unions which was simply ignored by the newly elected right-wing government that rose to power in late 2011 (Molina 2014). Although the European Central Bank did include liberalisation of the labour market in the famous letter that functioned analogously with the formal Memoranda of Understanding signed with other South European countries, this did not specify in detail the way to push through this. The Spanish government went beyond what the Troika was asking, acting in a sort of 'more royalist than the king' way (Int. 2, 2020). In Spain as in Italy, employers could barely dream of the legislative changes regarding employment relations that were adopted in 2012 (Meardi 2014).

The pressure from the Troika and especially from the European Commission cannot, on its own, explain the magnitude and the depth of the labour law reform. The trade union movement put the blame squarely on the Spanish government and although its immediate reaction with two general strikes proved insufficient to stop the reform, in the longer term it did manage to shape citizen attitudes and shift the attribution of responsibility from the international context to government policy (Molina and Barranco 2016). Anti-trade union views gained prominence in the Spanish right wing and this was reflected at policy level throughout the 2010s. Social dialogue, the main strategy on which trade unions had invested in, was side-lined as the modus operandi of the government shifted from negotiations and social pacts into legislative action and imposition (Molina 2014). There were variations across regions, but overall, it can be said that social dialogue was in a phase of retreat in Spain until 2018 (Int. 1, 2020; Int. 4, 2020).

The formal rationale of the 2012 labour legislative reforms was to 'create employment' and 'generate security for workers and entrepreneurs, markets and investors' in the context of the more general anti-crisis measures that were being adopted from 2008 onwards. There was some continuity in the attempt to increase flexibility which was the broader legislative tendency since the mid-1990s but there were also elements of rupture. At the surface level the effect of the labour law reform was contradictory since it both promoted and discouraged precariousness (Ginès-Fabrellas 2019). The capacity of the employer to modify labour conditions was enhanced, for example via the opt out from collective agreements, and through the reduction of wages and the increase of working time flexibility (Lopez-Andreu 2019b). On the other hand, fixed-term contracts were discouraged through the promotion of open-ended contracts, the employment of excluded workers was encouraged and a series of work-life balance measures were introduced including the right to reduce working time for care purposes and adapting the distribution of working hours subject to collective agreement regulation or employer consent.

When examined in more depth however and judging from the actual impact of the implementation of these measures, precariousness in the labour market expanded. Part-time work increased to 15% of the workforce, more than half of it involuntary, the reduction of fixed-term contracts was small with the proportion standing at 26.8% of the workforce and the average duration of temporary contracts decreased to less than 33 days. The effort to curb temporary employment failed completely and the small reduction in its percentage was largely because temporary workers were affected disproportionally by dismissals and because of the collapse of the construction industry which employed many of them.

Overall, the flexibilisation of working time was undertaken primarily unilaterally by employers offsetting and neutralising in practice the measures adopted to improve the work-life balance. The demand for employer consent made it impossible to implement the various work-life balance measures as there were hardly any collective agreements in the peak crisis years and where made, they were largely restricted to core issues and were defensive in form, while this right was further limited by the Courts and subsequent revisions in the legal text. The attempt to promote internal flexibility rather than external allowed the employers to unilaterally change labour conditions for example through imposing geographical and functional mobility in the interest of 'competitiveness, productivity, technical change or labour organization' (Ginès-Fabrellas 2019).

Traditional external flexibility was also enhanced by making firing easier and cheaper. Severance pay for unfair dismissal was reduced from 45 to 33 days per year and from a maximum of 42 monthly payments to 24. In addition to cheapening compensation the judicial review of the causes of dismissal was relaxed (Baylos 2015). This allowed employers to substitute some of their senior and more expensive workers with younger and cheaper workers with temporary contracts. With respect to redundancies although consultation in good faith remained obligatory, the consultation right was compromised, and its effect was neutralised. The prior administrative authorisation was removed and the scope of business causes allowing it was expanded from 'structural' to also 'circumstantial' situations, effectively increasing the capacity of employer unilateralism. The gap between temporary and permanent workers was reduced by increasing the vulnerability of the latter. Yet despite the lowering of the dismissal costs of permanent employees, the bigger trend was employers preferring to make temporary workers redundant first (Int. 4, 2020).

At the level of collective labour law, the 2012 changes were even more profound resulting in significant weakening of trade union rights (Fernandez Rodriguez et al. 2016). Bargaining decentralisation was promoted through placing priority in company-level bargaining. Moreover, the possibility of temporary disapplication of the collective agreements was opened up in cases where there were 'economic, technical, organizational or productive reasons' expanding the scope and expediting the procedure (Ginès-Fabrellas 2019). The post termination effect of collective agreements, their continued currency that is after their nominal end date, was reduced to the maximum of one year, allowing employers to subsequently modify unilaterally the terms of employment if a new collective agreement was not reached (Baylos 2015). Yet, it remained unclear which terms could be modified, and conflicts arising were increasingly taken to the courts (Banyuls and Recio 2015). Compulsory arbitration was also instituted as a means of resolving conflicts.

The abolition of the hierarchy principle among bargaining levels and of the post termination effect of collective agreements were the most important instruments through which the balance of power in Spanish industrial relations changed. Employers generally welcomed the reshaping of the field and the new freedoms they acquired in determining the terms and conditions of employment (Int. 2, 2020). Practically speaking, these legislative reforms were more important in less unionised settings, such as small businesses. There, workers lost the floor they had previously had, determined by the sectoral collective agreement, as employers dominated the company level bargaining (Int. 4, 2020). In bigger businesses where trade unions were more able to contest this, employers tended to be more reserved or less successful in instituting cuts to wages and benefits. Although in the immediate years after 2012 the trend was agreements stopping, there were soon some industry-level compromises, such as in chemicals. In weaker industries and many service sectors 'employers changed everything' (Int. 1, 2020).

In some regions, such as the Basque country, where trade unions had invested a sustained effort to grow stronger at the company level, it was not easy for employers to use enterprise-level bargaining to erode sectoral collective agreements. Similarly, the abolition of the post termination effect of collective agreements, although an important 'gift to employers' could not produce results automatically. Where trade unions and worker representative bodies were strong, they insisted on the validity of the terms of the expired collective agreement and contested the terms of employment reverting to the statutory minimum. When not able to force employers into a compromise and the signing of a new agreement, and where trade unions and workers were not cowed into signing away wages and benefits reductions, 'consolidated rights' could still be claimed via legal routes. This was not the case however with new recruits, primarily young, who were ultimately those bearing the brunt of the internal devaluation process.

Overall, the labour market reform measures were presented as both boosting employment and being an alternative to fixed-term contracts and redundancies. In the medium term, employment did go up, but most new jobs were temporary and the contracts short. By the end of the 2010s, the significant rise in the minimum wage also improved conditions for the low paid workers. However, the pre-crisis employment levels were not reached, many of the new jobs created after growth returned were low-wage and the power balance between employers and trade unions shifted as workers became more disempowered in and through the labour market reform of 2012. The full impact of the negative changes in the field of employment however cannot be assessed without also briefly examining the impact of austerity on social policy (Table 3.1).

*Table 3.1* Number of registered unemployed, Youth unemployment and Part time employment rates, Minimum wage in €, Spain, 2008–2019

| *Spain* | *2008* | *2013* | *2019* |
|---|---|---|---|
| No. of registered unemployed persons | 2 361 500 | 6 051 100 | 3 248 000 |
| Youth unemployment rate (15–24) (%) | 24.5 | 55.5 | 32.5 |
| Part time employment rate (%) | 11.6 | 15.7 | 14.5 |
| Minimum wage in € | 700 | 752.85 | 1050 |

Source: Eurostat.

## Austerity Social Policy without a Troika Support Mechanism

The attempt to keep the budget deficits low amidst a significant shrinking of public income as a result of the economic recession and the increasing pressure from the European Commission, which in the midst of the crisis instituted the balanced budget mechanisms in a legal form, led the Spanish government to the adoption of a series of austerity measures. As mentioned in the previous chapter, Spain did not formally sign up to a Troika support mechanism. It did receive support from the EU, however, implementing 'voluntarily', in the absence of a comprehensive Memorandum of Understanding, with its conditionality clauses and strict monitoring, a series of fiscal, institutional, and structural reforms. The two main parties, PP and PSOE after pressure from the EU and in the absence of a public debate and with almost no publicity, let alone a referendum, revised article 135 of the Spanish Constitution in August 2011, enshrining the principle of the balanced budget and the priority of debt payment within the state budget.

Austerity measures were adopted in waves initially by the PSOE government and after 2011 by the new PP government, resulting in the further shrinking of the Spanish economy and by 2013 enhancing and spreading poverty in society. Beyond the restrictive labour market and education reforms there were significant cuts in overall public spending, estimated at 8% while the infrastructure budget was cut by 30%. Money for long-term unemployment benefits and health care was reduced, early-retirement schemes were eliminated while the retirement age rose to 67. VAT was increased from 18% to 21% and from 8% to 10% for the basic goods while other consumption taxes were also increased (Toyer and Gonzalez 2012). Public sector salaries, often operating as a benchmark from the private sector were initially frozen and subsequently cut by 5% leading and pushing an average 10% wage reduction in general (León and Pavolini 2014).

More specifically at the level of social policy the crisis resulted in drastic cuts affecting gender equality and family-friendly policies, child-care and long-term care and curtailing of the rights to time off work. This reversed the expansion process in family support and care policy under way since the 1990s with which Spain was catching up with other EU countries such as for example in the provision of three years of pre-school universally provided education, enhanced maternity and paternity leave and subsidies to working mothers and to companies employing women. Social cohesion policies were also negatively affected as the cuts in the regional budgets brought cuts to minimum income and combating social exclusion programmes (León and Pavolini 2014).

Beyond the shrinking of central government health budget by 13.7% in 2012 and 22.6% in 2013 there was also a 5% decrease in the regional budgets in 2012 compared to 2010. More importantly the philosophy of the public health system shifted from one of universal health care of all residents to one restricted to those contributing to the social insurance system (Gallo and Gene-Badia 2013). This transition from a universalist to a Bismarckian welfare model inevitably excluded several groups, non-working as well as working occasionally and informally most of whom were especially vulnerable. The social insurance system, already inadequate in offering sufficient protection to the victims of the labour market in conditions of sky-rocketing unemployment was also used to decrease the coverage of the health system.

Operating in parallel to the declining employment conditions, the social policy cuts hit the most vulnerable groups in Spanish society hard. Already in 2010, people depending on assistance provided by the Ministry of Health and Social Services surpassed eight million while in subsequent years the number of people requiring welfare benefits increased and the budget for basic social services was cut by 40% (Oxfam 2013). Inequality increased substantially with the Gini coefficient rising above 34% in 2012 the highest since records were kept in Spain, and one of the highest in Europe. The high unemployment and the even higher youth unemployment provoked an exponential rise in the number of households unable to repay their mortgages, resulting in many young couples moving back with their parents. Parents' savings and pensions became a key safety net for a vast number of people in the peak crisis years as families pooled resources and shared housing (Int. 2, 2020). This added strains of the process of social reproduction as tensions were provoked between generations (Narotzky 2017).

Developments were broadly speaking analogous to those occurring in the rest of the crisis-stricken South European periphery (Cruces et al. 2015). What was to some extent different, or more enhanced compared to other south European countries, was the unwillingness to challenge the Eurozone project tout court, despite this operating as the framework within which austerity appeared as a one-way street. Although resistance to austerity at the social level was massive, its ideological scope, at least as the supra-national level is concerned, never extended to encompass the economic architecture of the EU. Discourses attributing the austerity policies to European economic governance and therefore suggesting, implying, or merely leaving open, the possibility of exiting the Eurozone were extremely marginal in Spain. This is attributed to historical factors – the contributing role of the EU in the democratic transition which has elevated the idea of the EU into a sort of a value in itself. Europhilia is thus relatively diffused in Spain, spanning the whole political spectrum and this was also reflected in the anti-austerity discourses in which Euroscepticism was too weak in contrast to other south European countries (Int. 1, 2020).

On the social level another dimension that differentiates Spain from the rest of the South European stricken periphery is the extent of the evictions carried out. By 2013 it is estimated that more than 600 000 families lost their homes (Oxfam 2013). This trend which continued in subsequent years, created the conditions for the emergence of the anti-eviction movement and the movements for the right of housing. These included not just the gathering of crowds resisting the ousting of people from their homes but also the squatting of empty buildings by people who lost their homes. The existence of numerous empty buildings whose ownership was entangled between bankrupt contractors and banks, and the presence of active strong solidarity movements facilitated this process. Over the subsequent years, many of these squatters came to agreements with the owners and partly or fully formalised their use of the empty housing in exchange for low or affordable rents (Int. 2, 2020).

The combination of reduction in public spending and the shrinking of welfare budgets, the housing crisis and the deteriorating conditions in the labour market created a 'brutal situation' (Int. 6, 2020). With more than six million unemployed, and with youth unemployment exceeding 55% at the peak of 2013, socio-economic conditions in Spain became bleak. To this should be added the substantially high percentage of part-time employment, largely involuntary and exceeding 15% of the formal labour market and those working in the traditionally large informal economy. Although some deflation in prices was observed, the cost of living in the urban centres where the mass of the population is concentrated remained high and the decline in wages led to shrinking purchasing power for most people. Like with the benefits of the economic growth of the pre-crisis period, the losses from the economic depression were not uniform – varying across regions and sectors, between and within occupational and social groups (Banyuls and Recio 2017).

## The Economic and Political System Crises

The signs of the development of a political crisis in Spain were present from the early stage of the unfolding economic crisis. PSOE, like all European social democratic parties had since the 1990s moved the full way along the path of neoliberalism of the 'third way' type and its connection with the labour movement became weaker not only in organisational terms but also ideologically. After it adopted the first austerity measures signalling that it was the world of labour that was to pay the cost of the economic crisis, its relationship with UGT, already weakened since the early 1990s became even more strained. UGT in 2010 participated after a very long time in the general strike against a PSOE government. By 2011 it became obvious that the PSOE was seriously damaged, seen as a central part of a failing political system. The defeat of PSOE in the late 2011 elections was much more than just its penalisation for its initial handling of the economic crisis. It was something much bigger as the following years demonstrated.

The 15M or the Indignados movement that had emerged in mid-2011 both expressed and accelerated the delegitimisation of the political system. Taking by surprise the Spanish Left and the trade unions, the 15M has been a milestone in Spain's recent history. Under the slogan 'Real Democracy now! Take to the streets. We are not merchandise in the hands of politicians and bankers' a series of mass protests spread in numerous cities and towns in Spain producing political developments (Perez de Guzman et al. 2016). The increase in electoral abstention and the blurring of the Left-Right cleavage was the immediate and direct political impact of the action of this mobilisation. Although the 15M initially damaged more the then ruling PSOE, it was the whole political system that came under attack and which became destabilised. Furthermore, it brought new people into movement politics and new ideas were formulated, older ideas were rearticulated, leading a few years later into the creation of new political parties (Flesher Fominaya 2020).

The occupations of the public squares did not last long as repression followed but the movement did not die out. The focus shifted to neighbourhood assemblies and the anti-eviction initiatives that sprung up in the main cities, especially Barcelona. Older and more experienced activists assumed leading roles as they were able to bring in their organisational capacity as well as their political understandings and exert significant influence (Flesher Fominaya 2017). However, it was not just old activist networks expanding and ultra-left views becoming mainstream again. There were new people, new content as well as new forms.

As the impact of austerity deepened in 2012–2013, the focus shifted from the radical democracy orientation to anti-austerity. The purely political demands about the reform of the political system, the elimination of corruption, the more direct participation of the people in decision-making were not scrapped, but took a back seat as the economic situation deteriorated, unemployment sky-rocketed and the welfare state shrank. Mobilisations took place against public spending cuts, against privatisations and opposing austerity policies and the neoliberal framework in which they were enshrined. The most impressive anti-austerity actions of this period were the so-called Marea Verde (Green Tide) and Marea Blanca (White Tide), a series of mobilisations, protests and strikes against the cuts in the education and health sectors, respectively. Trade unions supported these actions and were involved in them – in the health sector more centrally than the education sector – but were not the leading forces in these broader social coalitions (Molina and Barranco 2016)

The social movements that sprang up in 2011 were ambivalent if not hostile to the main trade unions, seen as part of the system and thus as part of the problem. Perez de Guzman et al. (2016) identify three sources of the hostility to trade unions – the radical political orientation of some core activists deriving from autonomist post workerism, the inter-class profile participants and the post-political general suspicion about trade unions emanating partly from the anti-union campaigns of the right-wing press. Trade unions were also ambivalent towards the citizen initiatives sometimes supporting, co-organising and co-existing with them in the streets while at other times keeping their distance. Although, as the discourse shifted to anti-austerity, a convergence between trade unions and social movements became gradually possible, the uneasiness deriving from the major trade unions' loss of monopoly over social protests remained, as evidenced in the Dignity Marches of 2014 (Perez de Guzman et al. 2016)

Sensing the limits of their own power after the failure of the two general strikes of 2012 to produce a direct impact on government policy, UGT and CCOO avoided overt antagonism with the other anti-austerity actors, which were its de facto allies. The agency of some activists situated politically at the intersection of trade unions and social movements was important as well as the open-mindedness shown by some trade union leaders (Int. 5, 2020). In any case social dialogue was no longer a viable option, blocked by the government. UGT and CCOO were already pushed from the road of competitive consensus and corporatism to confrontation (Köhler 2018). Yet after decades of overt reliance on the institutional power resource did not lead into significant gains in associational and societal power resources, they entered the confrontation field insufficiently prepared (Sánchez Mosquera 2018). And trade unions felt the constant pressure from 15M and the anti-austerity social movements. While they refrained from calling further general strikes, they did throw their weight often behind other citizen movements and initiatives – this de facto co-existence generally reduced mistrust and allowed UGT and CCOO avoid a major crisis of representation (Perez de Guzman et al. 2016).

By 2014 the anti-austerity mobilisations had managed to produce their own political expression in the form of new political parties. PODEMOS, was the key party that emerged and although initially attempted to present itself as being beyond Left and Right, was soon positioned de facto at the left of the political spectrum. Ciudadanos was the other significant new party formed, positioned itself at the centre-right of the political spectrum while the substantial loss of the votes by the traditional parties and the rise of the new parties resulted in the fragmentation of the political system and the difficulty to form stable governments from 2015 until 2019. Moreover, the crisis of the political system was conducive to the resurgence of regional nationalisms, the prolongation of instability but also the shifting of the attention from the socio-economic realm and class politics to national and territorial questions (Int. 6, 2020). In Catalonia, the attempt to push through an independence referendum resulted in polarisation and repression while at the same time facilitating the rise of the far right expressed through the right-wing populist party VOX which stands for the abolition even of the existing regional autonomy. The emergence and speedy growth of VOX effectively ended the Spanish exception of not having an electorally significant far-right party influencing domestic political dynamics. Since the end of the 2010s, VOX exerts significant ideological pressure to the political system and induces the centre-right parties to adopt a more nationalist, nativist and authoritarian stance.

PODEMOS, the new political actor at the left-of-centre political spectrum, has elements of both continuity and change. It exhibits a new type of techno-populism, combining the embrace of digital technology and its harnessing for the purposes of radical democracy as well as appealing to the people against 'the system' (Kioupkiolis and Katsambekis, 2020). At the level of policy proposals, it put forward an egalitarian welfarism and was able to capture a significantly large space left vacant as Social Democracy moved to more centrist positions. However, PODEMOS as a project was enmeshed in its own contradictions and was not able to rise to a hegemonic position in Spanish society like SYRIZA was in Greece.

Although PODEMOS did ultimately manage to rise to executive power in 2019, this was only after merging with the Left and as a junior partner in a coalition with PSOE, something that it had vehemently opposed in its early years. The two main contradictions of PODEMOS are between the horizontality in its ideology and its de facto centralism in terms of political operation and action and the antagonistic conceptualisation of the existing political institutions yet at the same time the focusing of all its energy, attention and address to those same institutions. Although by no means new phenomena, these were complemented by another contradiction also a frequent aspect of movements turning into political parties – that between the simultaneous projection of a technocratic orientation and people-centrism. Overall PODEMOS constituted a speedy institutionalisation of social movements and the transfer of contentious politics from the streets into parliament (Int. 6, 2020).

Initially PODEMOS's relationship to the trade unions was tenuous and even competing as they constituted different forms of attempts of representing the subaltern. The mutual suspicion between trade unions and social movements, inherited from the historical juncture of the 15M, PODEMOS' precursor lingered on. If within PODEMOS there was the view that the trade unions are too traditional and systemic, within trade unionism there was the view that PODEMOS is like a student movement that doesn't understand the realities of the world of work (Int. 4, 2020). Gradually though as PODEMOS allied with the Left and took its place in the political system, relations with the trade unions, especially CCOO, improved.

Taking a longer-term perspective, the 2010s was a transformative moment for Spain. In several ways the sustained upheaval provoked by the economic crisis signalled the end of the system established in the democratic transition. Even the elements of continuity, processes under way since the 1980s and 1990s such as for example the neoliberal paths of economic management, the liberalisation of the labour market gained such depth and intensity that appeared to be new phenomena. The re-politicisation of young people through the 15M movement, the emergence of numerous social movements with a diverse repertoire of action and the consequent restructuring of the political system constituted a historical rupture. The resurgence of regional nationalisms, the aborted attempt for Catalan independence produced an additional cleavage casting its shadow on the reshaped Spanish political landscape and affecting its dynamics and balances.

## Trade Unionism and Class Relations Amidst Political Upheaval

The economic crisis constituted a main challenge not only for the workers but also for the trade unions as organisations. As recession set in and unemployment rose, their structural-economic power resource, already significantly reduced after decades of neoliberal globalisation pressures, shrank even further. Their institutional power resource, on which they had placed their emphasis for decades suffered a major blow as a result of the emergency situation which created a context in which the government could afford to simply ignore them. The most characteristic example was the agreements reached with employers in the early years of the crisis which were sidelined by the government choosing instead to reshape the industrial relations system through its own legislative initiative. Nevertheless, their institutional power resource also exhibited resilience and despite the labour market reforms, there was also substantial structural continuity, and the trade union role in the worker representative system was retained (Rigby and García Calavia 2018).

By the end of the 2010s the main trade union confederations have recovered much of the ground they lost in the institutional realm. Yet this recovery was neither comprehensive in scope, nor complete in terms of content and depth. Social dialogue suffered blows across many countries during the crisis years although in different ways and to a different extent. In countries where trade unions were mostly dependent on their institutional power source for their function like Spain, and even more so like Greece as shown in the following chapter, the blow they suffered was considerable. There was also a retreat in terms of their associational power – they lost more than half a million members between 2009 and 2015 (De Rio Loira and Fenger 2019). The mass redundancies in the early stage of the crisis provoked a further decline in already relatively low trade union density, as the new jobs created in more recent years tend to be in sectors with low and no unionisation.

The image and reputation of Spanish trade unions, already declining in the neoliberal age also suffered additional damage in the initial stage of the crisis. As the economic crisis developed and expanded in scope encompassing the political system, trade unions were not spared as they were seen to be, to some extent at least, part of the discredited system. Their relative passivity in the face of deteriorating conditions in the labour market brought to the fore accusations by social movements of being insiders, and of representing the interests of better off groups of workers at the expense of the increasing portion of the excluded, the unemployed and the precarious workers. There was also the post-political view emanating from the media invoking the image of the established trade unions as outdated institutions, enmeshed in corruption. Yet the same people that would express this narrative '*would turn to a trade union when they get a job in big company*' expecting the union to protect them, offer them subsidised legal advice and so on (Int. 2, 2020).

While social movements coalescing into the 15M movement in 2011 were developing a new concept and a new narrative of the people against the establishment, trade unions in the best case were absent from the forces constituting and representing the people and in the worst featured as part of that establishment (Köhler and Calleja Jiménez 2017). However as mentioned earlier, as the battle of social movements and citizen initiatives against austerity climaxed in 2012–2013, UGT and CCOO joined in and despite tensions and ambivalence, the major trade union confederations were socially registered as a core part of the anti-austerity milieu. The fact that they proclaimed three general strikes between 2010 and 2012, both against the PSOE and against the PP governments, even if albeit short ones, allowed them to retain their image as working-class organisations (Las Heras 2018). At the same time the conservative institutionalist inertia of trade unions inhibited the development of full synergies and a more comprehensive revitalisation through the strategy of social movement unionism (Köhler and Calleja Jiménez 2018).

Most of the resistance to austerity policies and struggles in defence of worker rights and welfare took place in the public space rather than the workplace and the industrial relations field. Conflicts producing demonstrations increased from around 3000 each year in the period before the crisis to 45000 in 2013 (Fernandez Rodriguez et al. 2021). It was through street protests and popular mobilisations that UGT and CCOO sought to mobilise their members and supporters and targeted the state rather the employers. During the crisis years, however, new worker initiatives emerged in various industries and workplaces, some of which were able to challenge UGT and CCOO as well as the employers winning small victories through adopting a more radical stance (Int. 1, 2020). Works councils in Spain have bargaining powers and while trade unions dominate the regional and sectoral level bargaining, at the enterprise level it is the works councils that bargain and sign the collective agreements. As a result of the unified delegate elections often the traditional trade unions came under increasing pressure from their competitors, both smaller unions and non-union delegates (Las Heras and Ribera-Almandoz 2017).

Regional trade unions such as the Basque sovereigntist unions ELA and LAB engaged in frequent strike activity throughout this period and this has effectively also served as a strategy of revitalisation and expansion (Las Heras and Rodriguez 2020). This included both strikes at the company as well as at the industry level but also general strikes – whereas there were only three general strikes in Spain, there were eight in the Basque country during the crisis years. The March 2012 general strike in Spain was precipitated by the Basque trade unions who led the initiative and whose competitive pressure on UGT and CCOO was constant. The small Galician trade union CIG, also embracing a more combative stance engaged in several strikes including the metal sector and general strikes in Galicia. Smaller radical trade unions also engaged in numerous local struggles while there were workers' mobilisations including strikes even in the gig economy (Fernandez 2017).

The new worker initiatives and grassroots resistance movements emerging in the crisis years indicate that although a macro-societal level resistance to the shifting contours of class relations was not possible, it was not the case that there was generalised passive acceptance of the deteriorating conditions. Small local workplace struggles and urban initiatives beyond the workplace at the level of neighbourhood solidarity networks, movements for the right to housing in the face of mass evictions at the municipal level, pensioners and public sector movements against privatisations at the regional level were the political forms that social discontent assumed (Díaz-Bara et al. 2018). Some of these struggles were successful directly while more importantly in an indirect way they exerted pressure on the big unions and the left-wing political parties, old as well as new though creating and sustaining a milieu for an alternative politics.[1] Some of these struggles received much public attention, as they were amplified through skilful use of social media communication strategies such as for example by small radical trade unions in Andalusia (Int. 4, 2020). Others however did not, and there are not many references about them in the academic literature (Int. 3, 2020).

Examples of important successful strikes, and worker campaigns during the crisis decade include the Movistar's contractors' and technicians' long strike in Telefonica which was able to break the prevailing workplace fragmentation through spontaneous mobilisation bringing together employees and self-employed in different subcontractors (Lopez-Andreu 2019a). The occupation, boycott, and legal battle in Coca-Cola against forced redundancy and plant closure is another such example of worker struggle whose importance extended much beyond those directly affected (The Local 2015). The 21-month campaign not only ended victoriously but illustrated that organisational restructuring cannot be automatically and lawfully used for strike-breaking purposes (Fernandez and Delgado 2014). Important successful strikes took place also in street cleaning services in the Madrid Municipality in 2013 and in also in hotel cleaning services in later years (Int. 5, 2020).

Overall, when the crisis decade is examined as a whole, it is evident that the power balance at the employment and social reproduction level shifted in favour of capital. Employer unilateralism was boosted both via the increased unemployment which exerted pressures on the wages and through legal means which contributed to the erosion of collective bargaining and the weakening of the institutional power of trade unionism (Int. 2, 2020). Trade unions were generally on the defensive in the first stage of the crisis at the political level trying to prevent governmental unilateralism in the fields of policy and law and rescue social dialogue and their role in it. At the industrial relations level trade unions were even more defensive trying to challenge redundancies or at least negotiate milder terms, prevent, or reduce cuts in wages and benefits often with increasing resort to the courts. It was only in more recent years that offensive strategies were adopted attempting to win back what was lost during the peak crisis years in the form of wage raises. This is evidenced by the increasing number of strikes, strike days and number of people participating in strikes reported after 2016 (Int. 4, 2020).

Despite the fact that the social resistance to austerity was not effective enough at the national political level, in the sense of being unable to block or even substantially moderate the austerity measures at the labour market and social policy domains, it should be emphasised that there was no overhaul of the industrial relations system nor a collapse of trade unionism in Spain (Fernandez Rodriguez et al. 2021). While it is true that the legislative reforms of 2012 were unprecedented in their scope and pro-employer partisanship and they both expressed and facilitated a shift in class relations reinforcing the political position of organised capital vis a vis organised labour, in reality the actual change occurring at least as far as collective labour relations is concerned was smaller than anticipated (Lopez-Andreu 2019b). Trade unions retained substantial institutional resources, and although not able to operationalise them, especially at the political level, during the crisis years, they were able to do so increasingly in the post-crisis years and especially with the current PSOE-PODEMOS government. In the context of the handling of the Covid-19 crisis in 2020 a national agreement was made, transposed also into law reinstating fully social dialogue.

While at the beginning most employers went on the offensive after 2012, gradually at least some of them became reluctant or unable to use their newly acquired powers and adopted a milder stance and/or continued to be oriented to collective bargaining rather than imposing managerial unilateralism. There were various different reasons for that – in some cases they wanted to avoid strikes and the rise of conflict-oriented unions, in other cases they wanted to avoid getting entangled in legal battles, in yet other cases they did not want to disrupt too many existing relations with their staff (Int. 1, 2020). The uniformity and universality of the legislation should not hide the diversity and significant differences across industries, firms, and regions in Spain. The recession was general, but it did not impact to the same extent and in the same way industries and the labour force. This was because Spain has an essentially fragmented labour relations system, segmented further as a result of the crisis (Lopez-Andreu, 2019b). Whereas the more secure workers in big, unionised firms were subjected primarily to a long period of sustained wage moderation and minor cuts, the more precariously employed workers typically suffered more from unemployment, under-employment, and low wages.

Precarious and low-paid workers were in any case insufficiently protected. While they were not the main targets of the legislative reform, they suffered the brunt of the changes of the collective bargaining structure, partly because of their weaker positioning in the labour market, partly because of the objective difficulty to pursue their rights to the courts (Int. 6, 2020). Even in the relatively improved conditions after 2015, when economic stabilisation and growth brought about a reduction in unemployment and youth unemployment and when trade unions were able to push for moderate wage increases, there was little containment of labour market precariousness. Part-time employment remained close to 15% even in 2019, and in conjunction with the fact that most jobs created were at the low paid end, the increased population of 'working poor' indicates that although the crisis was over by the end of the 2010s, its impact on Spanish society was not (Int. 4, 2020).

## Note

1 Worker mobilisation in Amazon culminating in strike action in early 2019 is an illustrative example of this (Reuters 2019). Unrest had been growing since 2018 over long hours and stressful working conditions while further unrest arose in 2020 over working conditions during the Covid-19 crisis.

# 4 Greece. Suppression, Contestation, and Levelling

Greece was the first country where the economic recession turned into a full-blown crisis, where the Troika management was the longest in duration and the harshest, and where the crisis consequences were ultimately the most severe. The contraction of the economy was accompanied by the dismantling of the industrial relations system, substantial cuts in social policy and an unprecedented political upheaval. Over a period of less than a decade, Greece effectively experienced a rough process of economic shrinking, tearing down of its labour market institutions, political system restructuring and lowering of the overall standard of living. SYRIZA which emerged as the major political force promising the end of austerity and an alternative policy assuming executive power in 2015, not only failed to deliver this, but in fact ultimately served to stabilise, legitimise, and normalise the degenerate labour market and industrial relations conditions that had been established.

The management of the Greek crisis was in many ways a drama that dragged on for many years, capturing the attention of the whole of Europe and at times provoking or precipitating developments extending beyond Greece itself. From 2010 until 2015, the crisis management was framed as the effort to avert state bankruptcy and consequent exit from the Eurozone. As this, defined as the worst scenario, was ultimately avoided, as the humanitarian crisis was dealt with, and as the economy started expanding again, it can be said that the crisis has been overcome. Yet after a decade of crisis, Greece became essentially a poorer country, with inferior working conditions, weaker and even more fragmented trade unionism, reduced employment protection, and limited social welfare available.

While social contestation of the austerity policies was huge in the early stages of the crisis, it was unable to block them and the success of mobilisation has been restricted to the overhauling of the political system which was initially fragmented and subsequently reshuffled. SYRIZA, both the main beneficiary, and the protagonist of this process is examined more closely at the end of the chapter to shed light on deeper on-going developments in terms of class relations and the politics of the crisis period.

Trade unionism is also discussed in the light of the comprehensive restructuring that took place in the field of individual and collective labour law and the increased precariousness prevailing in the labour market.

This chapter, contributing a second national case study to the book, serves as an example of comparative contrast to the previous one. Liberalisation, employment deregulation and market enhancing reforms in general, although securing the support of national elites were not sufficiently owned by them and were largely seen as being imposed from the outside. Thus, whereas for Spain, compression is the word more aptly describing the treatment of employment and social rights, for Greece suppression and levelling more vividly describe the means with which labour was devalued. The legal order of the labour market was effectively suspended as a frontal attack was waged against collective bargaining. The extensive and thorough intervention on the industrial relations and welfare systems was unprecedented in scope and depth and its impact proved in many respects outlived the long crisis period. At the same time, the treatment of Greece and the level of political contestation it gave rise to extended beyond its national borders raising broader questions about the EU, the Eurozone, the Left, and the future.

## Recession, the Threat of Collapse and the Troika Support Mechanism

Up until the eve of the crisis Greece boasted a significantly high collective bargaining coverage despite its comparatively low trade union density. Wages were not particularly high, and the welfare state in place was not overtly generous, but for the majority, wages were sufficient to make ends meet and social welfare was organised according to principles of universality. Although neoliberalism was entrenching itself as an overarching frame in the Greek political system since the 1990s and was strengthening its appeal as a social ideology, its encroachment in the sphere of social policy, labour law and industrial relations was relatively slow (Int. 10, 2019). Labour market flexibilisation was introduced in the 1990s and this trend continued in 2000s with a series of laws deregulating and re-regulating aspects of the labour market through the creation of new type of employment contracts. However, the regular open-ended employment contracts enjoyed by the vast majority were left untouched (Vogiatzoglou 2017).

Despite the low and declining trade union density, the institutionalisation of flexible employment and the creeping rise of unemployment and involuntary part-time work already before the turn of the Century, the high economic growth also boosted by the 2004 Olympic Games resulted in rising standard of living and declining of overall income inequality. Tourism and construction were expanding, and the structural weaknesses of the Greek economy did not prevent it from growing and improving in all measures. There was both an increase in real wages without negatively affecting profitability and an increase in productivity (Tombazos 2018). To be sure, there was poverty and marginalisation in the labour market and in addition to migrant workers it begun to be increasingly also felt by younger nationals. However, up until the outbreak of the crisis in 2008 the trend at the level of society was for the majority largely positive.

At the level of the economy, it is important to stress that Greece's growth in the decade before the crisis was largely based on capital inflows from strong European states and the United States and that this resulted in rising public and private debt. When the global recession hit the European economy, systemic risks begun to pile up and the financial sector was in danger of collapsing. Within the Eurozone there were no mechanisms for the transfer of resources and Greece with its high public debt and bigger external deficit became the weakest link in the crisis of the European periphery (Tombazos 2018). The chronic problems of high public deficits and debt in conjunction with Greece's inadequate state infrastructure, low capital accumulation and weak export orientation rendered it very vulnerable very quickly. The increased credit flow from the north, mainly through Germany worsened further the trade balances (Theodoropoulou 2016), while the use of the European Central Bank cheap liquidity support by the Greek banks to buy government bonds tied the Greek state to the fortune of the Greek banks. As the Greek banks were already on the brink of collapse, this increased the vulnerability of the Greek state.

Foreign banks were also tied to the Greek state and the Greek banks and the collapse of the Greek economy was averted through the Troika Support Mechanism which initiated the first round of the austerity cycle. However, the first bail-out programme effectively transformed the Greek public debt from debt to private investors, foreign as well as national to debt to European states (Siani-Davies 2017). This made the option of default a more difficult one to choose and the management of the crisis more complex. Although in the beginning this enhanced tension, and increased the risks within the Eurozone, its longer-term impact was to isolate Greece at the inter-governmental level. More importantly it exacerbated the problem of public debt as the economy contracted while non-performing loans in the private sector also multiplied necessitating a second bail-out programme this time involving a 'voluntary' private sector haircut, the Public Sector Involvement scheme, which reduced public debt, without restructuring the banking sector and without bail-in procedures of the sort later used in Cyprus. The second bail-out programme led to much harsher austerity provoking a social crisis and led to further economic decline.

George Papandreou's government, that agreed the first bail-out programme was not in a position to implement it and after toying briefly with the idea of a referendum, to which EU leaders responded with a direct threat of exit from the Eurozone and for which domestic support was lacking, resigned (Siani-Davies 2017: 181–183). The austerity measures of the first programme and the transition to the second one were undertaken by the technocratic government of ex Central Bank Director, Loukas Papademos who took over in conditions of emergency and supported by the two main parties PASOK and New Democracy (ND) as well as the far-right party Popular Orthodox Rally (LAOS). By the end of 2011 however and as it was becoming clear that more drastic measures were needed and harsher austerity was to be imposed, a political government was needed that was to take direct ownership of the new bail-out programme. This became possible in mid-2012 when the leader of ND Antonis Samaras was able to head a coalition government of including PASOK and the Demacratic Left (DIMAR) a party formed after a split from SYRIZA.

## Contesting Austerity and the New Political Frames and Narratives

A bitter ideological struggle, or really a political struggle framed in and shaped by ideology was waged before the bail-out programmes were enforced. The media had a central role in building some support and directly or indirectly legitimising the economic and social policies adopted and the management of the economic crisis in general. Although this can be the subject of another book, and the communication politics surrounding the crisis does warrant a book-length analysis which cannot be undertaken here, some key elements of how the crisis was conceptualised are necessary in accounting how the recession was experienced and how austerity management was pushed through. The framing of the crisis was a battle fiercely waged throughout crisis-stricken Southern Europe and beyond and the media in many respects paved the way for neoliberal crisis management and austerity politics. In Greece where the crisis was deeper, its management harsher and the contestation greater, the conflict between competing frames and narratives was also more enhanced than the rest of Southern Europe (Teperoglou et al. 2014).

In the early stage, the media focused on the phenomenon of the crisis and on its consequences as a tool to avoid the discussion of its causes (Pleios 2013). Where the causes of the crisis did enter the frame of analysis and the narrative accounts, there was often a resort to cultural and social explanations with stereotypes of lazy and spoiled Greeks. This was in line with sensational articles produced in the mainstream international press, often approaching the grotesque in tabloid media. Although the master frame was really the classic and global neoliberal schema of the 'wasteful spending' and 'inefficient' state, in narratives more focused on and attuned to 'Greece' the neoliberal discourse also incorporated references to the Greek particularity, essence or soul.

The 'Greek soul' for example was to blame according to pop philosophers like Stelios Ramfos, as the crisis was seen really as a 'Greek phenomenon' while smart public relations and marketing media personas suggested 'positive action' through a sort of national re-branding in order to improve the image of the country and its self-confidence (Mylonas and Kombatsiaris 2013).

The development of moralist and culturalist explanations on the Greek crisis served to mask its systemic character and contain it as a national issue. It was about 'people living beyond their abilities' not about the contradictions in the nexus of capitalist relations in which Greece was implicated, and it was about corruption rather than market failure. More importantly the neoliberal construction of the crisis was eschatological – harsh austerity was necessary to avoid immanent destruction. Austerity, privatisations, the curtailing of social and political rights were in this narrative, necessary evils for Greece to become 'true European' and 'modern' (Mylonas 2014). In this way the Greek mainstream media effectively converged with the north European media and the racist and the neo-colonialist overtones of the PIGS narrative, developed regarding the South European periphery (Van Vossole 2016).

Although the depictions of the financial crisis varied in the international media with the emphasis and the focus shifting according to the level of involvement of each major country and the evolution of the crisis, there were some recurring themes and tropes built through a series of metaphors. The most common of these were the depiction of the financial crisis as a contagious 'disease' that needed to be contained and the debtor countries as its helpless 'victims' that needed to be rescued. The 'rescuers' were the strong Eurozone countries and the EU institutions that were able to confront the 'natural disaster' and provide therapies akin to a 'mechanical repair' of a technical fault. This process was also a 'learning experience' whereby the pupils had to be disciplined by their teachers for their own good in order to learn their lessons and avoid their mistakes in the future (Bickes et al. 2014). Variations of these hegemonic north European frames were adopted, adapted, and used to build hegemonic narratives in the European periphery which were diffused.

At the same time, these hegemonic narratives emanating from politicians, technocrats and the media were contested by a growing mass movement at the level of society composed by anti-austerity initiatives and expressed through diverse, popular mobilisations (Diani and Kousis 2014). 2010 was a year of numerous mass protests and general strikes as well as a variety of citizens' initiatives of resistance and solidarity. These continued in 2011 and escalated further before slowing down in 2012 and subsiding in 2014 after leaving their imprint on the Greek political landscape. Trade unions, although significantly delegitimised in the previous period as well as during the crisis years played a central role in the anti-austerity mobilisations as the general strikes they proclaimed, although typically lasting one and sometimes two days and with participation in the private sectors being much lower than in the public sector, served most times as rallying points for mass protests (Serdedakis 2018).

Although there were several strikes in this period, peaking in 2011–2012, the main field where contentious politics was played out was the streets rather than the workplace. As the crisis deepened and unemployment rose, workers and trade unions were less able to maintain a balance of power in the industrial relations field and turned their attention to the political level and seeking solutions from the state (Vogiatzoglou 2018). Amidst numerous bankruptcies, restructurings and threat of bankruptcies, trade unions waged primarily defensive battles regarding redundancies and trying to restrain wage and benefits cuts while often the most critical issue was the delays in wage payments (Papanikolopoulos et al. 2018). Precarious workers, students and the unemployed, primarily young, for whom it was impossible or too difficult to engage in workplace struggles were more enabled to join the anti-austerity street protests. While the first mobilisations in 2010 were organised and attended primarily by the usual suspects of left-wing parties and groups, social movement activists and trade unionists, the also attracted new participants or novice-protesters with different profiles, more alike to non-protesters (Rüdig and Karyotis 2013).

The peak of the anti-austerity mobilisations was the 'movement of the squares' in mid-2011 in which citizens from various political and social backgrounds without any organisational support coalesced in the squares of the main cities, in protest against the austerity policies and the politicians implementing them (Diani and Kousis 2014). Taking their example and name from the Spanish 'Indignados' (15M) the Greek 'Aganaktismenoi' (outraged) set up popular assemblies and put forward an alternative conception of politics emphasising direct democracy and citizen participation not only as a means to prevent austerity but as an end in itself. Although more diverse, politically inchoate, ideologically fragmented, and ultimately short-lived than the Spanish precursor, the Greek Aganaktismenoi had equally profound repercussions on the Greek political system and at a faster speed. Both movements expounded an anti-oligarchic view of citizenship, understanding it as the power of the dispersed 'citizenry' against the concentrated power of economic and political elites (Gerbaudo 2017). This was a departure from the anti-statism of previous social movements and the attempt to redefine the state as the basis of social cohesion, re-appropriating it for the purposes of 'people power'.

Coming after more than a year of frequent mass protests and strikes led by the 'usual suspects', the 'Aganaktismenoi' constituted both a rupture and a qualitative leap in the anti-austerity milieu (Sotirakopoulos and Sotiropoulos 2013). Although unable to articulate in a systematic manner, a coherent counter-narrative or put forward a set of proposals, it attracted many new people that were first-time protesters, it contributed to the re-politicisation and radicalisation of young people and it facilitated significant shifts in electoral behaviour in the subsequent months. Although the movement was brutally repressed in June 2011 and the squares ultimately cleared of the few remaining activists by the police around a month later, and although it proved impossible to prevent the approval of the 'second memorandum' by the parliament the 'Aganaktismenoi' constituted a critical event and in many ways a climax of the contention cycle that had begun in early 2010 (Serdedakis 2018).

In the public squares, radical economists, constitutional lawyers, and political activists blended their cognitive arguments with the affective and moral arguments emanating from citizens about the primacy of people and the right to defend popular sovereignty threatened by external forces (Aslanidis and Marantzidis 2016). As such the Aganaktismenoi movement contributed decisively in provoking mass defection from the two main parties dominating the Greek political system for three decades and in the crystallisation of the deep cleavage that was being formed between that section of society opposing the bail-out programmes and those supporting them. The political system was substantially delegitimised and in such conditions SYRIZA, established less than a decade before as a coalition of a small left-wing party with several far-left non-parliamentary groups, was able to come to the forefront as an alternative political force, the strongest and the most viable one among the 'anti-Memorandum forces'.

It is important to stress that there were numerous social movements active in the period 2010–2013. The discourse developed by these anti-austerity movements more broadly, also included appeals to the law as part of the mobilisation repertoire and the putting forward of alternative interpretations about the lawfulness of policies, constitutional rights and justice (Rethymiotaki et al. 2017). Like was the case with the 15M in Spain, the 'Aganaktismenoi' created a milieu in which many people, especially younger ones were politicised, repoliticised and radicalised. After the summer of 2011 when the public squares were emptied, the mobilisation energy that was accumulated did not fizzle out and much of it was directed into neighbourhood assemblies, self-help groups, and alternative structures with which people attempted to address their immediate needs. As the crisis deepened and unemployment and poverty soared, numerous solidarity initiatives and networks sprang up on a primarily informal basis. These were cooperative structures and social enterprises including housing and health care provision while more elaborate and sophisticated ones included solidarity-based exchanges such as barter clubs and time banks, credit unions and ethical banks even alternative social currency initiatives (Kousis and Paschou 2017).

At the political level SYRIZA was able to absorb the energy of these citizen movements incorporating in various ways and to different degrees numerous activists but more importantly successfully framing itself as the political and institutional answer to the problem of austerity, and its own narrative as the dominant one within the polymorphous anti-Memorandum bloc (Sotirakopoulos, and Ntalaka 2016). The mass mobilisations of the 2010–2012 period were not able to prevent the adoption of austerity policies at the level of the state. They did however erode the legitimacy of the political elite, exerted pressure on numerous parliamentarians who refused to vote the austerity bills and were ousted from the two mainstream parties and ultimately reshaped the political landscape (Siani-Davies 2017). The anti-austerity movement brought about the implosion and the fragmentation of the Greek political system. The 2012 elections, the first producing a fragmented parliament rendering the formation of a government coalition impossible and the second one which brought the ND led coalition to power and SYRIZA as the 2nd biggest party in opposition testify this trend.

## The Watershed in Labour Law, Employment Relations and Collective Bargaining

While the first bail-out programme focused primarily on public sector employment relations and had a primarily fiscal rationale, the second bail-out programme was a watershed at all levels – employment, collective bargaining, social policy – effectively dismantling the institutional order of industrial relations in Greece (Yannakourou and Tsimpoukis 2016). Unlike the case with Spain, whereby only a general framework of labour market policy reform was suggested and the national government was left to fill in the details, in Greece the Troika was more explicit in its 'suggestions' which constituted not only macro-economic goals that the Greek authorities had to set for themselves but also the means with which these goals were to be achieved. Greece was absolutely dependent on a new loan to avoid default and lacking any alternative means to refinance its debt, from the moment that the refinancing of the debt was understood to be necessary, had no other option than to comply with the suggested structural reforms. The conditionality mechanism was effective because it was at the same time both material and normative, a case of 'dominium over imperium', based on the disequilibrium between the two parties whereby the 'wealth of government was used to secure the legislative change' (Katsaroumpas 2018).

Numerous posts in the public sector were abolished through a variety of measures such as redundancy, reserve placements, early retirement, and the establishment of ratios from 1:10 to 1:5 between entry and exit into public sector employment. Essentially new hiring was almost blocked and in a period of few years there was a 22% decline in public sector employment. Wages were cut and the 13th and 14th salary[1] in the public sector was abolished by law, resulting in an average of 30% reduction in total earnings (Kouzis 2018). Working time increased from

37.5 to 40 hours per week, while stricter disciplinary measures were introduced resulting in work intensification and generalised insecurity. At the same time where new public sector hiring did occur it was mostly done via private law, raising the proportion of private law status employees in the public sector from 10% before the crisis to 28% after the crisis (Kouzis 2018).

In the private sector the most important measure was the abolition of the national collective agreement as the determinant of the minimum wage, 751€ before the crisis, and the establishment of a new minimum wage by law at 586€ and 510€ for those under 25 years old. This had a profound impact not only in economic terms with the more vulnerable workers paid at the minimum wage rate having their monthly earnings substantially reduced, but it also structurally eroded collective bargaining and by extension trade unionism (Int. 9, 2019). More broadly the state strengthened its role in the regulation of industrial relations while practically remaining a weak enforcement agency. The treatment of collective agreements as a private rather than a public good and the encroachment of the state was based on, and facilitated, the weakening of trade unionism (Koukiadaki 2019). In 2019, the 'under-25 category' was abolished and minimum wage rose to 650€ but remained determined by law.

Equally significant along this trajectory was the abolition of the favourability principle between overlapping existing collective agreements. This allowed firm-level agreements stipulating worse terms and conditions of employment to prevail over sectoral ones – and the national one – operating that is as a key deregulation instrument. Firm-level collective agreements increased from 170 in 2011 to 976 in 2012 (Katsaroumpas and Koukiadaki 2019). Extension clauses in sectoral and occupational collective agreements were abolished along with several benefits and yearly raises accruing from accumulated years of service. Furthermore, the scope of the national collective agreement was restricted to cover only signatories. Although this resulted in a temporary boost of trade union density as some workers joined trade unions to gain coverage, numerous employers withdrew from their associations to be no longer bound by collective bargaining (Int. 8, 2019).

More broadly labour market flexibility was promoted directly and indirectly through a series of measures the most important being the decrease in employment protection and the easing of dismissals (Yannakourou and Tsimpoukis 2016). The probationary period was extended from 2 to 12 months, notice periods were shortened, the maximum redundancy remuneration for long term employed was reduced from 24 to 12 monthly salaries and compensation payment instalments were spread in time (Koukiadis 2017). Collective redundancies were also eased through increasing the monthly number allowed from 4 to 6 and from 2% to 5% for firms employing 20–150 workers (Kouzis 2014). Working time flexibilisation measures were adopted eroding further over-time remuneration, extending the working day in retail trade and promoting part-time and rotational work. Agency work was also promoted through allowing its operation in the public sector and extending the maximum time from 12 to 36 months (Zambarloukou 2014). The conversion time of a fixed term to an indefinite duration/open ended contract rose from 2 to 3 years and special 'work experience contracts' were instituted for young unemployed persons with 20% lower wages (Kouzis 2018).

In the domain of dispute resolution, the right to unilateral resort to arbitration was abolished, effectively giving employers the right to block that route, a power which they have used systematically for several years before the jurisprudence of the Constitutional Court cancelled this in 2015 (Koukiadis 2017). Significant confusion continues to surround this issue though even among trade unionists and the broader real and perceived negative balance of power results in less frequent exercise of that right (Int. 7, 2019). The scope of mediation and arbitration services was also significantly curtailed to the finding of 'objective solutions' for which references are made to the firm viability and competitiveness but not to wage sufficiency given cost of living and worker living standard in general. Dispute resolution procedures between employers and non-striking workers about the non-payment during strike days were speeded up and in conjunction with recent case laws this indirectly brings back the right of employer 'lock-out' (Kouzis and Kapsalis 2020).

Trade union rights were severely weakened in many respects as the collective bargaining system was shrunk and restructured. The most extraordinary measure adopted was the one allowing employers to sign collective agreements with an 'association of persons' which represented 15–25% of workers in a firm and thus in conjunction with the abolition of the favourability principle, to completely by-pass sectoral collective agreements. There was a conscious attempt to provide employers with an overriding mechanism allowing them to introduce policies that could not be negotiated with trade unions or works councils (Voskeritsian and Kornelakis 2019). These were a key instrument through which bigger wage reductions were achieved (Giannakopoulos and Laliotis 2019). Although used extensively during the peak of the crisis years when the rapidity of deterioration of labour market conditions spread despair among workers, in more recent years the 'association of persons' instrument became much less widespread. This was probably a combination of workers' regaining some confidence and not consenting to the formation of such 'associations' and labour market conditions stabilising at a new lower level rendering such mechanisms less necessary for employers.

The other important vehicle through which trade unions were weakened was the shortening of the post termination effect of collective agreements from 6 to 3 months and restricting the post termination effect scope to the basic wage and some benefits. Higher-level collective agreements were not renewed resulting in the shrinking of their number from 100 sectoral and 90 occupational ones before the crisis to less than 20 in 2013 (Ioannou 2019). This was instrumental both in promoting individual bargaining and pressurising the trade unions to rush and reach a deal with the employer before the expiration of the 3-month period to avert the worse (Int. 10, 2019). The bargaining power of the employer and his ability to set the terms, already increased due to market conditions, was significantly enhanced through institutional means as well.

In addition to the above the protection of elected trade unionists from redundancy was lifted and some leading trade unionists were made redundant while the overall time allocated for trade union duties was restricted (Int. 7, 2019; Int. 9, 2019). In the third bail-out enforced by the SYRIZA government the participation quota for trade union assemblies deciding strike action was raised from 20–33% accordingly, to 50%, which in the conditions of general demobilisation and surmounting trade union difficulty, effectively restricted severely trade union capacity to strike. This was regarded as an additional attack on trade unionism and as a hypocrisy of the politicians who are elected in positions of state power with lower percentages (Int. 8, 2019; Int. 9, 2019). In 2019, the newly elected ND government pushed through a framework bill making obligatory an electronic database registration record of trade union membership, instituting electronic voting for decision-making and increasing the powers of the Ministry. These were seen by trade unions as additional attacks on trade unionism, further boosting the individualisation of employment relations.

At the level of social policy which is also directly connected with labour policy and needs to be taken into account when discussing employment relations since it structures the broader context in which workers meet employers in the labour market, there was also significant change during the crisis years. Overall per capita expenditure on social policy in Greece decreased from being at 72% of the EU15 average in 2008 to 57% in 2014. Per capita health spending shrank from 71% of the EU15 average in 2008 to 39% in 2015 while various fees were instituted at the point of delivery (Petmezidou 2018). However, it must also be said that the SYRIZA government in its attempt to deal with the 'humanitarian crisis' did extend health coverage to the unemployed in 2016. Unemployment benefit shrank in duration (to a maximum of 450 days in 4 years and to 400 days from 2014 onwards) and amount to 360€. Means testing was introduced for the long-term unemployed and active labour market policies were adopted, effectively establishing new subsidised posts substituting regular employment.

More broadly in addition to shrinking, the framework and philosophy of social welfare shifted from universalist principles to more market-centred ones. Means testing was expanded as the disability and family benefits were re-organised, stricter criteria were instituted involving both income and property and the process of benefit claiming was made more complicated and more unpleasant. Pensions were reduced on average by 30% and the overall level of protection and support to recipients was decreased (Demoulas 2018). In this context, the most important development was the introduction of a minimum guaranteed income scheme based on the neoliberal idea of the 'negative tax' which was named Social Solidarity Benefit by the SYRIZA government. This offered a very basic level of protection, dealing with cases of extreme deprivation and addressing the humanitarian crisis.

The Social Solidarity Benefit was really the epitome of neoliberal welfare in crisis-stricken Greece. On the one hand it helped many people gain the bare necessary means of subsistence and on the other hand it served as an adjustment tool to conditions of permanent precariousness (Spyridakis 2018). This is in line with the general function of welfare in neoliberal policy, as a disciplining mechanism, easing the adjustment of a group of people, who experienced rapid downward social mobility into their new place in the bottom of the social pyramid. On a more practical level, its insufficiency in lifting people above the bare minimum level of subsistence in conjunction with its strict eligibility criteria and restrictions and the sorry state of the formal labour market pushed many recipients to occasional casual undeclared work. In this vain like all poor welfare schemes, it increased the willingness and propensity of recipients to attempt to top up their limited income through the informal labour market (Table 4.1).

## Coping in Precarious Conditions

The rise of unemployment and underemployment in Greece constituted not only the most severe and direct repercussion of the contraction of the economy but also the setting in which the crisis was managed through austerity politics. Unemployment and involuntary part-time work or underemployment was already higher than the EU average before the crisis and as the crisis unfolded, they sky-rocketed. At the peak of the crisis years the unemployment rate rose to 27.5% in 2013, from 7.7% in

*Table 4.1* Number of registered unemployed, Youth unemployment and Part time employment rates, Minimum wage in €, Greece, 2008–2019

| *Greece* | *2008* | *2013* | *2019* |
|---|---|---|---|
| No. of registered unemployed persons | 364 300 | 1 330 300 | 819 000 |
| Youth unemployment rate (15–24) (%) | 21.9 | 58.3 | 35.5 |
| Part time employment rate (%) | 5.4 | 8.4 | 9.1 |
| Minimum wage in € | 794.20 | 683.76 | 758.33 |

Source: Eurostat.

2008, with half of the youth unemployed and one third of society in poverty (Kouzis and Kapsalis 2020). As the GDP decreased in volume by 25% from 2008 to 2013 whole industries such as construction, manufacturing, wholesale trade, and retail trade came to a halt while the downturn affected almost every sector. The economy shrank and the country entered into a recessionary spiral with the first austerity measures provoking a further drop in demand and further worsening of state finances leading into new austerity measures. Thousands of small firms closed down and thousands who stayed afloat had to downsize and lay off personnel.

Young people, already in a comparatively difficult situation before the crisis as they tended to be over-represented in precarious and low paid jobs, were severely hit by the crisis (Kretsos, 2014). In public discussions before the crisis, the concept of 'the generation of 700 euros' was popularised, to denote the average monthly salary on the market available to young workers most of whom had university qualifications. In the peak of crisis years young people who had full-time jobs and who had a regular monthly income of 700€ were considered among the better off. The structural obstacles faced by young people in the labour market, even in the relatively prosperous times of the mid 2000s, were instrumental in the growing political unrest. The movement of extended student occupations had also served to radicalise Greek youth as the spontaneous revolt of 2009 sparked by the killing of the high school student Alexis Gregoropoulos by the police, attests to this (Broumas et al. 2018).

The internal devaluation process during the crisis years was a particularly long and painful one in Greece resulting in rising inequality, through the 'second order macro-economic effects' (Perez and Matsaganis 2018). There were less jobs and less money around for everybody but as expected for those already worse off and vulnerable before the crisis, coping through the crisis became much more difficult (Markantonatou and Kennedy 2019). Involuntary non-standard employment grew substantially transforming the labour market (Livanos and Pouliakas 2019). A lot of people who has access to family dwelling in the countryside, moved there as it was impossible to sustain themselves in the cities and attempted to get by through setting up vegetable gardens, doing some casual agricultural work if, and when, available and generally get by with less.

Many more migrated to northern European countries, usually to cities where they had some contacts to host them for some time while looking for jobs, and experience reminiscent of older times. This time, however, it was not only semi-skilled and unskilled workers migrating. It was also and perhaps more so, young persons with a university education, often postgraduate and PhD qualifications (Labrianidis and Pratsinakis 2017). While the crisis magnified the 'push' factors that already existed in Southern Europe, it was not only unemployment, or narrowly labour market conditions that nurtured this migration wave, but also more general disillusionment with the quality of life prospects ahead. The negative factors of corruption, nepotism, and lack of meritocracy at home combined with the search of new experiences and professional opportunities abroad to drive the highly skilled youth to emigrate, in a combination of relative deprivation and cosmopolitanism (Triantafyllidou and Gropas 2014).

It is difficult to make generalisations about which social groups were hit the most by the crisis. Obviously, those employed in more volatile sectors, sectors overtly hit by the crisis and those occupying precarious job posts already were the first to face unemployment and underemployment often for longer periods (Gialis and Tsampra 2015). Women and migrants, already over-represented in the precarious segment of the labour force in Greece, became more vulnerable during the crisis years. Yet at the same time, the generalised depression of the wages as the recession deepened and the laying off of older, often skilled and/or experienced men workers resulted in the decrease of the gender pay gap as an aggregate whole (Liapi 2016). Similarly, with less jobs around, less migrants came and less remained in the labour market with many of those remaining being those who had established sufficient solidarity networks in the previous period and were more well integrated in Greek society.

Among the more relatively better off sections of the Greek labour force, the group that suffered a violent downward social mobility was older men who lost their jobs and whose age was far from that making them eligible for a pension and far from that which most employers would consider. Those were also often people with increased social and financial obligations who saw their life plans seriously disrupted. Many skilled workers, professionals, and small businessmen whose enterprises went bankrupt suddenly lost the status they had before the crisis as they were pushed down to the ranks of the poor. Among this social group those that had little savings and big mortgages and business loans found themselves trembling down the social ladder, losing not only the economic means with which to sustain their lifestyles but also their social network and esteem and their morale and confidence. Spyridakis (2018) captures in his interviews in very vivid terms the frustration and disappointment experienced by such people trapped in a condition that allows them neither to progress nor regress further. This entrapment in the world of precarity is felt as a sort of stagnation and liminality, learning to live on the margin, adjusting to a life with no visible prospects and killing time doing at most simulations of work that could hopefully sometime in the future become employment.

As known from decades of literature, unemployment is always more than an economic condition, having consequences which are also social, psychological and in the broad sense political, not only to its victims but to the whole of society (Karakioulafi and Spyridakis 2017). It raises questions of social justice and the distribution of resources among industries, regions, and generations, it weakens social bonds and participation in civic life, it leads to the increase of indifference and withdrawal. It exerts a type of psychological violence on its victims who not only come to blame themselves, but it also results in the lowering of their self-esteem and motivation and the decrease of their capacity for socialisation (Panayiotopoulos and Schultheis 2015).

It is not only that the unemployed of the Greek crisis had less material means with which to leave their home setting, although this was a key issue for people living in the countryside or away from urban centres, but also that their propensity to engage in social interactions decreased. In the narratives presented in Panayiotopoulos and Schultheis (2015) a sort of oscillation between despair, entrapment and resignation comes out vividly and repeatedly. In some cases, in the attempt to become accustomed to the reality of the material circumstances, subjects immerse themselves into a process of immiseration, which the authors consider to be the ultimate result of the pain inflicted by long term unemployment and associated poverty.

The expansion of unemployment was a foundation pillar upon which the new post-crisis labour field was built in Greece. It contributed to the collapse of collective bargaining or in the best cases its shrinking and erosion, it socially legitimised under-employment and normalised low wages and employment insecurity. Precariousness was no longer a condition of the labour market periphery but a condition to be also found within the bounds of regular, permanent work (Koukiadaki and Kokkinou 2017; 2016). Employment flexibility was pushed through a variety of measures at the institutional and policy level that facilitated and directed the shift in the labour market. For example, the spread of agency work contributed not only to the expansion of low wage work, but also added one more layer of difficulty in unionisation and the challenging of these conditions. An analogous result was achieved via subcontracting and outsourcing, occurring even in settings such as major hotels which also expanded substantially in recent times (Int. 9, 2019). These were developments preceding the crisis but exacerbated in the new deregulated framework and operating as an instrument through which employers could circumvent the national and the sectoral collective agreements, even in sectors where they had survived (Papadopoulos and Lyddon 2020).

Precariousness was not only an objective reality in the crisis labour market but also gradually internalised, subjectivised and ideologically consolidated. Bithymitris and Papadopoulos (2017) illustrate how subsidised training programmes accustomed young people to precarity through 'learning' liminality. In the hospitality industry, these programmes aimed to develop a professional ethos, social skills in dealing with customers and adaptability capacity, the soft skills that the employers believe to be lacking. Yet based as they are on precarious conditions, such programmes cannot really promote a professional ethos and their success is in strengthening a non-reflexive adaptability and a willingness to conform to a conjunctural scenario. Far from empowering the unemployed and equipping them with the skills and determination to forcefully enter the labour market, these sort of programmes do the utmost to instil low expectations that facilitate the acceptance of low wage jobs or any jobs irrelevant of content and enhance feelings of frustration and resignation (Bithymitris and Papadopoulos 2017).

Informality in the labour market, which is a diachronic feature of Mediterranean countries, especially high in Greece as the state was underperforming, increased further during the crisis (Siani-Davies 2017). Beyond the increases in taxes and social insurance payments and the imposition of stricter conditions and controls on benefit recipients, which increased the incentives for both employers and workers to opt for informal arrangements where that was possible, the more general disruption occurring via the rapid shrinkage of the economy was conducive to a preference for informality. Gradually, however, at least as far as the state was concerned, and in the context of the attempt to fight tax evasion, a set of new rules and practices were instituted making electronic payment of wages obligatory and improving the social insurance registration and payment procedures allowing better monitoring. Although the driver in this process was the need for improvement of the tax-collecting capacity of the state, it did also have a positive impact on the labour relations domain as it helped to some extent in arresting the spread of informal employment (Int. 8, 2019).

However, in some industries, hospitality being the prime example, a new hybrid regime has been established at the employers' initiative but, significantly, tolerated by workers and by the state. This involves mixing formal with informal employment and using part-time work as a vehicle with which to limit employment rights and benefits (Int. 10, 2019). Typically, in the hospitality industry workers work many more hours, above those which are registered and insured for and receive the wages corresponding to the extra working time as cash payment. In many restaurants, cafes, and bars in Athens most workers have part-time work contracts yet work almost full-time hours. Informality is also present in hotels, although these tend to be usually more regulated and typically covered by the sectoral collective agreement. In the islands during the tourist season, informal work encroaches through excessive unregistered and uninsured overtime work, also paid cash in hand. There, hospitality workers are typically registered for 40 or 48-hours per week but tend to work above 60, sometimes even above 70 hours per week for the whole duration of the summer. Not enjoying adequate rest time during the tourist season, not even the legal minimum, is quite a prevalent phenomenon (Int. 9, 2019).

## Politics, SYRIZA, Class Relations and Trade Unionism in a Crisis-stricken Setting

SYRIZA emerged as the political force representing primarily the losers of the crisis and expressing their desire to undo its consequences. A few years later it ceased to represent its electoral basis and to function more than a party mediating between particular interests and the state, converting itself effectively from a movement party, or rather a party flirting with the various anti-austerity movements into a cartel-party of austerity management (Seferiades, 2018). During the period of SYRIZA rule (2015–2019) not only was there no substantial reversal of the dismantling of collective bargaining and wage-setting mechanisms, but in the context of the third memorandum the new inferior for labour normal, was consolidated (Kouzis 2020).

This relatively rapid, compressed in time, transformation of SYRIZA which spread disappointment among left-wing circles in Greece and indeed throughout Europe, defies easy and uni-causal explanations (Charalambous and Ioannou 2015b). Terms such as 'betrayal' and 'capitulation' although carrying some descriptive relevance and a great emotional load, cannot really help understand the why and the how of the shift in the politics of SYRIZA, a process sealed after the referendum held before the 3rd bail-out programme in July 2015. Afterall the discrepancy between what parties declare and what they do has been observed long ago. This is much more complex than a matter of hypocrisy or cynicism of leaders; it involves constraints and different operational modalities (Morlino and Raniolo 2017: 79). To explain the political transformation of SYRIZA from a left-wing force promising the end of austerity to a social democratic or centrist social liberal force enforcing in government austerity 'with a human face' one needs to adopt a slightly longer-term viewpoint and examine in some more depth both the social dynamics prevailing in the crisis period and the conjuncture of 2015, but also the internal processes within the 'SYRIZA world'.

Kotronaki (2018) is an activist in addition to a scholar of social movements, with an inside knowledge of the trajectory of SYRIZA's rise from a small left-wing political coalition into a party heading the government. She argues convincingly that there is an organisational story at play. By examining the whole process of the evolution of SYRIZA from 2004 to 2015, Kotronaki argues that the shift in the discursive domain evidenced through the public proclamations of SYRIZA was paralleled by organisational changes of de facto centralisation which effectively preceded the formal centralisation occurring after the 2012 elections. SYRIZA became so easily a leader-centred, cartel party in 2012 because all the elements needed for this were already there, namely weak party structures, insufficient processes of internal debate and democratic decision-making on difficult topics and diverging views between factions too weak to challenge the leadership.

However, if the organisational dimension can answer the 'how question', how that is Alexis Tsipras and the top party leadership were able to prevail and electorally win, amidst such a U-turn in policy, it cannot on its own answer the 'why'. That is a more directly political question and is related with a contradictory political plan that characterised the whole path of SYRIZA from its beginning, even if that contradiction was revealed in its entirety just before its rise to power which also brought its resolution. Although possibly predictable, the path of SYRIZA was neither predetermined nor inevitable and the agency of different protagonists, acting and omitting to act, must enter the analysis (Seferiades 2018).

SYRIZA's contradictory political plan, involving both rupture and accommodation, both condemnation of the ills of the Eurozone and unwillingness to seriously consider an exit option, both supporting a democratisation process and remaining state-centred and leader-centred can only be explained in sufficient depth if the class dynamics of the crisis period are analysed. SYRIZA's adoption of populism, and more broadly its successful elaboration of the connection between left radicalism and populism goes some way to explaining its rise to power, and indeed the history of the European left (Stavrakakis and Katsambekis 2014). Yet, however useful the theories of populism may be in explaining the unfolding political dynamics and the shifts at the discursive and electoral levels, they often omit to ask the questions and provide answers as to the class nexus that structures the 'people', that ultimately the populists of both the Right and the Left refer to (Charalambous and Ioannou 2020a).

Undoubtedly SYRIZA's Europeanism played a role in its turn to pragmatism once in government (Kioupkiolis and Katsambekis 2020). However, its relationship to the social movements and the anti-austerity protests needs to be interrogated more thoroughly in the light of the shifts occurring in the class structure of Greece. SYRIZA's model of a 'mass connective party' linking together a diverse set of social groups and gradually unifying and representing them at parliamentary level was both successful and spectacular. The political strategy of party activists '*in* the movements' leading to the party '*with* the movements' did ultimately lead to the claim of the party being the 'voice of' the movements producing a shift from a horizontal to a vertical form of representation (Kioupkiolis and Katsambekis 2020). However, the discursive and electoral success of SYRIZA was not accompanied with the social, organisational, and political depth necessary for such an ambitious course of action in such difficult conditions. Anti-austerity and a clash with the EU were easy to proclaim but hard to achieve as a political stance amidst prevailing domestic and international conditions. Put in schematic terms, SYRIZA was too easy an answer to too difficult a question – and as such it proved insufficient.

In as early as 2010, it was obvious that the crisis of the Eurozone was not merely a financial one developing into an economic one but had also political and geopolitical overtones. Not merely in the sense of delegitimising governments and political systems and tarnishing the image of the EU but also straining relations between core and peripheral states and threatening the EU's cohesion. Greece was directly threatened with an exit from the Eurozone if it did not collaborate with the Troika in the context of the first bail-out programme. And this threat, although repressed and largely hidden from the front stage, returned with vengeance in 2015 before the third bail-out programme (Siani-Davies 2017). Although occasionally some viewpoints were articulated arguing that an anti-austerity programme in Greece presupposed defaulting on debts and exiting from the Eurozone, or at least the willingness to take such a risk this was never seriously considered by SYRIZA leadership.

This inability of SYRIZA to think through alternative and possibly initially painful scenarios left it with little options when the EU elites refused to back down in the 2015 negotiations. The solidarity from the people of Europe was more symbolic and emotional rather than political and effective in provoking policy shifts. SYRIZA's ultimate Europeanism, has already been mentioned as the key factor driving it to a pragmatic stance of compromise in 2015, really accepting from a point of weakness the dictates of the EU elites. Yet that needs to be unpacked, as it is much more than just an ideological issue. SYRIZA's unwillingness to seriously, even consider, taking the risk of an exit from the Eurozone, must also be read in geopolitical terms determining not just SYRIZA's leadership but also Greek elite thinking throughout the 2010–2015 period. Exiting the Eurozone in a conflictual manner, though defaulting on public debt would have entailed a serious risk of Greece being pushed out of European Union as well, with all the consequences that could involve such as furthering of instability in the Eastern Mediterranean and possibly fueling a resurgence of antagonism with Turkey.

There were also domestic concerns behind the unwillingness of the SYRIZA leadership to carry the clash with the neoliberal project to its conclusion. By the time SYRIZA was able to assume executive power in 2015 Greece was already a largely devastated economy. There was a genuine fear that it would have been unable to cope in conditions of state default. At the level of society, it was uncertain whether there was available political will to support a radical rupture with the European Union through a conflictual exit from the Eurozone and the printing of a new currency with no value in the international markets. In more practical and organisational terms, it was uncertain whether it would have been possible to sustain economic transactions and food distribution networks in a transitional period that seemed to be of unknown length and characteristics. Nevertheless, what is important to note, is that these scenarios with their difficulties and potentialities were not seriously considered. The leadership of SYRIZA, aided by an insufficient internal opposition, opted to not cross the line, validating, and reinforcing the famous neoliberal mantra of TINA (Seferiades 2018).

The contraction of the economy in the crisis years brought about the shrinking of the middle class as numerous small employers and professionals lost their firms and their jobs and suffered a decrease in their income. However, there was no major reversal in the pattern of social stratification – it was income that was affected most, less so the positionality in the class structure. The most important development in social stratification in the crisis years was the acceleration of the already pre-existing trend of the decline of the traditional middle class and the rise of the new middle class of professionals (Sakellaropoulos 2014). Yet this quasi-disintegration of the petty bourgeoisie did not lead to political polarisation in social class terms. Although SYRIZA attracted a substantial section of the middle strata who experienced a compression of their standard of living and life chances, another section of these strata turned to more apolitical, conservative, and far-right directions.

The small employers who survived, although sharing opposition to austerity policies, were at the same time eager, as eager as bigger employers to preserve the drop in the labour cost effected during the crisis years. Pensioners who experienced a substantial reduction in their income, and who were also hit by the social policy and health cuts felt they stood to lose more in condition of state default that SYRIZA policies risked throwing the country into. Even the middle-class strata of small businessmen and self-employed professionals who initially supported the anti-austerity programme of SYRIZA and who contested the rising taxation were gradually alienated as austerity and the tax-burden remained high throughout the period of SYRIZA rule.

SYRIZA's failure to implement an anti-austerity set of policies while in government must neither be underestimated nor overestimated in its significance. Its re-election to power immediately after its capitulation to the Troika and its being able to complete its four-year term in office, a rare achievement for a Greek government in such conditions, illustrated both the weakness of its left-wing defectors and critics but also of its maintaining of the image of decency among the electorate. That it was a political force who tried something alternative and failed, rather than a political force who cheated the electorate. Although the disillusionment that spread to the left, the demobilisation and the depoliticisation has been massive and did contribute to the erosion of its political hegemony and electoral support, SYRIZA's defeat in the 2019 elections cannot be explained merely by this. The refugee crisis in 2016 and its management and the conclusion of the trivial, banal nationalist, yet long-troubling Macedonian issue with the agreement with its smaller neighbour state to be renamed North Macedonia in exchange of full recognition were also important factors. The tarnishing of SYRIZA's image was also due to its handling of the crisis of the deadly fire in Mati (Hope 2019), as well as due to more routine administration issues exploited by a resurgent ND with a new leadership boosted by the media.

SYRIZA's challenge to the neoliberal austerity order effectively peaked in 2012 and subsided in the next years as it was preparing to govern. By the time it assumed power in 2015 the anti-austerity mobilisations had petered out while the social movements so active in the period 2010–2013 had clearly retreated. Protest fatigue and a mixture of disillusionment with direct action and the expectation from the institutional order to deliver solutions have undoubtedly played a significant role in the societal demobilisation. There was also the unwillingness of SYRIZA leaders and cadres to develop, strengthen, and sustain the social movement milieu and the citizen resistance environment which was the key to their political rise in the first place. Most attention and energy were invested in the establishment of a positive public image of SYRIZA and communicating this through the alternative and social media with the purpose of building electoral strength rather than developing elaborate political thinking and practical plans for the day after or even pure organisational consolidation. The inability of SYRIZA to build a solid presence within Greek trade unionism, with PASOK and KKE remaining the dominant players despite the damage they both suffered as parties – catastrophic in the case of PASOK – reflects that.

As mentioned above trade unionism in Greece, already substantially weak and discredited suffered further decline and delegitimisation during the crisis years. Although the general strikes proclaimed in the period 2010–2012 were the most frequent, massive and combative ones since the 1970s, allowing workers to express their rage and demands involving direct action and street battles, Greek trade unionism was not revitalised but sank instead into a deeper crisis (Broumas et al., 2018). The leadership of GSEE which distanced itself from PASOK was able to survive but conventional trade unionism retreated into deactivation. PAME retained its strength and mobilisation capacity but was unable to expand to such an extent as to play a significant role in the socio-political field or to dominate within the trade union landscape. Bureaucratisation and distancing of the leadership from the rank and file members, representation and confidence crisis, corruption, political fragmentation, close interrelation of the union bureaucracies with the state and the bosses, even infiltration of employers within the trade union leadership brought stagnation, erosion of trust and paralysis (Int. 7, 2019; Int. 10, 2019).

At the structural level, conventional Greek trade unionism has been and remains based on regularly employed workers and is stronger in the public rather than the private sectors. The flexible, precarious, and unprotected parts of labour, as well as the unemployed and immigrants have been systematically excluded (Broumas et al. 2018).

This 'insider-outsider' approach did not change much during the crisis years when the 'peripheral' segment of the labour force expanded so much. The refusal of the biggest trade union federations to open-up membership rights to agency workers for example illustrates the maintenance of the narrow, insider rationale. Needless to say that the stance of official trade unions to reject agency work in principle, cannot really challenge the normalisation and the de facto social acceptance of this ultra-flexible, employer suiting, form of employment and only leads irregular workers to form other separate trade unions bringing further fragmentation (Koukiadaki and Kokkinou 2017).

At the same time, the crisis years also brought a convergence of labour issues with wider social movements and the needs and aspirations of the oppressed classes. Numerous initiatives of grassroots unionism appeared, connected with citizen anti-austerity mobilisations, cooperative networks, and solidarity initiatives. Most of these focused on precarious workers and developed a strong working class-oriented identity, discourse, and framework of action. Grassroots unionism attempted to place rank-and-file activists at the centre of union's organising and mobilisation activities (Kretsos 2011). Typically initiated by left-wing radicals, these new trade unions, often informal and at the margins of conventional trade unionism, have been active and successful in waging local struggles, building solidarity, and sustaining collectivist spirit in the employment field. This essentially social movement unionism remains however weak and lacks the infrastructural, material, and political resources to offer sufficient practical help to workers, let alone representation rights and incorporation into regulatory structures (Karakioulafi 2019).

The crisis has significantly and violently transformed the employment field in Greece. It spread poverty, accustomed a large section of society into low wages and precariousness and marginalised trade unionism by stripping it of its legislative and institutional support. In the extraordinary conditions that emerged, politicisation and radicalisation processes were unleashed, class polarisation and new cleavages. Yet while the mobilisation wave of the period 2010–2012 left its mark on Greek society and socialised a new generation into activism, the crisis decade also socialised people, especially the younger ones into austerity. Despite some continued mild improvement in the labour market conditions, labour market precariousness remained high in 2019. Unemployment fell, but most new jobs created were low paid and wage moderation remained the norm of the post Memoranda labour market. The rise of ND to power, with at best an agenda indifferent and at worst hostile with respect to labour rights, largely oriented to maintaining labour market deregulation makes the revival of trade unionism, labour-centred movements, and class politics an ever more urgent matter.

## Note

1 These consist of the institutionalised Christmas and Easter bonuses which are however obligatory, and not at the discretion of the employer, as part of annual salary.

# 5 Cyprus. Shock and Resilience

Because of its small size, geopolitical positioning, and particular historical trajectory the Cyprus crisis although part of the broader Eurozone crisis and sharing the severity with which it hit the European periphery, also had some unique elements in terms of its origins, handling as well as its aftermath. The rapid modernisation process that escorted its transition from a colony to an independent state in the mid-20th Century, its on-going ethnic conflict, frozen but not resolved since the mid-1970s, its positioning as a small island on the south-eastern corner of the West and its maintenance of political and economic relations both with the Eastern bloc and the Third World all left their mark on how the Cyprus economic model was shaped by the close of the 20th Century when its European path was consolidated.

The economic crisis in Cyprus arrived a bit later and was over a bit earlier compared to the rest of Southern Europe. This chapter focuses on area under the control of the Republic of Cyprus as the northern part of the country operates under different political and institutional systems and with other economic dynamics and temporalities. Some references to relevant developments in north Cyprus will be made but confined to the footnotes. Although the crisis' impact on the labour market and employment was significant and did weaken trade unionism and increased social inequalities, at the same time its management fell short of transforming the structure of its prevailing economic model or even the basic institutional framework of industrial relations.

The Cyprus crisis was effectively a banking crisis spilling over into the economy exacerbating fiscal imbalances and threatening the financing of the state. The Troika support mechanism included like the rest of Southern Europe a diverse set of austerity measures that had a deep negative impact on income and social welfare. However, they did not bring about a social or an institutional rupture and did not provoke a major political system crisis as was the case in Spain and Greece. The crisis management in Cyprus became dramatic only in the banking sector with the bail-in programme and even there, it was a swift operation reshaping the field but not really changing its structure and function.

The relatively quick return of growth and the resilience exhibited by trade unionism allowed the Cyprus society to overcome the shock, prevent the worst and maintain the institutional order of industrial relations. The chapter ends with a discussion of the survival of trade unionism and its political response to the changed conditions of declining density and lower collective bargaining coverage.

In the Cyprus case, and for the purposes of the argument of the book two things stand out. The first is the fact that despite the rapid shock and decline of the standard of living in a period of five years, the longer-term legacy of the crisis was milder, and more path dependent compared to Spain and especially compared to Greece. While the inferior terms and conditions of employment imposed on all those recruited in the public sector in the 2010s and more broadly on the younger generation extended further the fragmentation of the labour force and exacerbated social inequality, the already liberal system of industrial relations showed resilience. Trade union density and collective bargaining coverage decreased but trade unions maintained sufficient strength in several industries and were able in recent years to strike new compromises. The second is the limited societal resistance and the limited political contestation manifested in the crisis years. At the same time, popular resentment to austerity, liberalisation and the arbitrariness of crisis management, was present and although less massive and less visible compared to other South European countries exerted sufficient pressure on parliament and was successful in blocking the attempted universal bail-in of insured deposits and the privatisation of telecommunications and electricity.

## The Structure of the Labour Market and the Industrial Relations System

The industrial relations system in the Republic of Cyprus was consolidated after the division of the island in the late 1970s based on voluntarist principles, strong trade unionism, semi-institutionalised social dialogue procedures with the state limiting its role to coordination and mediation functions rather than direct legal regulation and overt interventions. Collective bargaining was the central regulatory mechanism, operating at sectoral and enterprise levels and was based on high unionisation rates which ensured wide coverage, peaking at 80% in the 1980s. Trade unions were connected to political parties in direct and indirect ways at the level of federations/confederations and with formally organised as well as informally operating factions within the public sector trade unions and banking (Ioannou, 2016b).

Gradually, however, by the onset of the 21st Century conditions in the economy and the labour market had changed and exerted pressures on the industrial relations system which remained unchanged. The decline of agriculture and manufacturing had already converted Cyprus into a service economy while the increased capital and labour flows and the entry into the EU in 2004 which accelerated them, created new realities on the ground leaving regulatory gaps and new inequalities amidst continuous economic growth. The distribution of wages differed substantially between the public and the private sectors and women were over-represented in lower-paid jobs (Ioakimoglou and Soumeli 2008). Although the three main industries that constituted the motor of the economy, namely tourism, banking and construction had sectoral collective bargaining in place and relatively strong trade unions, their overt expansion, the internationalisation dynamics and the overall neoliberal climate that was becoming entrenched gradually facilitated its weakening as the primary regulatory mechanism.

The decrease of trade union density and influence and the increase of immigrant workers exacerbated divisions and enhanced the fragmentation of the labour force and established peripheries of workers with limited rights and inferior terms of employment even in sectors where the general conditions were good (Trimikliniotis 2009). Outsourcing and new subsidiary operations in the financial sectors, subcontracting and informal work networks in construction and personal contracts and mass hiring of casual workers on a seasonal basis in the hospitality industry restricted the coverage of collective agreements (Yannakourou 2016). The fact that there were no extension mechanisms and no legally binding force behind collective bargaining, facilitated in connection with trade union weakness the conversion of many workplaces into hybrid spaces of dual or multiple terms and conditions of employment (Ioannou 2015).

As the overall balance of power between capital and labour was altered in favour of the former already before the crisis collective bargaining was undermined through employers' refusals to engage in and be bound by it, through exclusion of a segment of their workforce from it and through selective enforcement of terms agreed. In many sectors and firms, collective agreements do not exist. Even when there is a collective agreement in the sector or in the firm it does not automatically cover new recruits. Often not to be covered by an existing collective agreement is implicitly a condition for getting the job in the first place.

Thus, collective bargaining the key regulatory mechanism in the Cypriot voluntarist industrial relations system became relativised and less effective in protecting the workforce (Ioannou 2015).

The economic growth of the preceding decades was accompanied with ideological shifts, in line with broader West European trends. Beyond the expansion of the labour aristocracy and the middle class, the generalised improvement of the purchasing power of broader sections of the population which, in conjunction with the relative ease of borrowing, increased consumption, and consolidated the ideology of consumerism. This involved the demise of collective values, political engagement and social solidarity and the diffusion of rampant individualism and apolitical materialism. As most Cypriots occupied the increasing number of mental work and white-collar office jobs, sales, administrative, and professional jobs, manual and low skilled jobs were primarily taken over by the ever-increasing immigrant workers from South East Asia and the Middle East, from Eastern Europe, with and without EU passports, and more recently also from China and Africa who, in their overwhelming majority, remained little integrated in Cypriot society (Trimikliniotis and Demetriou 2011).

Immigrant workers, at the same time, embody not only the victims of employer discrimination in terms of wages, rights and benefits (Carby-Hall 2008) but also serve as the means through which employers threaten the long-acquired rights and benefits of Cypriot workers. The weak labour market position of immigrant workers and their even weaker social position renders them overtly dependent on their employer, often also their landlord, making their joining of trade unions almost inconceivable (Ioannou 2016a). Although trade unions were initially hostile to immigrant workers, tolerating their presence and inferior treatment by employers as long as they remained in the margins of the labour process and not affecting their members, as the number of immigrants increased, many of them with EU passports and automatic right of residence and work they started attempting to recruit them. However, the difficulties in linguistic and cultural communication, the transient and precarious nature of immigrant employment, the fear and the distance keeping of the immigrant worker themselves prevented unions from making breakthroughs and even sustaining such an effort (Ioannou and Sonan 2021).[1]

In addition to immigrants occupying primarily low-paid and unskilled or less skilled work posts and women, many of them concentrated in feminised and less well-paid occupations and being over-represented in the part-time labour force segment, by the first decade of the 20th Century the youth emerged as an additional distinctly disadvantaged and vulnerable group. The increasing unemployment, underemployment, and irregular employment amongst the youth have been observed as phenomena in the 2000s (Trimikliniotis 2004) and were not really contained leading the problem to escalate substantially once the crisis set in in the 2010s (Ioannou and Sonan 2016). Although the economy kept expanding and the number of available jobs increasing in the 2000s little was done to integrate the terms of employment as more and more new entrants in the labour market had to face inferior employment conditions, relatively worse than their colleagues and worse than a decade before. If one takes into account the relatively higher qualifications and expectations of the new generation of workers as a result of the generalised improvement in educational level and living standards in the preceding decades, the social frustration provoked in the crisis years looms large.

At the political level, the subjection of the country to international dynamics and forces in the setting of the EU accession process facilitated the slow yet steady development of the neoliberal discourse in Cyprus. This was further enhanced with the adoption of EU directives, the harmonisation of the national legislation and the further institutional integration in the context of the entry into the European Monetary Union. By the end of the 2000s on the eve of the crisis, the neoliberal logic entrenched in the mechanics of the EU system had managed to set the framework for policy in Cyprus, so that when the crisis arrived in early 2010s it became impossible to think outside the neoliberal mode. Although there were no significant substantive legislative changes in the realm of industrial relations in the 2000s, individual labour contracts clearly gained ground vis a vis, collective agreements (Emilianides and Ioannou 2016).

This gave rise to a trade union initiative to strengthen collective bargaining and collective agreements. This effort was only partially successful as employer resistance blocked the attempt to institute extension mechanisms in the form of a ministerial decree. However, the trade union law was reformed in 2012 giving the power to the Trade Union Registrar to issue a decree of obligatory recognition in firms employing more than 30 workers and where at least half are trade union members. The process for this also includes a secret ballot under the auspices of the Trade Union Registrar which can be initiated when trade unions produce evidence that they represent at least 25% of the firm (Yannakourou 2016). Although this law, also extending trade union rights, easing access to workplaces and expanding the time allocated to shop stewards, was beneficial to trade unions, it was not able to reverse the bigger trend of decreasing trade union power (Table 5.1).

## Recession, Austerity, and the Troika Treatment

The crisis arrived in Cyprus in 2009 in the form of mild recession that was dealt with in a quasi-Keynesian manner by the left-wing government

*Table 5.1* Number of registered unemployed, Youth unemployment and Part time employment rates, Minimum wage in €, Cyprus, 2008–2019

| *Cyprus* | *2008* | *2013* | *2019* |
|---|---|---|---|
| No. of registered unemployed persons | 11 500 | 68 900 | 32 000 |
| Youth unemployment rate (15–24) (%) | 9 | 38.9 | 16.6 |
| Part-time employment rate (%) | 6.8 | 11.9 | 10.2 |
| Minimum wage in € (not national – only 8 occupations) | 743 | 870 | 870 |

Source: Eurostat.

then in office. Although increased public spending in the sectors of construction, tourism, and banking seemed to be working initially as growth returned in 2010, by 2011 it was clear that the crisis was a much bigger thing. The structural imbalances of the Cyprus' economy in conjunction with its internationalised character made it especially vulnerable to the unfolding European crisis (Pegasiou 2013). The banking sector, already too bloated compared to the size of the country, was little regulated and engaged in yet more risky expansion and being drawn in the process into alignment with the collapsing Greek banking sector (Stephanou 2011). Construction, largely driven by the building of holiday houses for foreigners came to a halt as international demand shrunk, resulting in rising unemployment.

The economic downturn affected negatively state finances which deteriorated, provoking increase of deficits (Pegasiou 2013). The burst of the construction bubble provoked the burst of the financial bubble which produced and sustained it. Non-performing loans began increasing and the banking sector crisis deepened at a time when the Eurozone was preparing to adopt measures of stricter control of banks including both their operation and their capital sufficiency. As the grave condition of the two major Cypriot banks was made obvious, and on the basis that the state was in no condition to bail them out, the Cyprus economy was rapidly devalued and effectively ousted from the international money markets in 2011. The Cyprus government negotiated a loan from Russia and instituted the first austerity measures in late 2011, but this only postponed the crisis for a few more months.

At the political level, Christofias' government, already weakened after the Mari incident found it increasingly difficult to continue governing.[2] Already its 2010 attempt to institute a temporary mild increase in corporate and property taxation was blocked in parliament. Its hesitation to impose austerity measures was defeated before the end of 2011 (Charalambous and Ioannou 2015a). Although the austerity measures imposed then seem very mild when one compares them with what happened in the following years it must be noted that the way these measures were decided violating social dialogue and through a cross party alliance in parliament because there was 'an emergent necessity' foreshadowed what was coming. The unfolding pattern was that the crisis and the threat of economic collapse rendered social dialogue a sort of 'luxury' of the past. Trade unions remained opposed to austerity but soon in different ways all acquiesced to it seeing it as inevitable.

Already in early 2012 one of the two Cypriot systemic banks, Laiki was on the brink of collapse and resorted to the state asking for a bail-out. The government and the parliament fearing the repercussions its collapse would cause to the economy, recapitalised Laiki, creating further strains on the public debt which was rising and without capacity of being refinanced itself. When the second systemic bank, the Bank of Cyprus also proved incapable of attracting the new capital stipulated by the new Eurozone rules by mid-2012, the Troika was effectively called in (Panayiotou, 2013). As the economic situation kept deteriorating, the negotiations with the Troika resulted in an agreement about the fiscal terms in late 2012 but the Memorandum of Understanding (MoU) had to await until the new government was to come in office in early 2013. Beyond ensuring that the Support Programme was to enjoy the ownership and commitment of the new government, the other reason the Troika delayed for a few months was the completion of the investigation about the Cyprus banking sector was that was to determine the overall magnitude of the economic support as well as its form (Demetriades 2017).

When the MoU was formally signed a few weeks after the new right-wing government was elected to office, the developments were dramatic as in addition to the bail-out of the state, a bail-in mechanism was agreed with respect to the banking sector. Shareholders, bond holders, and depositors were to pay for the rescue of the banking system (Tsitsiou 2020). The initial suggestion of a universal haircut of all accounts in all banks with two rates for insured and non-insured deposits with the latter being slightly higher provoked popular reaction in Cyprus and anxiety to other European countries. The idea of instituting a haircut on insured deposits and extending this to all accounts in all banks, that is including banks that were not in financial trouble was unprecedented. Besides its unfairness and levelling character, it would have effectively severely undermined the confidence of people to the banking system across the EU – because it would have set a precedent (Demetriades 2017).

After significant pressure from the electorate no parliamentary party in Cyprus supported it, as even the governing party DISY abstained from voting. In the next round of Eurogroup negotiations, a week later while the country was under strict capital controls, the Cyprus government agreed with the Troika to limit the bail-in to the two problematic banks and to uninsured deposits (above 100 000€) and this was able to pass through parliament. Although both systemic private banks were effectively bankrupt, it was decided to keep one of the two alive (Demetriades, 2017). Laiki Bank was liquidated, and its 'healthy part' was transferred to the Bank of Cyprus which effectively changed its ownership structure while the Cooperative Bank was nationalised and brought under the full control of the European Central Bank.

The austerity measures decided in late 2012 were implemented immediately adding their weight to the milder ones imposed in late 2011 and involved social policy cuts, increased taxation, and public sector wage cuts. After mid-2013 when the support programme begun formally and in the context of monitoring its implementation and re-assessing the economic progress some of these were further specified and reconsidered. In addition to the increase in VAT, and other indirect taxes, the general wage freeze, the 10% wage decrease for all newcomers to the broader public sector, the introduction of temporary and scaled special contributions on all wages including the private sector and the increases in public sector workers' contributions to various state and social insurance funds, the 2011 measures included some structural and permanent changes which set the pattern for the further more severe ones implemented in subsequent years. These included the abolition of state pension for newcomers and the introduction of taxation on state pension for existing civil servants, and full social insurance contributions from thereafter, penalties against early retirement and salary cuts for all public sector health professionals and reduction of their night shift benefits.

The most important structural changes in the 2012 austerity package was the increase of the statutory retirement age to 65 and the introduction of 12% penalty to all those retiring at 63. Further indirect taxation was introduced, and further budget cuts were made in various social provisions and welfare benefits (Christou et al. 2016). Freezing in wages, pensions and COLA was extended, further reductions in state pensions and associated benefits continued, the increase in contributions to social insurance was instituted. In the field of taxation further increases were imposed in 2012 and 2013 primarily on indirect taxes but also in the statutory corporate tax raising it from the ultra-low 10% to 12.5% (Ioannou and Charalambous 2017). A property tax was also instituted by in its final form was amended keeping it low and not sufficiently progressively scaled. Although there were no redundancies in the public sector, a system was put in place allowing one new hiring for every five retiring in the broader public sector reducing employment by 5000 by 2016. In the realm of social policy, already weak before the crisis, there was a blanket 10% reduction turning various universal benefits into means tested and the introduction of fees or increase of existing ones, for various public services (Charalambous 2014).

## Economy in Shock, Society Paralyzed, Politics Muted

Although the bail-in plan stabilised the banking system at least in the medium term, the shock provoked in the economy because of the capital controls in the immediate term was huge. Many small and medium firms closed, unemployment rose, and disposable income decreased further. A significant section of the middle class lost its savings while collective savings in the form of Provident Funds and Pension Funds also suffered damage, although they were ultimately treated a bit more lightly compared to private savings. Overall GDP decreased 12% from 2011 to 2015, employment shrunk by 11% in the period 2012–2014 and registered unemployment rose to 16% (Ioannou and Charalambous 2017). It is important to stress that since unemployment was traditionally low in Cyprus and up until 2009 was as low as 5.4% its rapid rise provoked significant social dislocation. Youth unemployment rose to record levels, involuntary part-time work increased and an emigration trend, of primarily young and highly qualified people surfaced both as a reality and more so as a desired plan (Ioannou and Sonan 2016).

Real wages dropped in all sectors and industries, in some cases as much as 20%. Beyond the pressure on the wages, the high unemployment spread job insecurity to previously secure and well-paid workers in many firms and occupations. Even the public, semi-public, and banking sector employees, previously seen as, and to a certain extent really constituting, a labour aristocracy was negatively affected (Ioannou 2016a). Inter and intra firm upward mobility froze and in addition to the cuts in wages and benefits, expectations were frustrated. Regular jobs became more and more scarce and the new wave of entrants into the labour market faced lower starting wages and limited prospects of advancement while for many, what was on offer were precarious jobs. For employers, the substantial decrease in labour cost also reinforced a negative stance vis a vis the prospect of the country's reunification.[3]

The huge and sudden rise of unemployment and youth unemployment, rising from 5.4% and 13% in 2009 to 16% and 32.3% respectively in 2015 (Ioannou and Sonan 2016) facilitated the expansion of irregular employment (fixed term, part time and other essentially precarious employment regimes) and diffused the feeling of insecurity to broader sections of the labour force including the well paid and more secure segments (Soumeli 2014; Ioannou, 2016a; Trimikliniotis 2016). The overall decline in disposable income eroded savings, increased social inequality, and increased the number of people in poverty and in danger of poverty. It also helped in normalising the low starting wages in all jobs, and temporary, low paid, publicly subsidised employment through the various active labour market schemes aiming to combat unemployment and youth unemployment that proliferated during the crisis years.

The shock from the dramatic developments of early 2013, with the bail-out and the bail-in agreement, enforced while capital controls were put in place and which were only gradually relaxed thereafter was not restricted only to the economy. These were unprecedented times reminding people of the emergency conditions after the 1974 war. Although there were some mass protests, aided by the fact that AKEL moved from government to opposition, there was no fundamental change in the pattern observed in 2012. The majority of citizens disliking the austerity measures but either judging them as necessary or considering the resistance to them a futile matter. Some sporadic protests did take place by groups directly impacted by the welfare cuts and the extra-parliamentary left-wing initiatives and these became bigger during the dramatic spring of 2013. There was nothing analogous however to the mobilisations that happened in the rest of southern Europe (Charalambous 2014). The 'paralysis' of the society which effectively allowed the smooth and speedy implementation of all the austerity measures and more importantly without any significant challenges to the political system can be explained with respect to particular dynamics operating within the political system and between the political system and civil society (Charalambous and Ioannou 2017).

As soon as AKEL moved to opposition, PEO took the initiative and organised a couple of major demonstrations, building also the umbrella group 'Society resists' which brought together in addition to its front organisations, DEOK but not also SEK, and from the public sector trade unions only POED (Charalambous and Ioannou 2017). This was more an exercise for AKEL flexing its muscles, testing the continued mobilisation capacity of its apparatus and controlling the damage of its image being the party that negotiated and agreed the fiscal aspect of the Memorandum of the Understanding with the Troika. These protests aimed more to register disagreement rather than really contest the implementation of austerity policies (Ioannou and Charalambous 2016). In any case AKEL's votes in parliament were not needed for the passage of the various bills from 2013 onwards as DISY could count on the support of DIKO which even after withdrawing from the government coalition continued to vote through the bills.

PASYDY, while being the most vocal against austerity in 2011 also organising strike action, restricted itself to rhetorical objections in 2012 and from 2013 onwards attempted instead to wage a legal battle against the salary cuts of its members. Although the judgements of the district courts and the Supreme Court in the initial stages of the crisis had upheld the constitutionality of the cuts conforming to the state's endeavour to save the economy and fulfil the conditions set in the Memorandum of Understanding with the Troika, in subsequent years the Administrative Court found cuts to pensions and salaries to be unconstitutional (Tsitsiou 2020). PASYDY had encouraged many of its members from early on to file individual cases in the courts using them as a substitute for further mobilisations and as an instrument of political pressure. The whole edifice backfired however in early 2020 when the Supreme Court overturned the decision of the Administrative Court ruling that there was no violation of constitutional rights.[4]

By 2015 the economy was back on the path of stabilisation aided by the more general improvement in the international conditions and the further expansion of tourism facilitated by the continued unrest in the competing neighbouring countries. It was to be sure a new low, as the full brunt of the economic contraction and the austerity policies were felt by society. Yet Cyprus' small size and external orientation allowed its economy to 'restart' relatively quickly while the strong family networks averted the worse in the field of welfare provision. Active labour market policies of sponsored temporary employment and the reluctance of the banks to proceed to foreclosures and forced evictions at a mass scale also aided to dampen further social dislocation. So was the introduction of the Guaranteed Minimum Income in the realm of social policy which extended coverage to longer-term unemployed but at the same time wholly restructured welfare provision aligning it with the contemporary European (neoliberal) paradigm (Koutsampelas 2016).

While the Guaranteed Minimum Income did contribute to the reduction of the number of people visiting food banks, an unprecedent phenomenon in Cyprus reminiscent of the aftermath of the 1974 war and it did relieve families struggling with poverty, it should be clarified that this did not constitute an expansion but merely a rationalisation of welfare provision. The strict budgetary constraints set by the Memorandum of Understanding with the Troika and the difficulties in setting up the mechanism rendered it an insufficient instrument in conditions of generalised economic difficulty. More importantly its strict rules, means testing and delays in its provision did not lift the burden of welfare from families nor did it lift recipients out of poverty, although it did lift some of them out of extreme poverty (Koutsampelas 2016). Persons that had inherited a piece of land or had some limited savings were excluded from the GMI even if they had no income, while it was distributed on the basis of household treating unmarried persons up to their late 20s living with their parents as dependents and thus not eligible. The logic of GMI was neoliberal and its aim was to operate as a disciplinary mechanism, a function clarified further in subsequent years when tied to special training programmes and obligation of recipients to accept low paid work when offered or risk losing part of it.

In the domain of health care, the Troika did not make a forceful intervention, other that is from overseeing the cutting of budgets and instituting or increasing user fees (Petrou and Vandoros 2018). Cyprus did not have a universal health care system and after decades of delays provoked by conflicting interests was only able to institute one in 2017 and operate its first phase in 2019. Troika supported the introduction of a national health service, GESY constructed as it was on mixed principles of both public control, mutuality, and solidarity as well as the maintenance of private ownership, competition, and market efficiency. The Troika was also lenient enough to tolerate further delay in its introduction. Like with public education, the issue of public health did not attract special scrutiny and beyond some general suggestions about reducing wastage and tax evasion and technological updates there was no effort to push through a comprehensive restructuring. Like with the rest of the public sector external intervention remained restricted to cost-cutting and in that sense was no different to the policy already pursued before the arrival of the Troika – only deepening it and refocusing the cost-cutting effort on the payroll cost.

The other issue on which the Troika and subsequently the European Commission did not insist to the extent of making it unavoidable, was privatisations. In the MoU privatisations of public utilities were specifically mentioned as a means with which state finances could be improved but the conditionality clauses were restricted to the establishment of the legal framework allowing privatisations and not to the sale of the public companies per se. Out of the three main public enterprises targeted, that is the ports, electricity and telecommunications only one, the Ports Authority, was ultimately privatised. The framework for the restructuring of all three and liberalising the respective markets was marginally voted by parliament in 2014 but there was substantial resistance by the trade unions active in these semi-public institutions and the public opinion remained firmly and overwhelmingly opposed.

In telecommunications, already an open market, the government was only able to proceed to some restructuring and voluntary redundancies before losing the support of DIKO in parliament and remaining in a minority position by 2016. In electricity, after a diverse repertoire of action including strikes, protests and litigation, the process was bogged down in the attempt to split the Electricity Authority into two entities into one controlling the infrastructure and another one involved in production and distribution (Ioannou and Charalambous 2017). The Ports Authority was the only one fully privatised, resulting however in the increase of prices and provoking reactions even from the Chamber of Commerce itself by 2019, which was one of the champions of its privatisation.

## The Decline and Resilience of Trade Unionism

Although the crisis did lead to significant negative change in labour relations systems, excepting the public sector, this was essentially a market-driven process in Cyprus. Due to the voluntarist industrial relations system, wages in the private sectors with the exception of a scaled temporary tax contribution were not cut by means of a legislative change decreeing lower minimum scales, or a restructuring of collective bargaining. The causes of wage reduction were the declining market conditions and the emulation of the public sector example and the means were unilateral employer action or new collective agreements or new interim collective agreements. Trade unions adopted a defensive strategy and attempted an organised retreat which in many cases worked (Ioannou 2016a). This consisted of exchanging trade union consent to the cuts for employer commitment that these were to be temporary.

Unable to block wage and benefits cuts even in places were trade union density was relatively high, trade unions focused their efforts on guarding the collective bargaining institutions. They refrained from strike activity, except in sectors and firms where they were strong enough and where they had clear legal advantage, which is also one of the key reasons that trade unions prioritised the effort to enhance their legal tools throughout the 2010s (Int. 11, 2020). Overall although the number of strikes and the days lost from strike action increased significantly in 2012, most of them were about non-payment of wages and blatant violations of agreements and were largely localised actions (Ioannou 2016a).

Interim collective agreements, special memoranda of understanding and regularly renewed collective agreements signed during the crisis at both sectoral and firm levels all stipulated a wage freeze and/or decrease and various benefits cuts. Where trade unions had strength, they opted for reductions of indirect monetary benefits such as employer contribution to Welfare and Provident Funds (Ioannou 2016a; PEO 2017). The idea behind this was that retreating on the substantive terms where resistance was anyway bound to be difficult in the prevailing conditions of recession, while negotiating cuts on secondary terms could induce the employers to refrain from attempting to destroy the procedures of collective bargaining and its institutionalised status. Indeed, there was no collapse of collective bargaining despite the pressures it faced and despite the reinforcement of pre-existing trends such as decentralisation, declining coverage and control of collective agreements and of course deteriorating conditions (Ioannou and Sonan 2019).

However, although the worse was averted, the decline of trade unionism, a process on-going since at least the late 1990s, was accelerated in the crisis years. Whereas at the turn of the Century trade union weakness was manifested primarily in the form of a constant reduction of density, lagging organisationally behind that is in the face of economic expansion, by the end of the 2000s they had more serious problems to face (Ioannou and Sonan 2017, 2021). Their ability to win wage rises allowed them to continue attracting members but the precariously employed segment of the labour force was expanding much faster. More importantly, the bureaucratisation process, already several decades old, created a context whereby members were largely passive and new members were also accustomed to view trade unions in an instrumental way, in any case an international phenomenon (Danaj et al. 2018). Local workplace committees under-functioned and more and more was left to the professional salaried trade unionists, enhancing the image of the trade unions as a sort of external agency, autonomous from their rank and file members (Ioannou 2015).

The expansion of the scope, role and most crucially the image of labour legislation in the institutional order of the Cyprus labour relations system after the entry into the EU also eroded trade unionism as it created a climate in which the role of the trade unions as active agents in the determination and regulation of the terms and conditions of labour was underplayed and undermined. The primacy of the private contract and of the freedom to do business also inculcated a culture of individualism in labour affairs in line with the neoliberal spirit of the era (Int. 11, 2020). Among both employers and workers, the view that trade unionism was a thing of the past and that the law was really what mattered for labour regulation gained ground. This placed added difficulties on trade union recruitment in new workplaces and especially in sectors with limited trade union presence.

Corporatist tripartism, social dialogue, and collective bargaining were not directly challenged before the crisis but when employers resorted to unilateralism, trade unions found themselves too weak to counter this on their own and resorted to the state. As trade unions came to depend more and more on the state in order to secure the enforcement of the agreements they made with employers, the real weakness of the trade unions begun to be gradually also perceived as such by themselves and the others. More and more frequently trade union interventions, even at workplace level, assumed the form of reporting labour law violations and non-enforcement of collective agreement clauses to the Labour Ministry (Int. 12, 2020). This trend was further enhanced during the crisis and post-crisis years.

The reform of the industrial relations system that was attempted and only partially achieved in 2012 was precisely a result of the realisation that the voluntarist system could not properly function in the face of substantial power imbalance between employers and trade unions. Although the new trade union law was a useful tool in the hands of trade unionists and used in some cases in the subsequent years, it was insufficient in altering the general state of affairs in the labour field and arresting the decline of trade unionism. The other part of the bill that was blocked by employers in 2012, aiming to legally fortify and politically extend collective bargaining could have restricted the deregulation process and could even expand in both scale and scope the role of the trade unions in the labour process. There was however neither political will by Anastasiades' government to reopen the issue and no signs from the employers that they could compromise on this.

Ultimately there is no short cut to achieving or restoring power balance in industrial relations. Politics, policy, and legislation are important elements that shape the context, but one should not forget that they largely also condense dynamics operative at workplace, sectoral, and national labour market levels. The increased role of legislation as a means of labour process regulation both reflects and overshadows the existing reality of deregulation. Trade union weakness is at the same time both a cause and a consequence of the employers' offensive. Since this weakening was a gradual, historical process, there was not much trade unions could realistically do when the crisis hit the Cyprus economy. Having for decades accustomed themselves and their members to self-restraint and occasional mobilisation exercises aiming more to put some pressure in negotiations rather than to impose terms on the employers, a path dependency was established (Ioannou and Sonan 2017).

Striking has diachronically been used by trade unions primarily as a weapon of 'threat' and only secondarily as a weapon of 'method' for the achievement of bargaining goals. This practice which was largely successful in previous eras has set a pattern that was not easy to reverse when the conditions changed. While sectoral and company-level strikes have not been absent from the trade union repertoire of action, these tended to be most often short, symbolic stoppages sometimes not even publicised serving to send the message to the employer rather than to the state, the working class or society as a whole. The absence of a tradition of protracted strikes led to an insufficient experience of waging organised class struggle. The trade unions in Cyprus had in the decades before the onset of the crisis become more as institutions of labour services rather than vehicles of struggle. And beyond rhetoric, they came to perceive themselves as such, a trend that has been in any case international (Heery and Kelly 1994).

Trade unions defensive and largely timid stance during the economic crisis was thus both in line with their historical trajectory and a realistic stance based on their assessment of their power. The concept of the general strike is absent from the history of the Cypriot labour movement unlike Spain and Greece and even sectoral strikes have traditionally been short events rather than long drawn-out conflicts. Trade union ability to mobilise their membership basis was at best uncertain and their influence among non-members limited as their organisational inroads into younger workers and migrants was minimal. The rise of unemployment affected trade unions in a very practical manner as well – beyond that is the decrease of their bargaining power. Not only did they lose members and their valuable subscriptions and had to lay off some of their salaried staff, but they also lost local workplace committee members resulting in yet further difficulty in conducting everyday trade union work (Ioannou and Sonan 2021). Their connections to the main political parties proved incapable of exerting sufficient influence in labour and social policy making in the face of the 'emergent necessity' conditions provoked by the economic crisis.

Effectively adopting a conservative stance and avoiding the risk of attempting mobilisation and open conflict was a default position of the big trade union federations/confederations. Employer unilateralism in the crisis years was dealt with just like the issue of personal employment contracts encroaching upon the collective agreements in the hotel industry, subcontracting undercutting the collective agreement in construction, outsourcing fragmenting the workforce in banking and services before the crisis. With verbal opposition and occasional skirmishes and temporary compromises substituting for a decisive and sustained campaign to block these. Similarly, on the organisational front, the key victims of the crisis, the young employed on sub-standard terms were dealt with no differently than the precarious primarily immigrant workers in the pre-crisis years – open to them in theory but not making the extra effort needed to understand their particular conditions and needs, persuade them about the value of trade unionism and adopt measures to facilitate their meaningful inclusion in trade unions. Trade unions in Cyprus like elsewhere remained more effective in protecting the interests of workers who already enjoy some degree of labour market power (Simms and Charlwood 2010).

## Trade Unions and Class Dynamics after the Return of Growth

Growth returned to the economy relatively quickly and this made international commentators refer to Cyprus being a good example of crisis management (Persianis 2015), and this also contributed to Anastasiades' success in the 2018 presidential elections despite serious weaknesses in several other fields. Only three years after the peak of the crisis in early 2013, the government could boast a constant trend of growth, unemployment reduction, and predictions of further expansion in the years ahead. The exit from the Troika Support Mechanism in 2016 signalled a generalised euphoria and a cautious optimism that the crisis was over, or at least its effects lay behind. Indeed, the economic indicators continued to constantly improve in the following years but the conditions prevailing in the labour market and at the level of society, even in 2019, lagged-behind the pre-crisis ones (PEO 2019).

The devaluation of labour that occurred during the crisis years and subsequent drop in real wages and purchasing power was significant (INEK-PEO 2014). This was not reversed as there was no effort by the state towards that direction neither in terms of labour policy nor in terms of social policy. At the level of economy different sectors were hit to different degrees and in different ways and subsequently had different and often diverging paths to recovery. Although the expansion of the economy did result in an overall increase in the employment rate, the benefits of the growth were not evenly distributed between the different industries and sectors and between different occupational groups. Most new jobs created were relatively low paid and a substantial proportion of them precarious. More importantly aggregate profits expanded at the expense of aggregate wages as a share of the GDP reflecting the shift that occurred during the crisis years (INEK-PEO 2018; 2019). At the same time, many small businesses lost ground to bigger ones, especially in retail trade, while capital was destroyed and changed hands with the Cypriot bourgeoisie losing effectively substantial control of the remaining banks as foreign capital dominated the reformed banking system (Ioannou 2020a).[5]

As mentioned above the survival of collective bargaining allowed the trade unions to gradually start claiming back the wages and benefits cuts of the crisis years. Already by the end of 2016 PEO claimed in the first-year assessment of its 'dynamic offensive' launched in its extraordinary December 2015 conference, that in half of the collective agreements renewed there were full or partial restoration of the agreed wage and benefits cuts (PEO 2016). This trend continued in the next years and workers covered by collective bargaining were able to recoup their losses or at least most of them (PEO 2017; 2019). However, as the economy began expanding, inflation also returned, and this undercut some of wage raises achieved. The Cost Of Living Adjustment (COLA) mechanism, an indexation system which automatically adjusts wages to current inflation rates as estimated by a price index based on a bundle of basic consumption goods, frozen during the crisis years, was restored with an interim agreement negotiated by employers and trade unions under the auspices of the state in 2017 but could only partially cover the losses in real wages.

In the initial stage of the crisis the employers had brought back their diachronic demand for the abolition of COLA while the European Commission was also exerting some pressure in that direction. Its freezing in the broader public sector in 2011, was viewed as an opportunity by employers to finish with it, and in 2012 many included it in the context of their unilateral cuts to wages. However, as the crisis developed, the shift from inflation to a mild deflation meant that by 2013 COLA was effectively neutralised as an instrument also in the private sectors and surfaced only in 2017 when the growth brought with it inflation. The interim agreement reached in 2017 effectively ensured the survival of the institution, albeit in a reformed manner, reducing for a second time since the 1990s its capacity to support household income in the face of inflation.

The most significant development with structural consequences in the post growth context, has been the framework agreement reached in the semi-public sector in early 2017 instituting a mechanism whereby a ceiling is enforced in the total percentile salary increases at the level of the nominal GDP. This was then followed by a similar agreement with PASYDY in the public sector proper. After the failure of the government to push this mechanism through as a permanent and automatic one in the public sector via law, it was effectively forced to bargain it with the main trade unions. PEO and SEK in the semi-public sector saw this as a compromise worth making, opening the way to collective agreements that covered the three-year period of 2015–2018 and making the government reaffirm its promise of instituting Provident Funds to cover all those hired in the last decade who were excluded from the pension arrangements of their older colleagues. While indeed in 2018 collective agreements were renewed and an additional agreement was reached introducing a five-year implementation period and the gradual repeal of all pay cuts imposed in the public and semi-public sectors during the crisis by 2022 which was subsequently legislated, the Pension Funds for new recruits to the broader public sector remained at the dialogue stage (Kalosinatos 2019).

In the public sector, the main trade union PASYDY has been multiply challenged during the crisis period and its leadership discredited as it has been seen as unable to maintain the good working conditions prevailing for civil servants. The agreement PASYDY made with the government for example concerning the ceiling in future wage raises was opposed by the rest of the trade unions of the public sector, which were excluded from the negotiations seeing it as unfair and unbalanced and threatening with legal measures. PASYDY's close association with the state elite and its bias towards promoting the interests of a more privileged core against those of an expanding periphery of younger, newly recruited, and irregularly employed workers has significantly tarnished its image. Even when in 2011 its leadership clashed with austerity supporting parties, including DISY and DIKO which were more vocal on this than the government led by AKEL, it was unable to appear as a universalist labour force. When pushed into accepting some austerity measures and in its attempt to limit the cuts on wages and benefits it agreed to a 10% wage reduction in all new recruits to the public sector and the reform of the pension system in a way much more disadvantageous to newer employees compared to older ones.

The pre-existing trend whereby PASYDY was gradually but steadily losing ground among the public sector workers was accelerated during the crisis years. PASIKY among the public hospital doctors and even more so PASYNO among the public hospital nurses especially after the lengthy and successful strike it led in 2016 were able to establish themselves as significant challengers of PASYDY. Another civil servants' union, ASDYK which more ambitiously attempted to take PASYDY head on, was not able however to sufficiently benefit from PASYDY's decline and recruit all those withdrawing their affiliation from the historical public sector trade union. Thus, the loss of members by PASYDY has resulted in overall declining density in the public sector. It remains to be seen whether the new PASYDY leadership which took over in 2020 can bring back at least some of the members who left. The expansion of irregular employment in the broader public sector in the 2000s and the inability of PASYDY as well as SEK to protect substantially these workers despite some improvements achieved has led to the establishment of another new trade union, ISOTITA representing all the irregularly employed workers in both the public and semi-public sectors (Ioannou and Sonan 2021).

In the education sector, the traditional trade unions held their ground and were not challenged by any new trade unions. The fact that they supported the irregularly employed peripheral education workers in various instances insulated them from direct challenges by new trade unions, although many of these opted to join SEK rather than the education or other public sector trade unions (Int. 12, 2020). The more characteristic such example was the struggle of teachers in afternoon public schools in 2017–2018, whom the government had converted into 'self-employed' in 2013 to reduce its labour cost and avoid employer obligations (Kalosinatos 2019). It was the government that attempted to curb the education trade unions' power by imposing a set of organisational changes in public sector education against their will. After two large protests in the summer months of 2018 and with the threat of strike action in September the government was forced to retreat initially to a temporary compromise agreement and subsequently in 2019 to taking back most of its initial plans.

Social dialogue had a more dramatic fate compared to collective bargaining during the crisis years. As mentioned earlier it was effectively frozen and largely rendered irrelevant when the key austerity policies were being decided and implemented in the period 2011–2016. Being as it was, more a sort of semi-institutionalised process and a tradition rather than a fully institutionalised and legally binding framework, the demise of social dialogue in the crisis years was a kind of taken for granted development without necessitating decisions and decrees, bills and legislation. Even after the Troika left in 2016 however, the recovery of the social dialogue framework was gradual and partial. In its 2017 Report, PEO cited a series of issues concerning overtime pay, the combat of unemployment, Provident Funds, the operational time of retail shops, and the Minimum Guaranteed Income where decisions were taken without prior consultation while it complained about the rare convening of some of consultation bodies in the period 2013–2017 (PEO 2017).

More generally the weakened position of trade unionism in the new post-crisis labour market context has led PEO and SEK to prioritise the attempt to strengthen collective bargaining and set minimum standards via legislative means. In the two key industries of construction and hotels they have managed in the negotiations with employers in 2018 to have the idea of converting into law what they call the 'key terms' of the sectoral collective agreements accepted in principle by employers. Just as the operational framework of social dialogue structures needed to be strengthened, rendering it clearer and binding where necessary, the same was true for collective bargaining argued the trade unions (PEO 2017; Int. 12, 2020). This became more urgent as the interpretation of the laws, rules, and collective agreements, already somewhat ambiguous before the crisis, became more so in the conditions which prevailed after it. After a lot of back and forth, tensions while negotiating the sectoral agreements and claiming wage raises to cover what was lost in real income during the crisis years, progress was made in both the hotel industry and construction and new legislation passed in early 2020.

In the hotel industry an agreement with employers was made first and the five-day week, annual holidays and Provident Funds became regulated by law. Yet this did not remove tension during subsequent negotiations nor the problem of the lack of clarity as to what was obligatory and what was not. In 2016 trade unions became furious at state officials who accepted the interpretation of employers on the remaining issues as being regulated by the sectoral collective agreement as belonging to a 'non-obligatory' realm. Additionally, the diachronic problem of non-enforcement by some employers of the collective agreements, or some of their provisions, sustained tensions up the next round of negotiations in 2019 whereby a further step was made via the mediation of the Ministry of Labour. The problem was especially severe with respect to seasonal workers, primarily migrants who were offered very low salaries. Trade unions prioritised thus the issue of the starting wages in the collective agreement and minimum wages were set for nineteen different hospitality sector occupations and assigned legal status (Int. 11, 2020). The ministerial decree providing statutory regulation for a diverse set of occupational minimum wages was issued in January 2020 (Stockwatch, 2020a). This was a decisive step in the effort to set up minimum employment standards, and thus counterbalance the decline in collective bargaining coverage.

In construction, where PEO is much stronger than SEK, and where the major and lengthy strike of 2013 at a time when the recession was at its deepest point took place, developments were slower but ultimately also successful. The attempt to legally fortify clauses of the sectoral collective agreement was delayed as unlike the case with tourism, construction was severely hit by the economic crisis. It was only in 2017 that an agreement was reached by employers and trade unions at sectoral level providing minimum terms of employment. Although the employers withdrew their support from the agreement in 2018 leading into confrontation including some strike action, by 2019 and with the mediation of the Ministry of Labour a general, framework agreement was signed. The previous success of trade unions in getting the state to institute model rules obliging all contractors who won public contracts to abide by the terms of the collective agreement, operated as a precursor for this (Int. 11, 2020). It served as a basis for the general agreement reached with employers in 2019 and subsequently passed through parliament and became law and did not focus on wages, typically higher than hospitality, but on working time and other monetary benefits.

As of 2020 working time and over-time pay, public holidays, bonuses, and Provident Funds as stipulated in the sectoral collective agreement became legally enforceable (Ergatiko Vima 2020). This satisfied trade unions which sought for some success in difficult times yet the actual impact of this on the ground remains to be seen in conditions where trade unions lose members and find it increasingly difficult to recruit new ones. The booming of the construction industry from 2017 onwards after almost a decade of recession undoubtedly played a role in this, as major developers and contractors sought for stability and were keen on avoiding industrial unrest as well as unfair competition by smaller employers who typically kept their labour cost lower.

There were other successes of trade unions in the post-crisis period. As mentioned earlier a gradual timeframe was set in place, in line with the mechanism linking wage raises to GDP growth, for the crisis wage cuts to be reinstated by 2022. In the private sectors, the trade unions were able to block some potentially negative developments such as the promotion of outsourcing and subcontracting in hotels removing an ambiguous clause in the revised operational rules of the hotel industry in 2019. In the banking sector during the crisis years bank managements suspended sectoral bargaining with ETYK having to negotiate separately enterprise collective agreements (Ioannou and Sonan 2019). ETYK stood its ground in the long-drawn battle to defend and maintain the universalist logic of wages raises stipulated by the collective agreements in a context of collective bargaining decentralisation – sectoral collective bargaining returned at the end of the decade coinciding with enterprise-level bargaining.

There were also failures such as the shrinking scope of their political influence with respect to the political parties and the limited leverage they had on government policy. Just as PEO was unable to prevent AKEL while in government from pursuing austerity policies in the period 2011–2012, so was SEK in the subsequent years with respect to the ruling DISY and the other centre-right parties. The most spectacular failure demonstrating this was the delay in the establishment of an Independent Labour Inspectorate. As violations of the collective agreements and labour law, a diachronic issue in many industries, increased during the crisis years, trade unions pressurised the state to improve its inspection structures (Int. 11, 2020; Int. 12; 2020). After many years of delays, it was finally decided to set up an Independent Labour Inspection Service with a broad remit including an increased range, scope, and depth of its authority. When the bill reached parliament however in 2019 a parliamentary majority including the governing DISY party rejected it. This was a temporary setback as the bill after some further minor revisions did become law in 2020 – yet its implementation and effectiveness remains to be seen.

## Notes

1 In the northern part of the island, migrant workers, primarily from Turkey but in recent years also from Central Asian countries as well as students from Africa are even less well integrated in society and even more distant from trade unions. Trade unions in the north are largely restricted to the broader public sector with conditions prevailing in the private sectors being typically harsh and despotic.

2 After an accidental explosion in a military base near the village Mari, which resulted in the death of 13 persons and the partial destruction of the nearby main electricity station Christofias' government came under a devastating attack from the opposition parties and the media, lost its partner in government and was largely delegitimised.

3 In the northern part of Cyprus, austerity policies were also being implemented with the economic assistance offered by Turkey becoming since 2009 increasingly conditional upon the Turkish Cypriot statelet embarking on structural reforms involving wage cuts, fiscal restraint, and privatisations. In 2014–2016 when the

intercommunal negotiations restarted, there were hopes that the reunification of the island would also bring along growth and employment in the context of reconstruction. However, the dominant view in bourgeois circles was that the risk in such development was bigger than the benefit (Ioannou 2020a).

4 It must also be mentioned that there was substantial political pressure exerted on the Supreme Court by the government and the media painting the imagery of an impeding disaster if the state was to be forced to pay back all the cuts. Also, significantly some of the Supreme Court judges disagreed with the majority decision and offered a different reasoning.

5 Of the two major private banks of largely Cypriot ownership, one, Laiki closed and the other, the Bank of Cyprus came under the control of foreign capital. Foreign ownership expanded in the third smaller one, Hellenic Bank, as well. Furthermore, in the context of the crisis the Cooperative Credit Movement, completed its process of conversion into commercial banking, losing its autonomy and subsumed under the governance of the Cyprus Central Bank and the European Central Bank, while it was also nationalised as capital was provided by the Troika in order for it to meet the new criteria of the European system. After five years in public ownership, during which no substantial reform was made to make it viable it was sold cheaply to the private Hellenic Bank by Anastasiades' government in 2018, which took it over postponing its own evolving crisis.

# Part III

# Beneath and Beyond the Economic Crisis: Development, Contention, and Class Struggle

# 6 Comparing and Contrasting Experiences and Impact

Despite the significant convergences in the causes, the policy mix adopted, and the consequences of the economic crisis in the labour markets, class structures and societies of Southern Europe, as the analysis in the previous chapters demonstrated, there were also several divergences. The convergences and divergences, deriving from differences in the historical trajectories, the institutional contexts, the conjunctural political dynamics, and the agency of different players at both the levels of the state and society were identified in passing in the three country-specific chapters. A more systematic and in-depth comparative examination is needed now in order to illustrate the factors that can explain them.

This chapter takes a more holistic view of the process occasionally zooming in on the specifics but generally maintaining a broad lens to allow for keeping sight of the big picture in the whole duration of the crisis decade. With this analytic strategy the drivers of the process and the key social and political mechanisms directing and/or influencing the continuity and change can be distinguished from national specificities and secondary developments occurring. The aim of this chapter is to discuss how the combination of the external forces, both economic and political, interacted with the structural attributes of the three south European countries and the class dynamics in operation, shaping the outcomes.

Bringing together the empirical analysis of the country case studies this chapter begins with a theoretical point about the process of institutional change and the role of law and politics in bringing it about. Highlighting the role of agency in processes of restructuring as well as the inertia, the chapter accounts for the shaping of the ideological context in which the liberalisation policies and their contestation took place. The role played by the mainstream media, the process of undermining collective labour relations and the limits of that process, and the spread of precariousness as well as social solidarity are set out as key parameters of the crisis decade. Institutional and legal change and their outcomes are discussed with respect to the driving causes, the underlying forces, and the consequences at the level of society in the three countries. In this way the chapter makes explicit several theoretical insights concerning employment relations, the labour market, and the class structure during the crisis decade.

This chapter serves then as the lynchpin of the book because it is a place where the comparative institutional analysis acquires the most breadth and depth and where the South European crisis is most systematically framed within international political economy. Law and ideology are also examined more comprehensively in terms of their influence on political developments, societal processes and more specifically on shaping the employment field and securing sufficient consent or toleration to the shifting policy framework of market enhancing reforms and welfare cuts. This chapter then brings together the insights of the preceding ones and ties together concepts and themes, observations and explanations constructing a comprehensive analysis that advances the argument of the book. It answers thus the main research question which concerns the similarities and the differences of the crisis management and impact across national contexts. Moreover, this chapter opens up the book's third part which raises broader questions about the historical causality and significance of the crisis and its legacy.

## Law and the Politics of Institutional Change

Legislative changes cannot on their own produce results automatically. Both the making and the implementation of law derives from and depends on socio-political processes. It is through the agency of the different parties that the law is enacted and assumes its materiality and force. At the same time, however, law sends signals to the parties which adjust their behaviours accordingly, and in the process changing the social reality (Dukes 2019). And legal discourse and legal norms in any case co-evolve with the social relations that they describe and constitute (Deakin 2015). Prevailing political dynamics influence not only the directions of institutional change but also how social forces perceive the evolving institutional context and their political options within and outside it. At the same time political action and the interaction between different agents at the level of society are mediated by ideological and discursive conflicts through which interests are understood and preferences are decided based on assessments about the feasibility of paths and the likelihood of optimal outcomes.

Actors may defect from, or reinterpret rules, and through their action test the limits of institutions. Changes emerge out of such contestations between actors (Hall and Thelen 2009). The emergence and development of new industrial relations practices were also determined by the employers' readiness to risk conflict by adopting more aggressive stances. These depended on the specific circumstances of each case. Throughout Southern Europe, during the crisis decade the prevailing economic conditions of mass unemployment had an overwhelming, direct impact on workers' readiness to resist, frequently not to resist that is, orienting trade unions towards seeking class compromise (Wright 2000).

Yet class compromise was not really on offer, at least in the initial stages of the economic crisis, as European elites and national governments demanded heavy, immediate sacrifices of employment rights and social welfare. This is what sparked the anti-austerity social movements which shaped, in some cases more than others, the domestic political dynamics in Southern Europe. Undoubtedly the external political and economic pressure for market-enhancing reforms in employment and welfare systems was overwhelming and crucial in ultimately forcing the devaluation of labour, a process that went deepest and was most extensive in Greece. Although this overarching macro-trend largely prevailed everywhere, this did not occur evenly and uniformly, and was not achieved in the same way and to the same extent in different countries. Pre-existing institutional orders, national political traditions, pockets of resistance and social solidarity in various combinations had their own impact on the directions of change in different countries and different spheres within them.

The highly regulated industrial relations systems in Spain and Greece could not simply change overnight and could not be transformed in all their dimensions. Whereas the neoliberal political offensive against labour was both extensive and sudden, its capacity to really transform the field of employment was not as thorough as it seems when examining the changed legal order. This is because there is no clean slate in institutional and legal reform and the temporality of labour law cannot be entirely subsumed within the logic of political expediency. Where and when resistance proved difficult at the workplace, it was expressed in the streets. In Spain, and to a certain extent in Greece, some of the impacts of the reforms were challenged in court with mixed results. Even in Cyprus with its liberal order and weak collective bargaining institutionalisation, there were sectors were trade unions could draw sufficient resources from tradition and tread an orderly retreat ensuring that some of what was lost could be gained back in the near future.

Whereas the adversarial political systems in Spain and Greece facilitated an early, overt politicisation of the anti-austerity movement that traversed the political spectrum resulting in implosion, cleavage, and polarisation, in the consensual political system of Cyprus where a left-wing government happened to be in office initially, political conflict around austerity was restricted to questions of timing and form. Being too small to matter and experiencing the peak of its crisis a bit later than Spain and Greece, at a time when the EU stance was more mature, clear, and determined, the scope for successful political resistance in Cyprus was narrower. Yet while the consensual tradition within the political system and the strong connection of the political system to society eased the adoption and implementation of most of the Troika reforms, some of them such as the privatisation of telecommunications and electricity provision were stalled and obstructed, eventually in parliament as well, by the same dynamics that allowed the rest of the reforms through.

The EU intervention in its southern periphery imposed institutional and policy change using finance as its instrument. Loans became necessary to avert financial collapse and this seemingly simple fact afforded the EU substantial leverage in its demanding and securing of a series of reforms. Yet to reduce the story to this crude core, will be to miss the processes by which other concerns, issues and views were ignored, sidelined, and/or underplayed and ultimately subsumed within the dilemma of 'austerity or catastrophe'. For this to happen the EU elites needed the consent of national elites and a degree of toleration or acquiescence by at least a significant section of the population. For this to be achieved a substantial amount of discursive effort was expended, so as to shape the prevailing ideological context accordingly.

## Neoliberal Framing: The Media as a Key Pillar of TINA

The austerity measures adopted as a response to the economic crisis were essentially unpopular and unwanted by an overwhelming majority of society in all South European countries. In the early years of the crisis, the austerity policies provoked societal tensions and mass protests (Andronikidou and Kovras 2012; Baumgarten 2013; Ancelovici 2015). Elites faced an increasingly difficult task in their effort to achieve some minimum social consensus or at least restrain dissent from turning into open contention and threatening the political and social order. If something can be generalised in the way the crisis and its management was communicated in South European countries is the promotion of the idea of the inevitability of austerity as coined in the famous neoliberal acronym TINA. This view, both a position and a perspective, both politics and a frame of politics was a key staple in the mainstream media.

Although the economic crisis effectively undermined the neoliberal narrative which was established and diffused in the 1990s, the inability of articulation of a coherent and comprehensive alternative narrative by the anti-neoliberal forces led to the political strengthening of the neoliberal policy framework at the time of its apparent ideological weakening. Analysts and researchers talked about 'neoliberalism 2.0', or 'neoliberalism on steroids' while Crouch's formulation as 'the strange non-death of neoliberalism' became possibly the most famous (Crouch 2011). Beyond the political economy of the crisis and complementary to it, exists the cultural political economy of the narratives, the imaginaries and the construals about the crisis. The ability of neoliberal ideology to not only survive but continue to dominate, determine, and shape policy lay in the ability of the political agents who were its bearers to promote its reading as a crisis in, and not as a crisis of, neoliberalism (Jessop 2012; 2013).

The media as active agents in the discursive struggles in society (Hall, 2005 [1982]) were inevitably the key actor in establishing the basic understanding of the nature of the crisis and the available set of options about it. This was more enhanced in the early stage whereby public opinion begun to grapple with the basic parameters of the crisis and its management. The semiotic power of the media in contemporary times is essentially multidimensional. It involves simultaneously a power of position through their authoritative role and social function, a power of disposition through providing the access to information and cultural goods and determining their use, and a power of interpretation through their ability to define and distribute mentifacts and thus shape cultural mentality (Siefkes 2010). Mainstream media in all south European countries were not only the official providers of news to the public. They were also the main site where the analysis of economic developments took place, and the main source of explanation as far as the people were concerned. Economists and technocrats were offered ample space and time to elaborate their accounts of what happened and what should happen, while the credit rating agencies downgrading every now and then the various national economies of South European countries were setting the tone.

In the Western world, at least in the initial stages of the crisis, it was the finance sector that came in the spotlight as the collapse of Lehman Brothers set in motion the global depression and forced states to start bailing out their banks to avert the worse. There was criticism of the excesses of bankers and the big bonuses, calls for the regulation of the financial sector and condemnation of social inequality and this found its way, to some extent at least, in the mainstream media as well. Yet, the 'Keynesian moment' of the elite was not only too thin, restricted to the use of public money in the rescue of private banks, – it was also too short. By 2010 full attention had shifted to the fiscal domain. It was no longer about financial institutions failing but about the state over-spending, the households living above their means and the workers being not competitive enough (Basu 2018). Despite substantial contestation with the Occupy Wall Street in the United States and its global diffusion in the claim of 'the 99% against the 1%' constituting the symbolic peak, the reality was that the elite's narrative had made significant headway.

The temporality of the unfolding crisis differed across countries and this affected the dynamics of its development not only in terms of the economy but also in terms of politics and the tone of public debate. From the standpoint of more than a decade later this nuance might seem less significant, but there is one thing that is important to note, namely, that Southern Europe as an area belonging to the economic periphery of the 'West' or the 'North' experienced the crisis as simultaneously a financial and an economic one. As the fiscal situation deteriorated rapidly, the already consolidated narrative in the more advanced neoliberal and ordoliberal power centres of the EU about the overt public spending as the root of the trouble, and consequently austerity policy as the needed correction, gained credence. Although less hegemonic in the receiving Southern Europe end, this narrative was systematically propounded and undoubtedly found adherents as it was adopted by the conservative part of the political spectrum and by the technocrats staffing the ministries and the media panels.

By 2010 the shift to the right at the level of government policy was clear everywhere in Southern Europe irrespective of which government was in office (Bosco and Verney 2012). By 2012–2013 all governments in Southern Europe became right-wing smoothening further the austerity process which climaxed. Although these were times of unprecedented protests and sustained contestation in most of Southern Europe, opposition to austerity policies, even if widespread, was never overwhelming. A substantial section of society either accepted the core premises of the dominant narrative about fiscal trouble being the cause rather than the consequence of the crisis (Walby 2015), and/or viewed resistance as unlikely to produce policy change or simply refused to care about it. More importantly, however, the calculus of the game was only partially operative in the periphery. The crisis both unveiled and enhanced the substantial power disparity between and within state formations at the Eurozone and EU level in total. The control of the supply of money, was at the end of the day, sufficient to cow dissent, neutralise objections and impose a very narrow range of policy options to the governments of South European states who had the choice to play along or fall off the cliff.

The hegemony of the austerity route was thus never in the last analysis about convincing sceptic national elites or sceptic electorates about its value per se. It was always a relative matter, about convincing that the alternative was at best riskier and at worst a graver threat bordering social disaster. This was the 'preferred meaning' of the possibility or eventuality of states defaulting to international lenders, of the mainstream media coded message pounded repetitively and systematically and made into common sense (Gramsci 1972). To ensure that the message of impending disaster was decoded in those terms, a series of metaphors were used to construct the suitable frames. The Barthian notion of the myth as a system of values masquerading as a system of facts and more generally the naturalisation of social and historical processes (Barthes 1972 [1957]) can account well for the logic of the process under way. The euro crisis was abstracted into its technicalities, and subsequently simplified into interpretative schemata which condensed the 'reality' through selective punctuation, ordering, and sequencing to produce familiar frames. Frames of war, of disease and of natural disaster were for example accorded primacy in the mainstream press in northern Europe (Joris, d' Haenens and Van Gorp 2014), imported and adapted in South Europe as well.

There were to be sure alternative media that contested the dominant reading of the crisis, offered diverging explanations, and put forward different policy proposals. Connected to the social movements and participating in the citizen protests alternative, typically on-line media waged fiercely the communication battle against austerity and its international and national proponents. The terrain where the conflict of narratives was played out was often the social media platforms which were utilised at the same time as a mobilisation tool and as a public arena. Whereas anti-austerity activists were sufficiently successful in their use of social media for organisational purposes reaching out to wider sections of society, swaying public opinion was not an easy endeavour. While social media can be an ideal tool in multiplying quickly popular reactions and turning them into a snowball that can force its way through the mainstream media, it is less well suited to the slow pace, systematic narrative building necessary in shaping the common sense over the prolonged period of the crisis time.

The dilemma of either succumbing to austerity policies and deeper marketisation of domestic economies or face collapse was encountered by all South European states serving as the background for the period 2008–2015 and more starkly in key junctures in 2010 and 2012 for Spain; 2010, 2012, and 2015 for Greece; and 2012 and 2013 for Cyprus. In these exceptional times, social dialogue was essentially suspended, and public debate stifled. Politics itself succumbed to the logic of force majeure as legislative and even constitutional reforms were initiated despite social contention rising to levels bordering a popular revolt. The EU's ordoliberal, 'iron cage', proved immune to protests, because it was able to embed austerity into its constitutional make up and remove democratic controls over the economy (Papadopoulos and Roumpakis 2018). As such the hegemonic moment of the EU macro-economic governance did not derive from its content but rather from its form – more precisely its capacity to frame the austerity form, not as a universal good, but as the objectively 'least bad' option – and thus as the inevitable way forward (Tables 6.1 and 6.2).

*Table 6.1* Median income and % of wage share in GDP in Spain, Greece, and Cyprus, before and after the crisis

| | *Median income 2010 in €* | *Median income 2018 in €* | *Wage share of GDP in 2010 (current prices) (%)* | *Wage share of GDP in 2018 (current prices) (%)* |
|---|---|---|---|---|
| Spain | 14 605 | 14 785 | 57.2 | 52.7 |
| Greece | 11 963 | 7 875 | 54.3 | 49.6 |
| Cyprus | 16 180 | 15 336 | 54.3 | 49 |

Source: Eurostat.

*Table 6.2* Estimated collective bargaining coverage and Estimated total trade union density, Spain, Greece, and Cyprus before and after the crisis

| | *Estimated collective bargaining coverage 2009* | *Estimated collective bargaining coverage 2018* | *Estimated total trade union density (active employees) 2009* | *Estimated total trade union density (active employees) 2018* |
|---|---|---|---|---|
| Spain | 80–85% | 70–75% | 18–20% | 15–18% |
| Greece | 85–90% | 20–25% | 22–25% | 20–22% |
| Cyprus | 50–53% | 40–45% | 50–53% | 40–45% |

Estimates based on a range of diverging sources: Eurofound, ETUI, OECD, ILO.

## The Undermining and Resilience of Collective Labour Relations

The decentralisation of collective bargaining, the individualisation of employment relations and the pressures on the state and employers to increase competitiveness by introducing market-oriented policies and business strategies were trends pre-existing the crisis (Morlino and Raniolo 2017; Papadopoulos and Roumpakis 2018). In the whole of Southern Europe and even in many countries of Eastern as well as Northern Europe these trends were also observable before the crisis and accelerated during it (Kouzis and Kapsalis 2020). However, there were divergences in the ways and the extent to which this was made. Whereas for example in Greece and Spain this occurred primarily through legislation in the more liberal-voluntarist oriented industrial relations system in Cyprus this occurred through a combination of market pressure and employer and government agency. It was thus a less comprehensive development and of a more temporary character. Spain also differed compared to Greece because although the mechanism was the same, the changes in Spain were neither as wide in scope nor had as big an impact on collective bargaining and its coverage.

For example, the shrinking duration of the post-termination effect of collective agreements in both Greece and Spain may have increased trade union anxiety and willingness to compromise rather than risk losing everything if the existing collective agreement was left to expire, but it was still in their hands to decide their action vis a vis intransigent employers. The changing institutional context which weakened their leverage in collective bargaining, imposed dilemmas on trade unions to fight back or retreat, and the choice was often determined by the power correlation perceived as directly operable. The negative power correlation, militating against trade unions was not only reflected in the changed institutional context. In Cyprus where no substantial labour law reform took place, this was reflected in the worsening political environment especially after the new right-wing government took over in early 2013 which infused a new spirit in the Ministry of Labour in its early years whereby industrial conflict mediation was prolonged as a means to delay and where possible avert strike action.

Institutional change including legal reforms changes the context but cannot automatically change the content of existing social relations. For this to happen, social actors must act, adapting their action to the changed context. Take for example the decentralisation of collective bargaining. It was the action of employers and the acquiescence of trade unions, or in the case of Greece increasingly 'the association of persons' which sprang up during the peak of the crisis years, which shifted the levels of bargaining downwards once the legal reform abolished the hierarchy principle. In contrast, in Spain employers were not too eager to shift from industry and regional to company-level bargaining, opting instead for using the legislative reforms to secure temporary derogations, allowing industry-level bargaining to remain relatively important (Müller et al. 2019).

Other legal reforms, however, such as the lowering of the minimum wage in Greece, its removal from the body of the national collective agreement, and its setting as a separate order regulated by decree, had more direct impact. Not only was it immediately enforced on many workers whose wages were regulated by the minimum wage before the crisis, but it also became the standard wage for most of the new entrants into the labour market in the crisis decade. In addition, it exerted a strong downward pressure on the wages of many others already in employment especially in non-unionised settings. Worse still, in many industries where precarious work was prevalent, rather than serving as a floor, the statutory minimum wage served as a ceiling (Dukes 2018). The combined effect of low wages and part-time work for an increasing section of the workforce produced high levels of in-work poverty.

In Spain, the minimum wage was regulated by statue from before the crisis and during the crisis there was neither a reduction nor the instituting of a sub-minimum wage for younger workers as in Greece. It merely remained static until 2016 after which it started increasing while a relatively big increase took place under the PSOE-PODEMOS coalition government in 2019 and 2020. Thus, although the minimum wage in Spain was at an analogously low level with Greece at least during the peak of the crisis, it was not a key instrument in directly forcing wages down as in Greece. The same is true for Cyprus, which does not have a national statutory minimum wage, but a Ministerial Decree setting a minimum wage for merely nine occupations (Eurofound 2019). The minimum wage for those nine occupations in Cyprus was initially raised but the increase was below inflation and subsequently remained static during the deflation of the peak crisis years and the inflation of the post-crisis years. Although there was significant pressure from employers to abolish it or reduce it, they were not able to amass adequate political support. Wage compression in Cyprus, like in Spain took place primarily through employers' evasion of collective agreements.[1]

In all three countries the main trade unions lost members and their resources shrank as aggregate membership dues decreased while indirect state funding also became scarcer. Also, in all three countries some smaller trade unions were able to make inroads and compete with the more established ones while there were also new worker initiatives, in specific areas, industries and firms often engaging in radical action. However, there was nowhere a restructuring of the trade union landscape analogous to that occurring at the level of the political system in Greece and to a lesser extent Spain. Whereas in terms of the weakening of trade union influence at the institutional level the three countries converged, there were divergences in terms of their other sources of power and in terms of how the crisis affected their functioning and the trade union landscape.

In Greece traditional trade unionism almost collapsed along with the industrial relations system with which it was associated. Drawing most of its power and legitimacy from the industrial relations system, once that was swept away, trade unionism in Greece had little to hold on to. In Cyprus developments in the trade union field were more alike Spain rather than Greece: decline of trade union influence amidst an industrial relations system reconstituted in a more hostile context but a milder organisational retreat and relative resilience. Trade unions in Spain and Cyprus were less dependent on the state compared to their counterparts in Greece and although their public image was also tarnished, and their societal power weakened, their status never deteriorated as much as in Greece. Despite losing members and declining in density and having to economise through merges and reduction of salaried staff, Spanish and Cypriot trade unions retained adequate organisational resources allowing them to at least play the defensive role they opted for (Fernandez Rodriguez et al. 2021; Ioannou and Sonan 2021).

There were similarities in the industrial relations systems of Spain and Greece, but the better functioning of works councils at company level, in the relatively more numerous middle and large firms, played a role in preventing the collapse in Spain. While both systems were fragmented, and both depended on the legal force of collective bargaining, bargaining decentralisation curbed trade union power more in Greece. Company level works councils, exposed UGT and CCOO to challenges from both more radical unions as well as yellow unions but at the same time kept representation structures alive while the survival of the erga omnes effect prevented the disintegration of the system. In Greece on the other hand, the simultaneous abolition of both the hierarchy of bargaining and the extension of coverage of sectoral collective bargaining to non-signatories, left trade unions with little room to function. Where grassroots, radical unions did emerge in Greece, they tended to be too marginal and often unwilling to engage in the formal representation structures which continued to demise (Karakioulafi, 2019).

In none of the three countries examined were there significant shifts in the political and ideological orientation of trade unionism. Although new independent trade unions emerged in various sectors and settings, often positioning themselves as more militant than established trade unions, they were nowhere able to transform trade unionism. In Spain, where this was advanced, the new energy emerging was mostly absorbed by UGT and CCOO. Spanish trade unionism has been at least partially able to adapt to the changing context and adjust the framing of its public discourse form workerism to citizenism. Shifting also the emphasis of its set of demands from the promotion of full employment to the denouncing of precariousness (Barranco and Molina, 2019).

In Greece, trade union leaders dissociated from the crumbling and discredited PASOK with which they were historically affiliated, but this provoked neither a real change in the trade union landscape nor was it enough to save Greek trade unionism. They did save their own position however within Greek trade unionism as they retained some legitimacy, or at least survived because their challengers were too weak to oust them. Within GSEE, PAME in contrast to KKE in the electoral field, grew a bit stronger but neither tried nor was it able to take over the confederation. SYRIZA, which captured the centre-left space held by PASOK in the political spectrum, was neither interested nor capable of setting up an organisational structure in the labour field in parallel to the one it set up in the political field. It thus could not challenge effectively the leading (ex-)PASOK faction within GSEE. In Cyprus, new trade unions only emerged in the broader public sector and although damaging PASYDY, did not pose a serious challenge to PEO and SEK.

Overall, the undermining of collective labour relations was both a cause and an instrument in the relative decline of worker income at the aggregate level. While in Spain the median income remained stable when 2010 is compared with that of 2018, in Cyprus there is a substantial drop in the same period from 16 180€ to 15 336€. In Greece, where the devaluation of labour was monumental the median income dropped from 11 963€ in 2010€ to 7875 in 2018. Although Greece stands out in terms of the rapid and huge drop in collective bargaining coverage, there was a substantial reduction of coverage in Spain and Cyprus as well. In contrast to the drop in collective bargaining coverage there is no significant difference between the three countries in terms of the decline in trade union density. In all three countries trade density dropped as trade unions lost members and faced increasing difficulty to recruit new ones.

Yet when seen from a longer-term perspective the decrease in trade union density was nowhere monumental, not even in Greece and was effectively a trend not diverging too much from pre-crisis patterns. The loss of members by the trade unions was largely a result of rising unemployment but this cannot explain the decline in trade union density as the proportion of non-unionised workers made redundant tended to be higher. The mild drop in trade union density was primarily a result of rising non-standard employment and the prevailing conditions of precariousness which dissuaded younger and newly employed or re-employed workers from joining trade unions.

## Political Restructuring and Political Inertia

Morlino and Raniolo (2017) rightly argue that the impact of the economic crisis on the political systems of southern Europe was significant but should neither be over-emphasised as there are many elements of continuity, nor should it be discounted as inconsequential. The effect of the crisis on South European democracies was complex, diverse, and contradictory with the patterns and courses taken in different countries depending on their historical trajectories and traditions, but also opportunity structures. Citizen disaffection and alienation in some cases like Portugal and Cyprus lead primarily to electoral abstention while in others like Spain and Greece it was translated into social protests which were subsequently institutionalised and stabilised through the rise of protest parties. In Italy, the political system was destabilised earlier and possibly rearranged to a greater extent.

Whereas the economic crisis initially deepened the crisis of traditional electoral behaviour producing electoral volatility, the emergence of protest parties capable of transforming protest into institutionalised electoral participation, SYRIZA, the Five Star Movement, and PODEMOS being the key such examples, operated in the opposite direction strengthening the representation structures of southern European democracies. At the same time, the policy choices available to national governments during the Eurozone crisis were simply too narrow, thus reinforcing and substantiating the 'blame shift' discourse, discharging that is responsibility for decisions to the European elites (Morlino and Raniolo 2017: 111, 117). Yet the emergence of these movement parties has been a significant development in the political sphere. It both expressed and facilitated the more directly political orientation of social movements effecting a convergence between the logic of the party and the logic of the movement and revitalizing thus the political system as such (Della Porta et al. 2017).

The bigger political restructuring in Greece compared to Spain was due to the bigger vulnerability of the well-established clientelist system in Greece in conjunction with its adversarial character between the traditional parties which could no longer deliver citizen expectations. The mainstream parties were not flexible enough to collaborate at the right time, hence allowing rapidly a huge political space for protest parties (Morlino and Raniolo 2017: 45). In Cyprus despite the shock provoked by the crisis management which included capital controls and the unprecedented bail-in arrangement, and despite the discrediting of the political system, there were neither sustained massive protests nor any protest parties managing to constitute themselves in national organisational forms and in electoral terms. The consensual tradition in the Cypriot political system and the depth of the penetration of political parties in civil society as well as conjunctural reasons of government-opposition dynamics at key junctures in 2012 and 2013 can explain why this was the case (Charalambous and Ioannou 2017).

Across the board, the forces of social democracy had adopted the neoliberal framework in the previous decades (Moschonas, 2002), and were thus largely incapable of convincingly promoting an alternative conception in the crisis years. The radical left remained divided and lacking a unified understanding of the situation was unable to construct a coherent alternative policy framework. It was populism that emerged in the last decade as the key adversary of neoliberal ideas, yet again although an ascending trend, populism is neither unified, nor coherent and does not really have a comprehensive policy set to put in place once in power as the SYRIZA experience showed. The same applied for PODEMOS, the Spanish variant of left-wing populism, which after all the anti-systemic rhetoric and the discourse of radical change eventually settled for an alliance with PSOE. This was of course as much indicative of the limits of PODEMOS' strength, as it was of PSOE's weakness which also had to swallow its pride and accept the alliance. PODEMOS exchanged support for and participation in the PSOE government with pledges for some minor and mild policies in a progressive direction. In any case populism has never been more than a communicational frame and a political discourse rather than an ideological or political position per se (Charalambous and Ioannou, 2020a). This is what allowed and allows its adoption by both the far right but also by left-wing forces; yet populism despite its capturing of the contention space, has so far proved incapable of constituting itself as the force that can end the neoliberal project.

The economic crisis shook all the political systems of Southern Europe but did not lead to the restructuring of all of them. In addition to the force of change precipitated by economic hardship, citizen disaffection and perceived malfunction of the political process as policies came to be devised and decided in supranational and technocratic centres according to market whims, there was also a force of inertia in operation. The weight of custom and tradition, consolidated conformist views, blame shifting, and topic deflection, unconvincing new actors and perceived lack of alternatives prevented the deepening of the political crisis from fully overturning the political field. No political system came out of the crisis unscathed, not even Cyprus which exhibited the least change in that respect. The increasing tension between the executive and legislative branches of power is one example of this. At the same time even the political systems that were largely restructured such as that of Greece, were soon re-constituted in terms of their balance and operating logic, after the reshuffling of political parties and political personnel re-stabilised.

Undoubtedly the contestation of the societal impacts of the economic crisis in Southern Europe was based on, and at the same time propelled, a process of re-politicisation of various societal segments. Yet, this process was neither extensive nor intensive enough to produce a new paradigm of politics. While many people became interested and involved in politics there were also others that became disillusioned and resigned from politics and the prospect of political change. As social resistance failed to change the policy framework in the crisis years and as non-systemic parties became incorporated into the existing political system in the 'post crisis' years, this trend was further strengthened. Thus, from a longer-term perspective, the legitimation crisis of liberal representative democracy, observed since the 1990s was not really reversed in the 2010s.

In both Greece and Spain, the rise of SYRIZA and PODEMOS constituted a sort of regeneration of the Left. More so in Greece where SYRIZA, a pre-existing party of the radical left used the notion of the Left, and the slogan for 'a first time Left-wing government' centrally in its campaign. Yet the discourse that prevailed and the basis on which mass electoral support was won was not a revitalised fully fledged left-wing ideology. Although there was a plethora of references to socialist and social-democratic values, slogans that alluded to the traditions of the left including even the communist left, this was not the key element allowing SYRIZA and PODEMOS to amass enough popular support and assume executive power. Populist appeals against the elite in general, and championing the interests of an undifferentiated people, calls to defend national sovereignty threatened by international lenders and ousting the corrupt political establishment were far more significant. For many people, alienated by the political system, SYRIZA and PODEMOS represented above all something new, that could be tried since the old had proved unsustainable. It is not a coincidence that the rise of left-populist parties took place simultaneously with the rise of right-populist parties, extreme right parties as well as new centrist parties (Table 6.3).

## Precariousness, Vulnerability, and Solidarity at the Societal Level

As described in the three preceding, single-country chapters employment precariousness expanded both in terms of societal reach and in terms of depth. The deinstitutionalisation and weakening of organised labour relative to capital has been a central social condition exacerbating

*Table 6.3* Immigration and Emigration during the 5-year crisis peak, Material deprivation and Inequality rates at the crisis peak year, and At risk of poverty rate and Threshold in 2018 in Spain, Greece, and Cyprus

| | *Total number of persons immigrating during the 5-year crisis peak* | *Total number of persons emigrating during the 5-year crisis peak* | *Material deprivation rate at the crisis peak year* | *Income inequality during the crisis peak. Quantile share ratio (top to bottom quantile)* | *At risk of poverty and social exclusion % in the total population in 2018* | *At risk of poverty threshold in € (60% of national median income) in 2018* |
|---|---|---|---|---|---|---|
| Spain | (2010–2014) 1 622 315 | (2010–2014) 2 191 750 | (2014) 17.8% | (2015) 6.87 | 21.5 | 9 618 |
| Greece | (2011–2015) 299 694 | (2011–2015) 550 347 | (2015) 40.7% | (2012) 6.63 | 18.5 | 5 547 |
| Cyprus | (2012–2016) 70 411 | (2012–2016) 99 445 | (2014) 36.5% | (2014) 5.37 | 15.4 | 10 503 |

Source: Eurostat.

precarity, a process climaxing with the emergence of the new European economic governance as the response to the crisis (Pulignano 2017). While tens and even hundreds of thousands of regular jobs were destroyed as firms downsized, went bankrupt or shifted their operations to adapt to the recession, the new jobs created during the post-crisis years were overwhelmingly low-paid and most of them temporary and irregular. In Spain there were 5069 bankruptcies in the first half of 2013 alone, the biggest number on record since statistics began in 2004 (Fotinatos-Ventouratos and Cooper 2015). Tourism, the industry that was the least negatively affected was traditionally one where most jobs were already largely precarious. As collective bargaining coverage levels dropped, more workers were driven to individually regulated contracts of employment, meaning, in many cases, sub-standard terms and conditions. Involuntary part-time work expanded across the board while casualised and precarious employment became, at least for the younger workers, the norm of the labour market (Kouzis 2013).

It was not just the scale of precariousness that grew however, it was also its scope. This is because labour markets, although differently structured and reproduced, remain 'intimately connected to each other' (Fine 1998). As the crisis deepened in 2012–2014, even workers who retained their regular jobs began to feel increasing pressure and experience increased levels of insecurity. In conditions of overtly high unemployment and deep recession, losing one's job was a devastating prospect. With redundancy pay significantly reduced in Greece and Spain and employment protection undermined making dismissals cheaper and easier for employers, this became nightmarish. Besides the salary and benefits cuts that varied across countries, industries and firms, the increased taxation and the reduced social policy budgets and the deterioration of underfunded public services affected also the relatively better off section of the labour force. In the Mediterranean context of strong family ties and weak welfare states, persons in regular employment most often had to support unemployed or precariously employed family members, and this increased the dependence on their employers and their readiness to do more in order to maintain their jobs.

At the peak of the crisis all three countries experienced conditions akin to a humanitarian crisis with a significant and growing proportion of people at risk of poverty and social exclusion. During the worst year for each country, after savings disappeared, the material deprivation rate climbed to 40.7% in Greece and 36.5% in Cyprus. In Spain, the material deprivation rate remained substantially lower but the proportion of people at risk of poverty and social exclusion remained above 20% for much longer. In Greece, which suffered the worst and more generalised compression of living standards, the threshold of relative poverty, estimated at 60% of the median income, dropped to just 5 547 € per year in 2018. The number of people resorting to food banks expanded in all three countries. In Spain homelessness escalated before being, at least partially, dealt with by the movement against evictions. In Greece, it became common for many households to spend winters without heating and some without electricity as well. To this day many blocks of flats in the Greek cities do not use their central heating systems as most tenants cannot afford to contribute to the price of fuel.

Precariousness does not have only material consequences but also psychosocial ones. More importantly its impact is not restricted to people that are precariously employed but extends to broader social groups including students, the unemployed, even people that have regular jobs who see others among their family and social networks suffer from it. The lack of stability, the impossibility of longer-term commitments and the inability to plan one's immediate future is known to have negative health impacts (Lewchuk et al. 2008). As precariousness spread in society, a feeling of generalised insecurity prevails leading to the intensification of work as more effort is perceived to be necessary in order to retain the job. The extra effort does not necessarily lead to increased productivity as there are limits and various other factors at play for that, but over-work necessarily leads to the undermining of physical and mental well-being. The economic crisis which has exacerbated the already difficult conditions prevailing in the labour market has resulted in increasing levels of stress and anxiety (Fotinatos-Ventouratos and Cooper 2015).

Younger people in Southern Europe, suffering the brunt of the crisis as they entered the labour market during the crisis years, were left with limited options. For most of them, the choice was between unemployment or irregular employment in the hope of someday escaping the precarity trap (Pulignano 2017). Some of those with less qualifications and skills were driven into jobs previously occupied by migrant workers whose number shrank as the recession deepened. Many of those with higher qualifications, skills and confidence opted for trying their luck abroad. During the 5-year crisis peak period, emigration out of Southern Europe substantially exceeded immigration into it. Although the crisis brought about downward social mobility, this process did not lead to fundamental shifts in the division of the labour and the class structure. Migrants continued to be concentrated in low paid and menial jobs and when growth returned the immigration rate exceeded the emigration rate again.

The social policy cuts and the reorganization of welfare provision in a neoliberal direction increased not only the hardship and vulnerability of various social groups but also served an ideological function, that of accustoming society into a substandard level of public social provision. The spread of active labour market policies, operating as a substitute in the absence of regular employment had a complementary impact – not only normalising employment precarity but also intensifying market discipline among the workforce, and thus contributing to the erosion of the decommodification function of the welfare state (Greer 2016).

In the cases of Greece and Cyprus the Social Solidarity Income and the Guaranteed Minimum Income respectively, instituted in both countries after the return to growth, were important vehicles through which relief was extended to the most vulnerable groups bordering absolute poverty but was at the same time inadequate to lift them out of relative poverty. More important than the socio-economic, was the ideological function of this welfare reform; it contributed to the stabilisation of the humanitarian crisis and the habituating of society to the new post-crisis normal, whereby relative poverty was seen for many people as a permanent condition. The bureaucratic hustle of the application process which needed to be frequently repeated for this benefit to be continued was part of the disciplining role this policy was meant to play.

Trade unions and the Left were essentially trapped into this mechanism of neoliberal welfare. Pressed between the dire need to provide relief to those excluded from the existing systems, economic stagnation and fiscal restraint, the Guaranteed Minimum Income figured as the only game in town. In Spain, where no analogous universal mechanism was instituted, and welfare provision remained fragmented, non-systematic, and leaving some groups totally unprotected, the Guaranteed Minimum Income was even seen as a means of 'fighting inequality' and as an imprint of the return of progressive politics with the new PSOE-PODEMOS government instituting it in the midst of the Covid-19 crisis (Sánchez Nicolás 2020). The ability of the neoliberal logic to capture even the space of social policy, a realm traditionally associated with social democratic values, is indicative not only of an altered correlation of class forces but also of an ideological retreat.

## Class Dynamics and Ideological Shifts

While at the level of industrial relations, employers emerged out of the decade-long crisis with a clear advantage over workers and trade unions, changes in class dynamics and prevailing ideologies were more complex, varying across space and time, and contradictory. As mentioned earlier the economic depression primarily accelerated and intensified already existing trends in the labour market of Southern Europe of weakening trade union power, fragmentation, and precariousness. In Spain, and even more so in Greece, this process also involved institutional restructuring, weakening support for collective bargaining, and reducing employment protection. This was escorted by austerity policies which undercut social transfers and undermined the redistribution function of the state. As such, working class power was eroded both at the workplace and the macro-economy, both at the level of production and at the level of distribution (Silver 2003). The working classes of Southern Europe contested the changes in different and diverse ways and although forced to retreat, they did ultimately manage to signal that there were limits to the depth and the time length of that retreat.

Throughout Southern Europe, it was external pressure emanating initially from the international money markets and subsequently from the EU that provided the backdrop and influenced developments at the level of the national states. This was escorted with surveillance which increased when reforms were delayed or when they did not deliver the expected results (Theodoropoulou 2015). Yet austerity and internal devaluation policies were also adopted by national elites who willingly or less willingly ultimately took ownership of the process. This process was most advanced in Spain after the rise of PP to power in 2011 and in Cyprus after the rise of DISY to power in 2013. In Greece popular resistance to austerity led to the biggest destabilisation of the political system making national elites more reluctant as political legitimisation was weaker than ever. It took the election of SYRIZA to power and its capitulation to the terms of the Troika for stability to return to the Greek political system and for the national elites to become protagonists, a process completed as SYRIZA's power base was gradually eroded and ND returned to power in 2019.

Working-class resistance to austerity in Spain and Greece proved impossible to channel through the existing institutionalised forms. It was expressed in the early years of the crisis through new and revived social movements which were interclass in form embracing also middle-class strata and focusing on the political rather than the industrial relations sphere. The Indignados in Spain and the Aganaktismenoi in Greece in 2011 constituted a peak of the social contention which was speedily institutionalised in the form of SYRIZA and PODEMOS. Although incapable of blocking the pathway to austerity in the subsequent years, the rise of new left-wing parties to the political mainstream, demonstrated that the drift to impoverishment and immiseration could not continue indefinitely. In Greece, the rejection of the Troika plan in the 2015 referendum, was another signal of working-class insubordination (Seferiades, 2017: 361–367), even if in the absence of determined leadership with a willingness to face the consequences of a possible Grexit, manifested more an act of recklessness rather than of power. In Cyprus, the most spectacular intervention by the working class and allied middle strata was set in 2013 succeeding in the rejection of the universal bail-in, subsequently adopted in a less socially diffused form.

Although there were changes in the class structure of South European societies and shifts in the prevailing ideology during the crisis decade, these were multi-directional and contradictory and did not lead to any substantial rearrangement of class relations or any paradigm shift in the political culture of any country. In all three countries investigated in depth in this book, the middle-class strata shrunk in size and influence as there was a general polarising socio-economic trend (Eurofound 2017b). Many petty capital owners were led into bankruptcy or brought under the control of bigger capital owners through increasing capital centralisation and many professionals were proletarianised or more precisely many graduates were blocked from becoming professionals and most definitely from being remunerated as professionals. At the same time, the deepening of the labour force fragmentation prevented the integration of the working-class strata despite the unificatory trend of generalised, even if variable, deterioration of terms and conditions of employment.

The destruction of capital and the reshuffling provoked in the context of the reform of the banking sector produced winners and losers within the capitalist class but did not fundamentally change something in its character, societal positioning, dependence on the state, or political orientation. There was not even substantial change in the composition of the networks of the bankers and the financiers. After all the damage provoked to the economy by the banking system, the changes effected in its management personnel and operational structure were truly limited, restricted to some changes in the board of directors. The banks in Southern Europe were essentially rescued rather than allowed to collapse as in Iceland, and their continued fragility militated against the adoption of policies of retributive justice (Kovras and Pagliari, 2020). Just as the banks proved 'too big to fail', the bankers proved 'too big to jail'. The very few prosecutions for minor offenses and the handful of convictions effectively allowed the representatives of finance capital to continue their careers with minor disruption and the finance sector to maintain its privileged position in the political economy of South European states.

If something changed in relation to the capitalists as a class in Southern Europe is relative to their counterparts in the economically stronger states, in the international rather than the domestic field. In Cyprus for example, the national bourgeoisie suffered substantial loss of control of the reformed banking system. More generally in all countries there was also significant flight of capital provoked by the financial destabilisation and the economic recession. At the level of the real economy, the conditions of general de-investment during the recession, allowed some bigger and more internationalised firms to make headway in some sectors over smaller and more nationally focused businesses which had less capacity for resilience.

The need for speedy economic recovery that was to create jobs and bring tax money to the state relieving to some extent its social policy burden resulted in the further enhancing of the political standing of private capital. Although the taxation burden of the bourgeoisie also increased, this was relatively small compared to the taxation burden suffered by the middle and the working classes and was too little to offset the gains accrued from the reduction of labour cost. More importantly the reshaping of the economic field created more favourable conditions for businesses in the post-crisis years. More workers were available to work for less, the state was more ready to provide facilitations to capital to 'get the economy going again' while a series of public assets were put on sale to keep public debt under control and the lenders satisfied. The enhancement of the position of capital vis a vis labour is reflected in the decline of the wage share of GDP in all countries. Estimated in current prices the wage share of GDP dropped between 2010 and 2018 from 57.2% to 52.7% in Spain, from 54.3% to 49.6% in Greece and from 54.3% to 49% in Cyprus.

The biggest change in terms of positionality in the class structure during the 2010s affected sections of the middle-class strata and sections of the lower-class strata. While economic hardship was generalised throughout society, and as analysed above varying in magnitude as a result of a multitude of factors, for these two groups the shrinking of the range of opportunities and subsequently available income, was crucial in producing a social class shift. Although cushioned by family support networks and social solidarity initiatives the proletarianisation of some middle strata and the impoverishment of some working-class strata was a significant social development with political consequences. It accentuated the de-legitimisation of the political system, contributed to rising discontent which was channelled into protests and new parties and became both cause and effect in the rearrangement of social policy. Downward social mobility which swelled the ranks of the new poor and the working poor was to a certain extent temporary – yet it was a sudden and a relatively extensive process and as such it was a disruptive social trend that could not easily be framed in individualised terms.

At the ideological level the biggest shift that can be observed at the macro level in the crisis decade is the further weakening of the traditional cleavages of right and left and the further de-alignment of class positionality from the right-left axis. Conservative, liberal, and social-democratic ideologies became less appealing as comprehensive discourses, another process under way at least since the 1990s. However, this did not merely enhance depoliticisation but also the rise of new hybrid ideological discourses built after several and ever-changing mutations and cross-fertilisations of older ideological forms (Charalambous 2021). These were often incoherent and contradictory as diverging and conflicting ideas co-existed and interacted to build new frames and narratives. Against the EU and the national elites, but for Europeanism and the autonomy of the nation; against the market but sceptic towards state regulation; critical of technocratic authoritarianism but in search of a new technocracy; in favour of redistribution but against taxation; and so on. Populism is often used as a shorthand in the attempt to map out the fuzzy ideological space that does not conform to the known ideologies of the second half of the 20th Century. And it is the closest term that exists, able to capture the levelling, the blending, the simplification, and the blurriness that characterizes the discontents of liberal democratic systems. Yet the relativisation of political stance on the left-right axis and of class consciousness as a determinant of political views is more complex and beyond the analytic reach of the populism debate.

Part of the difficulty to come to grips with the issue of ideological shifts in general, and more specifically the ideological shifts manifested in the crisis decade, is the multiplicity of the contradictory trends in operation. Whereas for example the retreat of the axis of left-right polarisation which in Southern Europe also carries the marks of civil war or quasi-civil war experienced just one and two generations ago, is clear across the board, there were also signs of revival of that cleavage on several occasions. In Portugal, for example, the carnation revolution of 1974 served as a frame of reference for the anti-austerity protests (Amaral 2020). In Greece, the imagery, and metaphors of the German occupation years in the 1940s were frequently used blending the narrative of national independence and left-wing resistance (Theodossopoulos 2014). In Spain there was much talk of re-enacting the democratic transition of the 1970s, closing the epoch and bringing politics back in to take it further. In Cyprus, a deadly accident in 2011 and its bad handling by the left-wing government provoked the resurfacing of anti-communism while the economic collapse sustained for a few years, schemata likening it to the 1974 Turkish invasion.

The de-alignment of class positionality from the left-right axis is to be sure a longer-term process. Its acceleration during the crisis was facilitated by the negative notion of a corrupt and incompetent political class, a unified political elite comprising of both right-wing and left-wing politicians which gained prominence. A substantial section of the popular strata including the newly impoverished deserted the parties they traditionally voted for opting for new parties or in their absence abstaining (Lewis-Beck and Costa Lobo 2017). To the already increasingly inter-class appeals of the traditional mainstream parties, were added populism on the left and on the right as well as nationalist and xenophobic discourses, civic republican narratives embracing modernisation and enhanced use of technology in politics, direct democracy, revived statism, and libertarianism emanating from urban youth.

Overall, it can be said that while the crisis accelerated and precipitated shifts in the class structure of society and in the prevailing ideological constitution of South European politics, these seem less historical in the 2020s than they seemed while occurring in the 2010s. Even though the dominant policy framework was contested, no radical change was achieved. While collective labour relations were substantially undermined, in many respects and to a significant extent the structures underpinning them proved resilient. Political systems were to greater or smaller degree reshuffled but except for Italy, where instability also had a longer pedigree, new balances were consolidated. Precariousness, poverty, and deprivation grew, yet as growth returned the humanitarian crisis came under control. At the same time all South European societies came out of the 2008 crisis at least partially transformed – and the wounds inflicted were nowhere healed before the new crisis emanating from the Covid-19 pandemic hit them in early 2020.

## Note

1 As mentioned in chapter 5, this is what made PEO and SEK to seek and finally secure in 2019–2020 legal force on some key terms of sectoral collective agreements, including the minimum starting wages in the hospitality industry.

# 7 Covid-19 and the New On-going Crisis

After more than a decade of crisis whose development and consequences were analysed in the previous chapters, at the beginning of 2020, there was some room for optimism in Southern Europe. In Spain, the long-awaited PSOE-PODEMOS government raised the minimum wage, re-invigorated social dialogue, and pledged to reverse some of the labour legislation which had weakened collective bargaining. In Cyprus trade unions had some relative success in reversing some of the cuts instituted during the crisis years, some progress was made in the effort to legally strengthen aspects of the major sectoral collective agreements in hotels and construction and a pledge was made to institute a national minimum wage if unemployment continued its downward path. Even in Greece although far from reversing the economic and legal legacy of the crisis years, some mild improvement was achieved with the raising of the minimum wage and the reinstitution of the legal force of some sectoral collective agreements. Overall, it seemed for the first time that the crisis was over or was soon about to be over. And then Covid-19 arrived, sparking a new depression, much more sudden and deeper and at the time of writing bringing uncertainty as to what and how profound its consequences will be.

This chapter outlines the main developments of 2020, provoked by the global pandemic and especially the experienced and foreseen impacts from its management on the labour markets and societies of Southern Europe. The lockdown measures are described and their rationale and mode of enforcement in Spain, Greece and Cyprus is explained marking continuities and changes and accounting for the political dynamics at national and EU levels. The focus of the analysis is the field of employment and the economy more broadly and the aim is to examine the contribution of the temporary relief measures in averting the worse, but also their inadequacy to provide social protection in a universal and comprehensive manner. Some observations on the impact of the lockdown measures on people's lives, working conditions and socialisation are also made, based on the ten-month experience of intermittently imposed restrictions.

With tourism and services hit most as result of the social distancing measures, South European economies, especially those with limited manufacturing such as Greece and Cyprus, suffered a comparatively bigger blow. The shock to the economies and societies of Southern Europe is sketched based on available figures and predictions about the changing labour market conditions. The crisis provoked by the global pandemic is to be sure on-going and its full impact can only be sufficiently assessed in the years ahead. Nevertheless, by the onset of the second wave in the autumn of 2020, there have been some signs of adjustment to the new context. The unfolding labour market environment is outlined with reference to the responses and agency of employers and trade unions in navigating through the new terrain and moulding its texture and boundaries.

This chapter serves the dual function of both keeping the book up to date with on going developments and using the insights from the experience of the 2008 crisis to understand the current crisis. Although different in form and causality, scope, depth, and speed, and although provoking in many respects, responses by the national and EU authorities which diverge from the austerity paradigm of 2008, the 2020 crisis operates as continuity. Southern Europe is plunged into fiscal adventures once more while the threat of mass unemployment and huge national debt loom enormous in the years ahead. This chapter thus offers a concise account of the 2020 developments sketching the parameters of the emerging labour market context and the impact of the shock on the institutional economic and social policy frameworks, on employment and class relations.

## The Rationale and the Enforcement of Lockdown

As Covid-19 began to spread in Europe, by February 2020 with the situation in northern Italy becoming the paradigmatic case of tragedy as the public health system collapsed, governments across Europe begun reluctantly to take precautionary measures. By March, the term 'social distancing' became dominant despite it being sociologically inaccurate as it literally meant people keeping the physical distance of two meters from each other and avoiding all sorts of physical contact. Social distancing was promoted as a concept of social solidarity – that people should actively adapt their behaviour as if every person has the virus oneself and therefore taking care of not transmitting it to others. Mass gatherings were discouraged, and various public events started to be cancelled. As the number of people infected and the number of people dying increased cumulatively and as in many workplaces and leisure settings physical distancing was either impossible or too difficult to achieve, many governments began to take more radical measures in their attempt to impose it.[1]

These included erecting border controls and restrictions, prohibiting unnecessary movements and ultimately closing-down hospitality businesses and all workplaces where close contact was inevitable, leaving open only businesses that were essential to the food supply and those which serviced the health system. Schools and universities closed shifting in various degrees to on-line education and office work and all types of work that could be performed at a distance shifted to on-line operations. Those that could not work from home were generally furloughed and became eligible to state support. However, despite the governments' calls to avoid redundancies, many businesses used the opportunity to reduce their staff proceeding to lay-offs. In Spain, as unemployment started to sky-rocket the government proceeded to outlaw this practice by decree (Catalan News 2020; Keeley 2020). In Greece and Cyprus with right-wing governments in office, no such measures were taken and the state support to workers during the lockdown was much less generous.

The lockdown measures were supposed to prevent the collapse of the public health systems and allow the governments to buy time to enhance their capacity. Whereas emergency health spending increased, upgrading the health systems that have suffered from decades of underfunding, neglect and creeping privatisation remained a difficult endeavour. Although the Covid-19 crisis has demonstrated that health is too important to be left to the market, and it was acknowledged that more investment was needed in the public health systems, there has been no consensus about how this could be achieved and whether that is meant to be a permanent policy or merely a temporary, emergency measure. In fact, one may argue that the inadequate state of public health systems in several countries, including Greece and Cyprus, in the face of the second wave of the pandemic in the autumn demonstrated that what appeared in the spring as a quasi-consensus of prioritising public health was neither robust enough nor sufficient to affect the way governing elites whether at the national or the EU level operated.

It is clear now that contrary to all the talk about a so-called 'revived Keynesianism', there has been no comprehensive challenge of the notion of health marketisation at the policymaking level. In Greece and Cyprus with right-wing governments in office, it was the private health sector that was boosted more. Even in Spain where the government brought private hospitals under public control, it is unclear how this emergency measure will develop and whether this 'nationalisation' will outlive the current crisis. In Greece and Cyprus, the private health sector was brought in as a partner to the public health sector through agreements negotiated and private services bought with public money from day one. Testing which expanded exponentially as the Covid-19 crisis evolved, was surrendered to the private sector. In Cyprus this became a lucrative market from private chemists as the government made testing obligatory to various categories of people subsidising it in some cases and making the citizens pay directly in other cases.

At the political level, the lockdown signalled a turn to political authoritarianism threatening directly numerous civil liberties. Citizens were largely treated as inherently irresponsible and states attempted to discipline them through strict restrictions and police repression. Often these were measures imposed through executive decrees instead of proper legislation, rendering their constitutional basis shaky and their legality questionable. Despite the fact that a state of emergency was not formally declared, many governments invoked war-like language and imagery with Covid-19 portrayed as an invisible enemy, health professionals as the front-line soldiers and heroes, citizens as having the duty to abide by governmental instructions and not undermine the national effort and the governments' chief scientist advisors as the generals who strategised and oversaw the progression of the battle. In several variations this trope was propagated by the mainstream media and reproduced by a frightened public in the social media accumulating in force, stifling dissent, and impoverishing public debate. Opposition parties generally supported the lockdown measures and refrained from attacking the government restricting themselves to mild criticisms on methods and timing rather than their essence or means of enforcement.

As fear spread in wide sections of society provoking a 'rally around the flag' phenomenon, popular support for governments increased in polls and these legally questionable measures were socially legitimised even if only tacitly. Unlike the United States there was little political reaction to the spring lockdown in Southern Europe. In fact, a sort of moral panic against those deemed to be irresponsible and violating the lockdown was sustained for months. This allowed excesses and abuse of authority in some cases as well as measures whose rationale was at best dubious (Ioannou 2020c). By May after the peak of the first wave had passed and the relaxation of the lockdown measures began, it was the economy that attracted most of the attention of both governments and also of the public. As the impact of the lockdown was becoming measurable in actual terms and not just in terms of predictions, the politics of how that cost was to be paid took the front seat again both at the national and the EU levels, provoking cleavages and contention.

## The Temporary Relief Measures

In addition to emergency spending to enhance the capacity of the national health systems, all governments instituted various sorts of temporary relief measures aiming to support businesses and workers during the extraordinary period when lockdown measures were in place. These included temporary tax relief and emergency liquidity provision to firms in the form of very cheap loans guaranteed by the state, discouraging or even forbidding redundancies and covering with public money the overwhelming proportion of the labour cost during the period when the firms suspended their operation (Bonfert 2020). Irrespective of the means and the extent to which workers were supported, the priority for European states was to restrain the rise of unemployment and consequently the further burden on already strained social security systems.

Consumption also needed to be maintained to avoid a meltdown and that was the logic behind the readiness of national governments to simply ignore the Eurozone budget rules that became largely irrelevant inducing the EU to formalise the suspension of those rules (Valero 2020). The provision of liquidity however in the form of cheap loans and the temporary tax relief measures could not go far enough. As early as May talk about bailing out major corporations begun. However, as the lockdowns at least in their strict form ended by June, and as the EU states were able to agree on a major package involving both grants and long-term loans in July, most major corporations were able to survive the new conditions with downsizings and extension of state support rather than full-blown bail-outs similar to those given the banks a decade ago. Some major corporations, such as the internet giants, in fact made huge profits out of the lockdowns and the fact that many more people spent much more time on their computer screens for work, socialisation and entertainment purposes.

For the workers who shifted to on-line working maintaining their salaries, the cost was minimal in economic terms and a positive experience for many who avoided daily travel. In some cases though, the transition to on-line work was not smooth and required additional effort to adjust and increased operational expenses as the home was converted to a workplace while many employers did not offer the necessary equipment (Eurofound 2020b). In addition to the psychological and social burden provoked by the change and its rapidity, even if the pace of work slowed down, it was a draining experience for many. For those who had to combine full-time work with simultaneous full-time child-care at home the lockdown was exhausting. Women, burdened more than men with child care, were hit hardest by the nursery and school closures, while overall women lost as a result of the economic contraction since feminised sectors such as hospitality, retail, and personal services were hit more than other sectors (Pilavaki 2020). The gains employers made from the reduction of operational costs were probably offset by declining productivity while the prevailing uncertainty precluded any comprehensive strategy-making that could optimise efficiency.

Workers whose work was suspended temporarily receiving instead state benefit, suffered some economic cost as the benefit was typically a proportion of the salary lost but more importantly experienced major anxiety about the future of their employment. The social distancing measures had not only a direct effect on a series of industries and occupations but also an indirect on industries not affected by it (Laeven 2020). The decline in demand reduced the amount of work needed for many businesses both during the lockdown period and after its relaxation. Thus, although many people retained their jobs, a substantial proportion of them had their working time and hence their income reduced (Eurofound 2020b). It is also important to stress that in conditions of recession, and increased unemployment there was limited scope for challenging the reduction of working time and little options for additional, alternative casual employment to make up for the lost income.

Whereas some arrangements were made for reduction of mortgage payments and in some cases also rents, these were simply postponing the problem in household finance rather than resolving it. The same is true for the owners of small family businesses who typically got some sort of relief but often just enough to postpone rather than avert the threat of bankruptcy. Yet suspending evictions in Spain during the lockdown, a measure that the opposition managed to force the government of Cyprus to take as well in late 2020 was significant in a humanitarian sense, even if only temporary. An analogous buying time effect was also in operation at the macro level of the political economy. No structural measures were adopted, and the fiscal condition of states was left to deteriorate with debt piling only with a view to be refinanced by new debt (Streeck 2020b).

There were variations across countries in the scope and depth of state support offered. For example, in Spain, the furlough scheme Expediente de Regulación Temporal de Empleo (ERTE) covered 70% of the workers' salary for six months and 50% from there on if the employee paid insurance for 360 days within the last six years (Murcia Today 2020) and this was subsequently extended for four further months. In Cyprus this was 60% and was also subject to the regulations of the existing social insurance system. In contrast Greece had its equivalent scheme in the form of one-off special benefit payment of 800€ covering a period of almost two months rather than subsume it within the existing social insurance system. An analogous logic characterised the measures adopted by the Greek government during the second wave of the pandemic and the autumn lockdown while also extending unemployment benefits (Euronews 2020). The self-employed, typically enjoying less employment protection and employment rights were also in principle supported in these emergency schemes. In Spain self-employed workers were already entitled to unemployment benefit, in Cyprus where this was not the case, they were temporarily included while in Greece they were made eligible to the special one-off 800€ benefit.[2]

As was to be expected, although valuable to many workers and small businesses, these temporary relief measures could not and did not cover everybody. It was difficult to extend eligibility to some groups of workers such as seasonal and casual workers while for those working in the informal economy it was simply impossible. The weak welfare state in

Southern Europe, eroded further after a decade of austerity policies, was unable to offer a universal safety net in times of 'normality' – it was even more difficult to do so in exceptional times, even where there was a will such as in left-wing governed Spain. Overall, the Covid-19 crisis exacerbated existing inequalities as precarious workers suffered more than regular workers, while inequalities in housing became a more defining parameter as 'stay at home' became the new order (Bergamini 2020). Those that came out worse off were the informal or partially informal workers who lost their jobs and income during the lockdown period. Worse yet, the social distancing measures, the movement restrictions and the closure of the economy for several months meant that family support networks were also disrupted, while even work in the gig economy became more difficult to attain and more poorly paid (Fairwork 2020).

The Covid-19 crisis exacerbated not only existing socio-economic inequalities but also exposed different groups of people to different levels of health risk (Blundell et al. 2020). Beyond the distinctions of those that could shift to on-line work and those that could not, and from within the latter, between those who were obliged to continue working and those obliged to stop working, the distribution of health risk varied on the basis of geographic, demographic, as well as socio-economic factors. Especially vulnerable groups such as refugees in camps and migrant workers that shared accommodation in large number households could not practice social distancing and many of whom were often excluded from support measures (ILO 2020). In some cases, , such as Greece and Cyprus not only were they neglected but also occasionally profiled as a public health threat after being offered less access to testing. However, in other cases, such as Portugal where an active effort was made to include them, migrants were able to benefit from the expansion of the public health coverage and social security related benefits. Those already in unemployment became trapped moving further away from the prospect of employment as the labour market shrank. Long term unemployment in Cyprus, counting those without work for twelve months expanded by 315% by the close of 2020 while it is set to expand further in 2021 (Stockwatch 2020b).

Hospitality and entertainment workers were among the occupations hit most (Theodoropoulou 2020). Given the expanded significance of tourism in the recent decades for the economies of Southern Europe with millions of people directly and indirectly depending on it for their livelihood, this brought a major social blow. Southern Europe essentially has a mass tourism model based on 'sun and sea' operating on relatively low-paid work and which is substantially seasonal. Although there are numerous hotels and restaurants operating throughout the year, with several of them being expensive and offering better pay to their more skilled staff, the majority of tourist establishments in Spain, Greece, and Cyprus are in resort areas operating on the logic of mass international tourism in the extended Mediterranean summer. With quarantine measures and advice against non-essential travel from governments on the one hand, flights disruptions, fear and shrinking of disposable income, the volume of international tourism fell to very low levels despite active efforts by the EU and national governments to 'save the season'. The increase in domestic tourism, as expected, was too little to offset the damage.

## The Shock to the Economy

Even before the lockdown measures were adopted, the brewing crisis was revealed through the rapid drop in capital movement in the international stock markets, while the price of oil continued its downward path. From early on it became obvious that dealing with the Covid-19 public health crisis would involve major economic sacrifice, but it was not until after the lockdown measures were instituted in spring that the magnitude of that started to be conceptualised. Two major parameters of the crisis provoked by the management of the threat of Covid-19 was the rapidity with which it unfolded and its depth. This was unlike any other economic crisis of the past because the depression it brought about escalated not in months but weeks and it did not only involve finance or circulation, not even production per se, but the most central axis of capitalism – wage labour. The labour market was not merely disrupted – it was frozen as millions of workers had to withdraw their labour immediately and simultaneously.

Although the state did step in to prevent the collapse of the process of social reproduction, capitalism as a system suffered a major shock. Real economic activity dipped in the second quarter of 2020 by 21.5% in Spain, 17.9% in Italy, 16.3% in Portugal, 15.2% in Greece, and 12.3% in Cyprus. The budget deficit in the second quarter of 2020 stood at 11.4% of the GDP for the EU and at 11.6% for the Eurozone (Theodoropoulou 2020). By mid-November 2020, 90.3 billion worth of support was approved or requested by 18 EU states. In the first half of 2020 the rise in unemployment was restrained to a bit above one million persons but this figure is an underestimate of the real situation and is expected to significantly rise in the yearly figures while the 'bounce back' of the economy expected in 2021 and/or 2022 is now expected to be smaller than initially anticipated.

In the early phase of the crisis during the spring of 2020, this objective shock gave rise to some alternative thinking including some calls to use this crisis as an opportunity for broader change. To slow down the pace of economic life by changing lifestyle patterns, reduce travel and consumption and come up with a better balance in the relationship between humanity and nature. However, these views remained marginal and after around two months of the lockdown the dominant theme in the public sphere propagated by government and public alike was when and how to return to 'normality'. Normality was defined as the social status quo ante and was understood as such by both elites and the people.

Yet as some of the emergency measures adopted, such as on-line teleworking was really pre-existing at the margins and was seen by some businesses as the way forward from before, the Covid-19 crisis constituted an opportunity for more general restructuring. More importantly, although the lockdown ended by the summer, not all restrictions were lifted, and it became clear that some things had come to stay at least for the foreseeable future. Many restrictions returned in the second wave in autumn (Walker, 2020). This kept the issue of the sustainability of various aspects of the existing business models on the front line of economic and policy thinking.

The collapse of several markets and the massive intervention of the state in the economy neither signalled a change in hegemonic beliefs about the institution of the market, nor did it initiate new political thinking. Although both in the fields of labour and social policy, many measures undertaken pointed to the opposite direction of the hitherto national and EU mantra, the overall framework did not change (Streeck 2020c). Increased public spending remained focused on averting the economic collapse of businesses, not effecting any form of indirect income redistribution, or tackling with existing and exacerbating inequalities. The operation of the financial sector did not change – in fact in some cases like Cyprus it was the first sector to be supported through given a mediating role in the provision of government aid to businesses. No reform of the taxation system, to increase the tax contribution of accumulated wealth, was seriously contemplated even for merely symbolic reasons.

At the EU level, the prevailing political climate was analogous. After the initial shock, the EU apparatus began to adapt to the new situation of crisis and deal with the numerous issues that the rapidity and the depth of the Covid-19 challenge put forward. As mentioned above the relaxation of fiscal rules was a step taken with relative ease. Like with the closing of the borders, the national states had acted on their own accord with no coordination on this matter as well. However, current budget deficits meant public debt and as early as March the debate of how to deal with this opened up an intra EU rift between Germany and other economically strong states of the north and the weaker ones of the European south with Italy and Spain at the forefront but allied also with France. Italy already struggling with its public debt came to near-desperate situation with the Covid-19. Yet neither that, nor its coalition with the other EU states of the south was enough to strike a favourable compromise at the European Council.

The mutualisation of debt through the issuing of special European bonds, an idea rejected by Germany was repeatedly blocked by the 'frugal four' as they were called Austria, Sweden, Denmark, and the Netherlands which insisted that responsibility for debt repayment should lie with the member states. The liquidity aspect of the crisis was essentially dealt with, by means of a series of emergency measures including collateral flexibility measures (Surubaru 2020). The European Investment Bank took over guarantees and funding, the European Commission provided favourable loans through the Support for mitigation of Unemployment Risks in Emergency while the ESM ran a programme of general crisis support. The European Central Bank ran the Pandemic Emergency Purchase Programme as an extraordinary instrument of monetary policy for the euro area.

As the damage to the European economy was understood to be bigger than initially predicted and with the recovery looming as a long-drawn process, EU states were pushed into the logic of compromise. By June, the IMF revised its initial prediction, raising the predicted contraction of the GDP in the euro area to 10.2% in 2020 (IMF 2020). The EU leaders ultimately decided that the economic aid package was to involve a mixture of grants, loans and guarantees and that the European Commission would use the long-term budget as a security to borrow money from the markets for part of the funding (Gill et al. 2020). The understanding reached concerning the framework prevented the intra EU conflict from escalating and gave time for further negotiations and bargaining. By July, the final deal was reached raising the economic aid package to €750 billion, €390 billion worth of grants and €360 billion worth of loans (Gill and Chadwick 2020). More importantly, there were no serious conditionality strings attached, neither with respect to political matters nor specific economic policy frameworks relieving eastern and southern European governments from potential pressure.

Yet the compromise agreement did not end tensions that continued concerning the rebates budgets. Moreover, the €7.7 billion programme to improve the resilience and preparedness of national health systems was ultimately erased from the recovery package, and so was the solvency fund for businesses hit by the pandemic while humanitarian aid under the new seven-year budget was restricted to €9.8 billion (Peel and Khan 2020). The recovery effort of the €750 billion termed the Next Generation EU, was agreed in conjunction with the multiannual financial framework 2021–2027 (€1074.3 billion) raising the total EU budget to €1.83 trillion. What this amounted to effectively was the aversion of the worse by spreading the consequences of the economic melt-down further ahead into the future years.

The shock to the structurally weak economies of Southern Europe, which had not fully recovered from the previous crisis was huge. The drop in tourism in Mediterranean Europe was the second bigger of all world regions, above 70% (UNWTO 2020). The relatively central role of the tourism industry in South European countries meant that the contraction of the tourist flow resulted in spill-over in several other economic sectors. Agriculture and food production, geared to cater for a huge summer population also contracted, while all businesses that were directly or indirectly connected with and supporting hospitality suffered a drop in turnover.

Trade unions prioritised from the very beginning the protection of jobs and in that they had a common interest with governments. They were generally consulted by governments and, in Spain and Cyprus at least, they did exert some influence with respect to some of the general compensation schemes made available to workers (Int. 5, Int. 11). At the same time some of the gaps identified in the measures adopted, which left groups of workers insufficiently covered, remained as trade union efforts to pressurise the state for modifications were not always successful. During the lockdown trade unions were also approached by numerous workers searching for information and advice with respect to their rights, many of whom were not trade union members (Int. 12, 2020). It remains to be seen whether trade unions in Southern Europe will be able to recruit members, if anything, to offset their loss of members loss due to rising unemployment.

## Adjusting to the New Context

At the time of writing (December 2020) the adjustment to the new context is a process that has just begun and there is a huge level of uncertainty as to how this will develop in the following years. Essentially it is a constantly evolving situation and while the economic consequences of the pandemic are to some extent predictable and predicted according to numerous scenarios decision makers at the national and the EU level make, they have not yet taken their full toll at the social level of lived experience. It is one thing for people to stay with no income or with limited income for a period of some months and quite another if this extends to some years. It is one thing for workers to telework for a few months and a wholly different matter if that is to become the new modality of working life. Social distancing and wearing masks at work and in public space, avoiding congested places and the discouraging of 'unnecessary' movement places additional strains on people.

As the incidences and deaths attributed to Covid-19 subsided in Europe by June, and as the projected economic consequences from the lockdown became more and more threatening, one after the other Southern European countries begun to partially open up their tourist markets despite the fact that at least some of them, such as Spain for example, initially considered that impossible. The European Commission actively encouraged member states to relax the restrictions concerning internal movement, insisted that 'there will be a holiday season in the summer' and that there was plenty of scope to open up the economy and hospitality while taking sufficient health precautions (Keating, 2020). There was also pressure from hotel owners and hospitality businesses while after the experience of the lockdown demand for holidays was high among the public as well.

By July, a system of classification of countries and sometimes regions within countries was instituted whereby each state assigned other states into risk lists, allowing, discouraging, or forbidding entry according to epidemiological data taking of course into account other economic, cultural, and political factors. Like most of the measures undertaken by governments with respect to handling Covid-19 there was a significant element of arbitrariness as decisions were taken on a series of consecutive and accumulating abstractions. Worse still, national lists changed frequently, as Covid-19 incidences begun to increase again, with countries jumping from one category to another, maintaining the condition of unpredictability for people trying to plan their holidays. This led the European Council to attempt to put some order and a recommendation setting a common framework and common criteria for travel restrictions was adopted in October (European Council, 2020), but being non legally binding, it was not widely enforced. In any case air-travel remained disrupted and airline companies, especially the low-cost ones, found it unprofitable to operate various routes where restrictions were in place. Prior testing, voluntary self-isolation, special permission, and prior flight passes all discouraged flying and in conjunction with the deteriorating financial situation and the health anxiety of many people, shrunk the volume of air-travel and holidays abroad.

Greece was the first to open up and set in place minimal preconditions to international tourists. Moreover, insufficient controls and loopholes in the system meant that even some of the initial restrictions could be bypassed. Spain followed suit although keeping regional variation in the rules. However, as incidences spiked again, restrictions begun to be re-imposed by the countries of origin of the tourists such as the United Kingdom preventing the volume of tourist flow from becoming large. Cyprus took a more cautious stance, delayed opening-up and demanded prior negative Covid-19 tests even from countries such as the United Kingdom and Russia, from where most tourists traditionally originated, and initially at least 14 days of self isolation as well. This led to very few tourists coming and the government having to extend the temporary aid to the hospitality businesses and workers for the autumn as well.

By September, new restrictions begun to be re-introduced in many countries and by October most European countries were in semi lock-down conditions again. This brought a sudden end to the optimist mood and all attention was firmly anchored to the prospect of mass vaccination as the only way to return to 'normality' (Meyer 2020). It must also be said that unlike the spring lockdown which took everyone by surprise, in the autumn there was much more preparation by businesses which re-tooled their factories and offices and cushioned to some extent the impact of the new restrictions (Boston and Chaudhuri 2020). While it is now expected that the virus will be brought under control by the end of 2021 at least in Europe and North America, it remains unlikely that the experience of 2020 will become a distant memory in the following years. The shock the pandemic provoked is simply too big and its impact, not just economic, is already shaping developments in several fields.

Isolation, avoidance of public places and insufficient socialisation, curtailing of bodily contact and people keeping to themselves for long periods of time will inevitably have negative impacts on people's psychology, social and intimate relations, and lifestyles. Social solidarity initiatives have propped up and new sensitivities have arisen and some of the aspects of the 'slow-down effect' have been beneficial. Yet overall, the deteriorating economic conditions, the restrictions to civil liberties and the absence of hope to the prospect of prosperity ahead resulted in increased social discontent that was only kept under control by fear and repression. The right-wing governments of Greece and Cyprus for example outlawed street protests and repressed them with police violence and arbitrary arrests irrespective of the fact that protesters abode by the public health measures of wearing masks and maintaining physical distance. This included even symbolic street protests involving a few persons opening a banner or leaving flowers on a memorial. In Greece, three elected trade union leaders including the president of the Panhellenic Workers' Federation in Tourism and Catering were arrested for opening a banner reading 'we are hungry' outside the Prime Minister's Office (Npress 2020).

In addition to generalised repression, the government in Greece is currently pushing through further legislative change in field of employment in the direction of the Troika measures at the beginning of the 2010s. The bill currently being discussed in addition to updating trade union law, parental leave and regulating tele-working, also promotes further flexibilization and individualization of employment relations. It effectively constructs a new framework for over-time work further eroding the distinction of working time pay and over-time pay by means of individual agreement in the absence of an enterprise collective agreement (Foskolos 2020). Beyond flexibilising the time and place of work the new bill rearranges inspection and mediation functions and weakens dispute resolution services and places additional restrictions on strike action provoking strong reactions by the centre-left and left-wing parties (Livitsanos 2020). The lockdown context is seen as a convenient time for this, both because societal attention is turned elsewhere and because the rising unemployment spreads fear among the working class and further difficulty on the part trade unions to mobilise.

At the level of public discourse, despite the fact that the main economic impact of the pandemic was on the labour market in general and on employment in specific, employers and trade unions have not been particularly vocal. While they issued occasional statements about the grave situation, the need for continued generous state support to businesses and workers, about the value of being consulted with respect to the form and duration of the temporary relief measures and so on, there was little development in 2020 in Spain and Cyprus on the various issues that were open from previous times. In fact, if anything, planned developments and on-going conflicts, such as legislative reforms with respect to collective bargaining in Spain and the prospect of instituting a statutory minimum wage in Cyprus were suspended. The pandemic in some respects froze things, which to be sure are due to open up again soon in one way or another.

More generally, consecutive failures of the state have placed strains on trust to institutions and the Left has not managed to intervene and convincingly put forward alternatives. In these conditions it is conservative and reactionary narratives that come out strengthened, whether of the statist 'law and order', or the 'anti-science, conspiracy theory' variant. The vaccination programme currently under way is expected to bring Covid-19 pandemic under control, in Europe at least in 2021. Yet the 2020 experience has already scarred in many ways the politico-economic and socio-cultural fabric. The questions raised about democracy and authoritarianism, the form and scope of state regulation and the market, individual and collective rights, the public and the private remain unanswered. More than that, the rational, theoretical tools with which these questions can be debated have been undermined as arbitrariness and naked power emerged stronger amidst confusion, fear, and resignation.

## Notes

1 For a comprehensive coverage of the various policy measures adopted by governments across Europe and the world with respect to Covid-19 see the global directory of the University of Oxford (Daly et al. 2020).
2 Some professionals were asked to do special on-line training courses before they were made eligible but the whole training scheme proved to be of scandalously low-quality and the government had to withdraw it (Giokas, 2020).

# 8 The World of Labour in Southern Europe from Crisis to Crisis

While a lot has changed in Southern Europe since the onset of the financial crisis in 2008, much has remained the same. When writing at the time when institutional and even structural change is ongoing, it is common to exaggerate the implications of current reforms and to make projections that blur the distinction between the potential and the actual. Often it takes several years and sometimes decades before sober assessments of the significance of events, actions, and reforms can be made that situate them on the historical plane. At key junctures, historical time sometimes coincides with political time, but usually history and politics operate in different temporalities. Societies are always changing in one way or another, sometimes faster, sometimes slower, and new conflicts and new contradictions supersede older ones. Identifying the causes and the implications of specific changes in real time is not impossible, yet it is rarely straightforward either.

At the time of writing (December 2020), the new economic crisis provoked by the Covid-19 pandemic is still unfolding and it is difficult to assess its impact, let alone predict its consequences. What seems certain, however, is that the recovery from the 2008 crisis has been arrested and that new burdens have now been added onto South European societies. The 'Keynesian moment' of this pandemic crisis in 2020 might have saved the world of labour in Europe from the worse, but given the power correlation, the prevailing ideology and most importantly the structural realities and institutional orders, at some point soon sacrifices will be sought once again to make the numbers add up. This is at least the lesson that can be drawn from the management of the 2008 crisis as far as the elites are concerned. Unless there is indeed a reversal in multiple levels and ways.

This short, concluding chapter sums up the key insights from the analysis in this book and discusses the issue of continuity and change in the employment field in Southern Europe. The 2010s are examined in a historical frame, which includes all the dimensions dealt with in the preceding chapters: the institutional context and the societal dynamics, politics, and prevailing ideologies and their role in influencing law, economic policy, and class relations. Trade unionism and its potential, social movements and the discourses of the 'people', and the prospects of successful contestation of the neoliberal status quo are also revisited and some modest projections are made, not about the future per se, but about what can already be seen to constitute trends and what cannot. In the form of final remarks, the chapter goes beyond the key implications of the book into some comments of a more general and abstract character about the European Union and the Eurozone, neoliberalism, capitalism and democracy, and the prospects of the working class and class struggle.

As the final chapter of the third part, this chapter concludes the discussion that begun in Chapter Six with the aim of going beneath and beyond the economic crisis and assessing both what lies in its core and what its longer-term significance is. It thus maintains the broader analytic lens that overviews the region and the themes and moves from dimension to dimension rather than from detail to detail and from country to country. As the final chapter of the book, it revisits the key theoretical concepts and empirical findings and reiterates some of the key tenets of the argument articulated. Supranational dynamics are not simply translated on the national level and that it is the degree of their alignment with forces operative on the national level that determines the path of institutional change. Different political traditions and different constellations of power, including ideological and discursive ones, can shape policy priorities, implementation, and actual outcomes on the ground. And class relations and the shifts thereof are both cause and consequence of the regulatory regimes and the depth and direction of their change.

## Summing Up: Continuity and Change

Few will doubt that in the late 2010s the labour market in Southern Europe was a more difficult terrain compared to the 2000s. At the general level there were fewer jobs available and the real wages were lower. Employment protection was lower than it used to be, trade unions were weaker, and precariousness affected more people in both immediate and less immediate ways. Neoliberal social and economic policies assaulted collective bargaining everywhere, directly and indirectly, resulting in the weakening of its regulatory capacity (Müller et al. 2019). This took place in different ways and to different extents across countries, but the main trend has been organized decentralisation, reduced institutional support, and the shrinking of the scope and depth of collective bargaining.

The crisis decade has left labour in a weaker position relative to capital. At the same time, the crisis decade, or at least its first half, has been a time of enhanced contestation and repoliticisation, bringing to the fore popular mobilisations and progressive reform agendas, which challenged the EU edifice and its neoliberal logic. Social movements rather than trade unions took the lead, and the streets rather than the workplaces were the epicentre of contentious claims. Nevertheless, these were movements with materialist values and demands, anchored in the forces of labour, and pursuing increasingly universalist, and potentially universal, as opposed to sectional or single issue, demands. Moreover, trade unions were able to attune and adapt to the changing context of protest politics. Although ultimately not successful in blocking austerity or re-orienting policy, citizen resistance did set limits to the liberalization and deregulation processes. The significance of this became evident in subsequent years, when at least some of the degenerate conditions imposed were reversed and others kept being questioned.

The promotion of market-enhancing reforms in the fields of employment and social policy were processes long under way but occurring slowly as national elites were hesitant to push them through amidst opposition from trade unions, ambivalent political parties and a hostile public opinion. The crisis brought about such economic conditions that a state of emergency could be revoked and created a context in which national elites could align themselves with the EU elites, eagerly or reluctantly, towards that direction. Labour market liberalisation and deregulation processes were speeded up during the peak of the crisis, but they continued to be insufficiently legitimised and were contested on the ground. Market-enhancing reforms were largely promoted as a means towards an end rather than as an end in themselves. As such just as their adoption was made possible only by the mechanism of conditionality from above, their acceptance or toleration from below remained at best nebulous and not well grounded.

While the direction of the crisis management measures largely converged, their scope, depth, and means of enforcement diverged because countries differed in terms of their size and positionality in the European periphery and therefore structural and geopolitical significance and because they differed with respect to their economies and institutional orders. National government-opposition dynamics also played a role because they influenced the temporality and conjuncture of the EU intervention. So, did the slight variation in the timing of the crisis peak in each country because the stance of national and international actors took account of preceding developments and was adjusted accordingly. Consequently, while there was a convergence in the logic of the anti-crisis measures there was some divergence in the dynamics of their implementation. This was also dependent on divergences in terms of the actors which mobilised, the social coalitions built and the discursive framing of the stakes in each case and time.

Whereas the anti-austerity protests failed to block austerity at the national political level, just like the solidarity initiatives failed to establish permanent structures of an alternative, ethical economy even at the local level, they did contribute in the medium term to the moderation of the humanitarian disaster. Social movements, trade unions and left-wing political parties failed to establish a new paradigm of politics, or even to maintain the level of social protection existing prior to the crisis; yet seen from an historical perspective, their weakness, systemic cooptation and political retreat were of a partial, incomplete, and tactical type. As such, amidst their defeat they did hold some political ground, left their imprint on history and the legacy of resistance became a resource for societal resilience.

The decline of trade unionism has been a long-drawn process and although varying in terms of form and degree, its weakening in the first decades of the 21st Century compared to the late 1970s or the 1980s has been universal. Yet trade unionism has also manifested resilience almost everywhere. The revitalisation efforts undertaken in the 2000s and 2010s might not have produced spectacular gains, but in many cases the defences erected were successful enough to prevent major retreats. Public perceptions about trade unions have not deteriorated as much as it is often believed they have, and a substantial majority perceives a need for strong trade unions to protect their pay and working conditions (Turner and D' Art 2012). The crisis, for all its negative impact on the economic and institutional order, has not fundamentally changed that.

At the level of the EU policy, some mild and modest change is visible when comparing the beginning and the end of the decade of the 2010s. It is of course too early to say anything about a possible re-direction, re-orientation, or even mere change in a substantive sense, yet some modification in emphasis at least at the discursive level can be observed. The introduction of the European Pillar of Social Rights, the reduction of demands for greater flexibility and decentralisation of wage setting in the Country Specific Recommendations and the proposal for a Directive on adequate minimum wages before the outbreak of the pandemic may indicate something. The prioritisation of support of the real economy and the protection of employment, the absence of anti-social strings attached to the Covid-19 related loans, the renewed support for trade union involvement and the suspension of the EU fiscal rules which will probably be extended at least until 2022 could constitute an opportunity for potential change in a progressive direction.

Yet, the objective conditions shaped by the current crisis provoked by the pandemic are dire. Nominal and real wages have decreased, and the increased unemployment makes it difficult for trade unions to negotiate wage increases, while we have only seen the tip of the iceberg with respect to unemployment, with its rise temporarily halted with the furlough schemes and cushioned by the reduction of working time. The Directive on adequate minimum wages, currently surrounded by vagueness and ambivalence, can be a step in the right direction only if it acts as as 'ladder' supporting gradual wage increase. As Müller et al. (2020) argue there are conditions for this: a) that it incorporates the 'double decency threshold' of standing at least at 60% of the median and 50% of the mean wage b) that it is escorted by support for (cross-)

sectoral bargaining and c) that it respects and protects national bargaining systems. Unless collective bargaining is strongly supported both from above and from below, increasing its coverage and unless social rights are prioritised over economic freedoms, both politically and legally, it is doubtful that any real progressive change can be achieved.

As argued throughout this book, framed methodologically and articulated substantively, developments in the systems of industrial relations and employment law can only be explained by reference to the economic, social, and political dynamics in which they are embedded in. Shifts in discursive emphasis and public policy direction are connected with the outcomes of ever on-going battles waged in the realm of ideology and class relations. At the same time, the institutional order both enables and restricts action and institutional change impacts on the capacity of agents to mobilise and engage in antagonism as well as collaboration.

Whereas the legacy of the crisis decade has obviously been overall negative for the world of labour, in various domains and to various extents, the fragility of neoliberalism as a master narrative has been revealed. Increased levels of social contestation demonstrated the limits of legitimation, while the contradictions of the dominant policy paradigm became more visible and threatening for the system's stability. As is often the case in history, moments of rupture do not necessarily produce immediate change and key junctures are recognised as such only post facto. What is certain is that the Great Recession initiated and served as the backdrop for the multiple rearrangements in the labour market and political systems of Southern Europe. Which of these rearrangements will prove structural and historical and which temporary and contingent remains to be seen and will inevitably be influenced by the development of the current pandemic crisis and how this is managed in the medium term.

## Projecting Ahead: Ideology, Trade Unionism and the Politics of Class

In starker terms than ever before, the 2008 financial crisis brought to the fore the classic question concerning the relationship between democracy and capitalism, and whether and under what conditions the former can survive under the suffocating rule of the latter. The hollowing out of representative institutions, the rise of technocratic ideologies, the narrowing down of the framework of feasible politics, the loss of mobilisation power by political parties, the growing de-politicisation of the people through the rise of electoral abstention are phenomena observed since the 1980s and 1990s. As European expansion and integration progressed and intensified in the 2000s not only none of these were resolved but in many ways were exacerbated as another layer of governance and technocracy was added distancing further the locus of power from the people and insulating further economic elites from democratic control. The European Union evolved into a depoliticised space, allowing little scope for political opposition and this begun to reach down into the domestic sphere promoting democratic deficits at the level of the national state as well (Mair 2007).

The 2008 financial crisis and its management in the 2010s and now the Covid-19 crisis in the beginning of the 2020s is bringing these processes to their culmination. The rise of populism left and right is seen as a threat to democracy, yet it is also a consequence of the shrinking scope of democratic politics in liberal democracies. Lack of popular trust to the institutions does not only lead to the revival of politicisation of which the anti-austerity movements and later the radical environmental youth movements were a moment of, but also to the reactionary movements against vaccines and 5G technology, which now blend deniers of the pandemic with people who are angry with the lock-down measures and the management of the pandemic by governments. Increasing economic difficulty of people to make ends meet and ineffective, and unresponsive national authorities which are unwilling or powerless to act differently constitutes the backdrop behind growing popular alienation and disaffection.

The question about the compatibility of democracy and capitalism in contemporary times can only be discussed in a historical context and taking to account the institutional order as shaped in the preceding decades and its ideological legacy. The globalisation discourse predominating in the 1990s and the perceived need of the European Union to transform itself into a sort of 'United States of Europe' and constitute a global political power was instrumental behind the construction of the European Monetary Union in the 1990s, the EU's eastward expansion in the 2000s and the ongoing attempts of 'integration'. The ideology of Europeanism, however successful it was in superimposing itself upon the various national political systems of member-states before the crisis, was neither thorough nor deep enough to produce a transnational space for democratic politics that has the potential to reshape the institutional order of the EU.

As Streeck (2014) argues, the crisis has both accentuated and revealed the narrow limits of possible progressive change within the EU 'neoliberal cage'. The European Monetary Union, by centralising monetary control and denationalising economic policy has further sealed the bars of that cage locking member-states in a matrix of structural inequality within and between countries under German supremacy. The economic power imbalance between the core and the periphery of the EU, which was at the centre of the 2008 financial crisis, resurfaces again in the current ongoing crisis provoked by the pandemic. Just as crisis management resulted in devastation of the Southern Europe in the early 2010s, as its structural causes have not been addressed then and are not being addressed today, the possibility of another round of devastation in the early 2020s lies ahead (Streeck 2020a).

There is nothing inherently wrong or dangerous in the ideal of a united Europe, while there are numerous ills and dangers in an international system of antagonising national states. Yet the, actually existing, European Union is anything but a united Europe and worse, its foundational structure, institutional architecture, and political rationale is immune to democratisation, let alone substantively progressive reform. So long as transnationalism remains an imbalanced process decisively weighing to the side of capital's advantage, the national state inevitably remains the key locus for the defence of society and the revival of democratic politics. This is because only at that level can trade unions, social movements and other progressive forces still exert influence on political dynamics and policymaking. The experience of SYRIZA in government has revealed in a dramatic way both the limits and the illusions of left Europeanism. The Habermasian Europeanist vision has proved to be too idealist to stand a chance in the face of material realities. Austerity was revealed to be less a consequence of an insufficient ideally conceived European integration and more a prerequisite for the actually existing European 'integration' (Sumonja 2019).

21st-Century capitalism is aggressively authoritarian and austeritarian, and the Eurozone is not only its powerful instrument but its mode of imposing policy hierarchies and the might of stronger states of the core over the weaker ones of the periphery. While nationalism is a danger, the establishment of the Eurozone has not only not contained it, but in fact has given it space to grow as inequalities between and within Eurozone states are consolidated not reduced. It is in this context that the renationalisation of economic policy becomes a precondition for progressive change with respect to employment and welfare in the European periphery.

The renationalisation of economic policy, or more broadly subjecting economic policy and the economy itself to democratic control is a popular, not a populist demand. The rise of populism in recent decades in Europe is real enough and this has had repercussions in the political systems, in the public discourse and in societal ideologies. Yet the misuses of the term by journalists and politicians and its exaggeration in the public sphere and the liberal academia conflating it with anything that questions the economic orthodoxy, and the political status quo obstructs a sober discussion of the phenomenon theoretically, an assessment of its political significance and potential utility or negativity. For the broader Left, including political parties, trade unions and social movements, populism is a double-edged sword useful in tapping upon popular discontent, exploiting the system's legitimacy crisis, and bringing democratic renewal, yet at the same time carrying the danger to slip into simplistic levelling, catchy sloganeering, and emotional appeals. The line between appropriating populism and being appropriated by it remains thin (Charalambous and Ioannou 2020b).

In conditions of heightened social inequality within and between countries, the significance of class and class politics increases. This inevitably creates space for trade unionism and labour-based movements. Whether that space will be occupied and effectively utilised by South European trade unions remains however a different question. Visser (2019) suggests that in the changed contemporary conditions although the revitalisation of trade unions is both necessary and possible, the future of trade unionism is more likely to not be bright. Based on comparative observations of the current international trends, he lists four possible futures for trade unionism in which revitalisation comes fourth, after marginalisation, dualisation and substitution. Yet while signs of all these are visible today and plausible eventualities, from a historical perspective it should be reiterated that class conflict and class politics has predated trade unionism and is not reducible to it.

Trade unionism has throughout the 20th Century been the dominant form of representing the collective interests of the working class. As such trade unionism has also shaped the working class both in terms of its own political composition and in terms of its relationship with capital and the capitalist state. Yet the world of labour, and more broadly the subaltern classes across time and global space have found expression, representation, and agency in a much broader repertoire of action in multiple spheres beyond the workplace and beyond the institutional framework of state. If trade unions are further marginalized, restricted to a few sectors and social groups, or substituted by informal networks, NGOs, or other associational types, that will negatively impact the form but not necessarily the content of class struggle.

There are at least two lessons from the South European crisis for trade unionism. That in conditions of declining trade union outreach and generalised precariousness the scope of action and influence of social movements expands and covers partly what was in older times a social space and function performed by trade unionism proper. Social movement unionism is steadily on the rise and although with definite limits on how much it can contribute to the revival of collective bargaining, its mobilisational and discursive power is significant. Recognising this reality early on and orienting towards alliances in action rather than competition can benefit both trade unions and other forms of alternative or non-trade union, labour formations. The second lesson that trade unions need to take home is the fragility of corporatist arrangements and the risks entailed through the explicit focus on the institutional dimension. Having not invested enough and having not been successful in the organisational and societal dimensions, and given the gradual erosion of their power resources in the structural/economic domain, trade unions in Southern Europe had little to hold on to when the employers and international and national elites lifted their support for collective bargaining and social dialogue. It is true that as the crisis subsided by the end of the 2010s, trade unions regained some of their capacity to act in and shape the institutional realm, yet the eclipse of social dialogue and the sudden attack on collective bargaining in the peak of the crisis serves also as a warning for the future.

Class inequality breeds class resistance and it is inevitable that informal, unorganised, and non-politicised forms of workplace conflict will continue to emerge. Class resistance is always connected to social norms which allude to some notion of justice, and law and regulation need to remain oriented to these norms and understandings of justice if they are to retain their social relevance and hegemonic class function (Thompson 1971). This concerns the substance of institutions in general and the procedures of collective bargaining. Occupational and enterprise-level bargaining is more difficult to achieve, maintain, and extend but at the same time has the potential to be better adjusted to these social norms and to breed more participatory forms of worker representation. If sufficiently backed by both procedural and substantive law, worker agency and collective solidarity can re-invigorate industrial democracy (Dukes and Streeck 2020b).

The EU's neoliberal project involving deregulation and decentralisation of collective bargaining by stealth shifts the field from the legal procedures and legal formality into that of the political power (Ewing 2019). While this reflects and facilitates the declining significance of labour law in protecting workers, it also expresses the declining legitimacy of neoliberal politics and the contradictions that are inherent in it. More importantly the trend of the declining regulatory function of trade unionism and multi-employer collective bargaining while worsening employment conditions, also opens the space for the re-politicisation of employment relations. And consequently, both for defensive struggles that may draw upon remaining legal resources which European economic governance marginalises but also for more offensive struggles at the level of the state, prioritising the political function of trade unionism as a force of mobilisation force in the context of broader social coalitions.

This book, with its synthetic logic and comparative analytical edge, adds to the big and growing literature about the impact of the Great Recession in the European periphery. Its systematic examination of the link between employment relations and the south European crisis and its approach which combines industrial relations, labour law, and political sociology extends its relevance to multiple disciplines, sub-disciplines, and literatures. The three-level analysis employed discussing institutional frameworks, socio-political agency and class composition dynamics and outcomes at the structural level shed light on several dimensions, processes and trends shaping employment, trade unionism and class. Through exploring the crisis milieu and its external and internal dynamics, it was thus able to offer a comprehensive account of the changing conditions in the socio-economic landscape and the labour market of Southern Europe.

# References

Interviews cited:

*Spain (February–May 2020):*

Interview 1: Expert (Academic)
Interview 2: Expert (Academic/Trade Union Activist)
Interview 3: Expert (Academic/Social Movement Activist)
Interview 4: Trade union (Think Tank/Policy Level)
Interview 5: Government advisor/ex Trade union advisor
Interview 6: Trade union leader (national level)

*Greece (March–October 2019):*

Interview 7: Ex Trade union leader (sectoral and national level)
Interview 8: Trade union leader (sectoral and national level)
Interview 9: Trade union leader (sectoral and regional level)
Interview 10: Expert (Trade Union researcher/ex Labour Inspectorate)

*Cyprus (June–September 2020):*

Interview 11: Trade union leader/professional (national level)
Interview 12: Trade union leader/professional (national level)

Secondary sources:

Adkins, L. (1995). *Gendered work*. Buckingham: Open University Press.
Amaral, I. (2020). Citizens beyond Troika: Media and anti-austerity protests in Portugal. *International Journal of Communication*, *14*, 3309–3329.
Ancelovici, M. (2015). Crisis and contention in Europe: A political process account of anti-austerity protest. In H.-J. Trenz, V. Guiraudon & C. Ruzza (Eds.), *The European Crisis: Contributions from political sociology* (pp. 189–209). Basingstoke: Palgrave.
Andronikidou, K., & Kovras, I. (2012). Cultures of rioting and anti-systemic movements in Southern Europe. *West European Politics*, *35*(4), 707–725.

Anderson, B. (2010). Migration, immigration controls and the fashioning of precarious workers. *Work, Employment and Society*, *24*(2), 300–317.
Anthias, F. (2000). Metaphors of home: Gendering new migrations to Southern Europe. In F. Anthias & G. Lazaridis (Eds.), *Gender and Migration in Southern Europe*. Oxford: Berg.
Arrowsmith, J. (2010). Industrial relations in the private sector. In T. Colling & M. Terry (Eds.), *Industrial relations: Theory and practice* (pp. 178–206). West Sussex: Wiley.
Aslanidis, P., & Marantzidis, N. (2016). The Impact of the Greek Indignados on Greek politics. *Southeastern Europe*, *40*, 125–157.
Baccaro, L., & Howell, C. (2017). *Trajectories of neoliberal transformation European industrial relations since the 1970s*. Cambridge: Cambridge University Press.
Bailey, D. (2020). Mapping anti-austerity discourse: Populism, sloganeering and/or realism? In G. Charalambous & G. Ioannou (Eds.), *Left Radicalism and Populism in Europe* (pp. 183–203). London: Routledge.
Banyuls, J., & Recio, A. (2012). Spain: The nightmare of Mediterranean neoliberalism. In S. Lehndorff (Ed.), *A triumph of failed ideas European models of capitalism in the crisis* (pp. 199–218). Brussels: ETUI.
Banyuls, J., & Recio, A. (2015). A crisis within the crisis – Spain under the regime of a conservative neoliberalism. In S. Lehndorff (Ed.), *Divisive integration. The Triumph of Failed Ideas Revisited* (pp. 39–68). Brussels: ETUI.
Banyuls, J., & Recio, A. (2017). Labour segmentation and precariousness in Spain: Theories and evidence. In D. Grimshaw, C. Fagan, G. Hebson & I. Tavora (Eds.), *Making work more equal: A new labour market segmentation approach* (pp. 129–149). Manchester: Manchester University Press.
Barbieri, P. (2009). Flexible employment and inequality in Europe. *European Sociological Review*, *25*(6), 621–628.
Barranco, O., & Molina, O. (2019). Continuity and change in trade union frames: Evidence from general strikes in Spain. *Economic and Industrial Democracy*, OnlineFirst, https://journals.sagepub.com/doi/10.1177/0143831X19857791
Barthes, R. (1972) [1957]. *Mythologies*. London: Paladin.
Bartolini, L., Gropas, R., & Triantafyllidou, M. (2017). Drivers of highly skilled mobility from Southern Europe: escaping the crisis and emancipating oneself. *Journal of Ethnic and Migration Studies*, *43*(4), 652–673.
Basu, L. (2018). *Media amnesia*. London: Pluto Press.
Baumgarten, B. (2013). Geração à Rasca and beyond: Mobilizations in Portugal after 12 March 2011. *Current Sociology*, *61*(4), 457– 473.
Baylos, A. (2015). Changes in labour law in Spain in the wake of economic crisis. *Korean Institute of Labour*.
Beck, U. (1992) [1986]. *Risk society*. London: Sage Publications.
Beck, U. (2000). *The brave new world of work*. Cambridge: Polity Press.
Becker, U. (2009). *Open varieties of capitalism: Continuity, change and performances*. Basingstoke: Palgrave Macmillan.
Bergamini, E. (2020). How COVID-19 is laying bare inequality. *Bruegel.org*, 31/3/2020, https://www.bruegel.org/2020/03/how-covid-19-is-laying-bare-inequality/

Bertolini, A. (2020). *Temporary agency workers in Italy and the UK*. Cham: Palgrave Macmillan.

Bickes, H., Otten, T., & Chelsea Weymann, L. (2014). The financial crisis in the German and English press: Metaphorical structures in the media coverage on Greece, Spain and Italy. *Discourse & Society*, *25*(4), 424–445.

Bithymitris, G., & Papadopoulos, O. (2017). «Μαθαίνοντας» την οριακότητα: η περίπτωση ενός προγράμματος κατάρτισης ανέργων στον κλάδο τουρισμού ['Learning' liminality: the case of a training programme for unemployed in the tourism sector]. In C. Karakioulafi & M. Spyridakis (Eds.), *Κοινωνία, ανεργία και κοινωνική αναπαραγωγή* [*Society, unemployment and social reproduction*] (pp. 349–373). Athens: Gutenberg.

Blundell, R., Costa Dias, M., Joyce, R., & Xu, X. (2020). COVID-19 and Inequalities. *Fiscal Studies*, *41*(2), 291–319.

Bogg, A., & Dukes, R. (2013). The European social dialogue: From autonomy to here. In N. Countouris & M. Freedland (Eds.), *Resocialising Europe in a time of crisis*. Cambridge: Cambridge University Press.

Boltanski, L., & Chiapello, E. (2005). *The new spirit of capitalism*. London: Verso.

Bonfert, B. (2020). Political economy and politics – Covid-19, critical political economy, and the end of neoliberalism? *The European Sociologist*, 18/12/2020, https://www.europeansociologist.org/issue-45-pandemic-impossibilities-vol-1/political-economy-and-politics-covid-19-critical-political

Bosco, A., & Verney S. (2012). Electoral epidemic: The political cost of economic crisis in Southern Europe, 2010–11. *South European Society and Politics*, *17*(2), 129–154.

Boston, W., & Chaudhuri, S. (2020). For many European businesses, new lockdowns might not be as tough. *The Wall Street Journal*, 2/11/2020, https://www.wsj.com/articles/for-many-european-businesses-new-lockdowns-might-not-be-as-tough-11604322310

Braverman, H. (1974). *Labor and monopoly capital: The degradation of Work in the 20thcentury*. New York: Monthly Review Press.

Broumas, A., Ioakimoglou, E., & Charitakis, K. (2018). Greece: Grassroots labour struggles in a crisis-ridden country. In D. N. Azzellini & M. Kraft (Eds.), *The class strikes back self-organised workers' struggles in the twenty-first century* (pp. 56–81). London: Brill.

Burawoy, M. (1979). *Manufacturing consent: Changes in the labor process under monopoly capitalism*. Chicago: Chicago University Press.

Burawoy, M. (1985). *The politics of production: Factory regimes under capitalism and socialism*. London: Verso.

Burchell, B. (2002). The prevalence and distribution of job insecurity and work intensification. In B. Burchel, D. Lapido & F. Wilkinson (Eds.), *Job insecurity and work intensification*. London: Routledge.

Calhoun, C. (2011). From the current crisis to possible futures. In C. Calhoun & G. Derluguian (Eds.), *Business as usual: The roots of the global financial meltdown* (pp. 9–42). New York: New York University Press.

Campos Lima, M. P., & Artiles, A. M. (2011). Crisis and trade union challenges in Portugal and Spain: Between general strikes and social pacts. *Transfer*, *17*(3), 387–402.

Campos Lima, M. P., & Artiles, A. M. (2013). Youth voice(s) in EU countries and social movements in southern Europe. *Transfer*, *19*(3), 345–363.
Casey, C., & Alach, P. (2004). Just a temp? Women, temporary employment and lifestyle. *Work, Employment and Society*, *18*(3), 459–480.
Castells, M. (2000). *The rise of the network society* (2nd ed.). Oxford: Blackwell.
Carby-Hall, J. R. (2008). *The treatment of polish and other A8 economic migrants in the European Union*. Warszawa: Bureau of the Commissioner for Civil Rights Protection.
Catalan News (2020). Spanish government bans firing employees due to coronavirus, 27/3/2020, https://www.catalannews.com/business/item/spanish-government-bans-firing-employees-due-to-coronavirus
Charalambous, G. (2014). *Political culture and behaviour in the Republic of Cyprus during the crisis*, PRIO Cyprus Centre Report.
Charalambous, G. (2021). *The European radical left: Movements and parties since the 1960s*. London: Pluto Press.
Charalambous, G., & Ioannou, G. (2015a). No bridge over troubled waters: The Cypriot left heading the government: 2008–2013. *Capital and Class*, *39*(2), 265–286.
Charalambous, G., & Ioannou, G. (2015b). Fragmented we fight: What's Left in Greece in 2015? *Open Democracy*, 18 September 2015, https://www.opendemocracy.net/en/can-europe-make-it/fragmented-we-fight/
Charalambous, G., & Ioannou, G. (2017). Party-society linkages and contentious acts: Cyprus in a comparative South European perspective. *Mobilization: An International Quarterly*, 22(1), 97–119.
Charalambous, G., & Ioannou, G. (2020a). Introducing the topic and the concepts. In G. Charalambous & G. Ioannou (Eds.), *Left radicalism and populism in Europe* (pp. 1–30). London: Routledge.
Charalambous, G., & Ioannou, G. (2020b). Conclusions: Populism and left radicalism in Europe across time and space. In G. Charalambous & G. Ioannou (Eds.), *Left radicalism and populism in Europe* (pp. 257–265). London: Routledge.
Charles, N., & James, E. (2003). The gender dimensions of job insecurity in a local labour market. *Work Employment and Society*, *17*(3), 531–552.
Choonara, J. (2019). *Insecurity, precarious work and labour markets: Challenging the orthodoxy*. Cham: Palgrave Macmillan.
Christou O., Ioannou C., & Shekeris A. (2016). The Cypriot welfare state at a time of crisis. In K. Schubert, P. de Villota & J. Kuhlmann (Eds.), *Challenges to European welfare systems*. Cham: Springer.
Clarke, S. (1991). State, class struggle and the reproduction of capital. In S. Clarke (Ed.), *The state debate* (pp. 183–203). New York: Palgrave.
Clegg, H. (1976). *Trade unionism under collective bargaining*. Oxford: Basil Blackwell.
Colling, T. (2010). Legal institutions and the regulation of workplaces. In T. Colling & M. Terry (Eds.), *Industrial relations: Theory and practice*. West Sussex: Wiley.
Cranford, C., Vosko, L., & Zukewich, N. (2003). The gender of precarious employment in Canada. *Industrial Relations*, *58*(3), 454–482.
Crompton, R. (2010). Class and employment. *Work, Employment and Society*, *24*(1), 9–26.

Crouch, C. (1993). *Industrial relations and European state traditions*. Oxford: Oxford University Press.

Crouch, C. (2011). *The strange non-death of neoliberalism*. Cambridge: Polity.

Crouch, C. (2013). Entrenching neo-liberalism: The current agenda of European social policy. In N. Countouris & M. Freedland (Eds.), *Resocialising Europe in a time of crisis*. Cambridge: Cambridge University Press.

Cruces, J., Alvarez, I. Trillo, F., & Leonardi, S. (2015). Impact of the euro crisis on wages and collective bargaining in southern Europe – A comparison of Italy, Portugal and Spain. In G. Van Gyes & T. Schulten (Eds.), *Wage bargaining under the new European governance: alternative strategies for inclusive growth*. Brussels: ETUI.

Daly, M., Ebbinghaus, B., Lehner, L., Naczyk, M., & Vlandas T. (2020). Oxford supertracker: The global directory for COVID policy trackers and surveys. Department of Social Policy and Intervention, https://supertracker.spi.ox.ac.uk/

Degryse, C., & Tilly, P. (2013). *1973–2014: 40 years of history of the European Trade Union Confederation*. Brussels: ETUI.

Danaj, S., Çaro, E., Mankki, L., Sippola, M., & Lillie, N. (2018). Unions and migrant workers: The perspective of Estonians in Finland and Albanians in Italy and Greece. In V. Doellgast, N. Lillie & V. Pulignano (Eds.), *Reconstructing solidarity: Labour unions, precarious work, and the politics of institutional change in Europe*. Oxford: Oxford University Press.

Davies, P., & Freedland, M. (2007). *Towards a flexible labour market: Labour legislation and regulation since the 1990s*. Oxford: Oxford University Press.

De Rio Loira, P., & Fenger, M. (2019). Spanish trade unions against labour market reforms: Strategic choices and outcomes. *Transfer*, *25*(4), 421–435.

Deakin, S. (2015). Juridical ontology: The evolution of legal form. *Historical Social Research*, *40*(1), 170–184.

Deakin, S., & Koukiadaki, A. (2013). The sovereign debt crisis and the evolution of labour law in Europe. In N. Countouris & M. Freedland (Eds.), *Resocialising Europe in a time of crisis*. Cambridge: Cambridge University Press.

Della Porta, D. (2006). From corporatist unions to protest unions? On the (difficult) relations between labor and new social movements. In C. Crouch & W. Streeck (Eds.), *The diversity of democracy corporatism, social order and political conflict*. Cheltenham: Edward Elgar.

Della Porta, D. (2015). *Social movements in times of austerity: Bringing capitalism back into protest analysis*. Hoboken: John Wiley & Sons.

Della Porta, D., Fernandez, J., Kouki, H., & Mosca, L. (2017). *Movement parties against austerity*. Cambridge: Polity Press.

Demetriades, P. (2017). *Diary of the euro crisis in Cyprus: Lessons for bank recovery and resolution*. London: Springer Verlag.

Demoulas, K. (2018). Κρίση και κοινωνικό εισόδημα αλληλεγγύης [Crisis and Social Solidarity Income]. In Y. Kouzis & K. Demoulas (Eds.), *«Κρίση και κοινωνική πολιτική: Αδιέξοδα και λύσεις», [Crisis and social policy: dead ends and solutions]* (pp. 173–192). Athens: Topos.

Diani, M., & Kousis, M. (2014). The duality of claims and events: The Greek campaign against the Troika's Memoranda and austerity, 2010–2012. *Mobilization: An International Quarterly*, *19*(4), 387–404.

Díaz-Bara, I., Roca, B., & Martin-Díaz, E. (2018). Indignados, municipalism and PODEMOS: Mobilisation and political cycle in Spain after the Great Recession. In B. Roca, E. Martín-Díaz & I. Díaz-Parra (Eds.), *Challenging austerity radical left and social movements in the South of Europe*. London: Routledge.

Dickens, L., & Hall, M. (2009). Legal regulation and the changing workplace. In W. Brown, A. Bryson, J. Forth & K. Whitfield (Eds.), *The evolution of the modern workplace*. New York: Cambridge University Press.

Doellgast, V., Lillie, N., & Pulignano, V. (2018). From dualization to solidarity: Halting the cycle of precarity. In V. Doellgast, N. Lillie & V. Pulignano (Eds.), *Reconstructing solidarity: Labour unions, precarious work, and the politics of institutional change in Europe*. Oxford: Oxford University Press.

Doogan, K. (2009). *New capitalism? The transformation of work*. Cambridge: Polity Press.

Dukes, R. (2009). Otto Kahn-Freund and collective Laissez-Faire: An edifice without a keystone? *The Modern Law Review*, *72*(2), 220–246.

Dukes, R. (2018). From the labour constitution to an economic sociology of labour law. *Jurisprudence*, *9*(2), 418–423.

Dukes, R. (2019). The economic sociology of labour law. *Journal of Law and Society*, *46*(3), 396–422.

Dukes, R., & Streeck, W. (2020a). *From industrial citizenship to private ordering? Contract, status, and the question of consent*. MPIfG Discussion Paper 20/13. Cologne: Max Planck Institute for the Study of Societies.

Dukes, R., & Streeck, W. (2020b). Labour constitutions and occupational communities: Social norms and legal norms at work. *Journal of Law and Society*, *47*(4), 612–638.

Edwards, R. (1979). *Contested terrain: The transformation of the workplace in the 20$^{th}$century*. New York: Basic Books.

Emilianides, A., & Ioannou, C. (2016). *Labour law in Cyprus*. Alphen aan den Rijn: Walters Kluwer.

Erne, R. (2015). A supranational regime that nationalizes social conflict: Explaining European trade unions' difficulties in politicizing European economic governance. *Labor History*, *56*(3), 345–368.

Ergatiko Vima (2020). Η δικαίωση των οργανωμένων αγώνων των εργαζομένων στην Οικοδομική Βιομηχανία [The victory of the organised struggles of workers in the construction]. *Ergatiko Vima*, 11/6/2020.

Esping-Andersen, G. (1990). *The three worlds of welfare capitalism*. Cambridge: Polity Press

Eurofound (2020a). *Labour market change: Trends and policy approaches towards flexibilization*. Luxembourg: EU Publications Office.

Eurofound (2020b). *Living, working and COVID-19*. Luxembourg: EU Publications Office.

Eurofound (2019). Cyprus. Country Profile, https://www.eurofound.europa.eu/country/cyprus

Eurofound (2017a). *Involvement of the social partners in the European Semester: 2016 update*. Luxembourg: EU Publications Office.

Eurofound (2017b). *Income inequalities and employment patterns in Europe before and after the Great Recession*. Luxembourg: EU Publications Office.

Eurofound (2016). *Role of the social partners in the European Semester*. Luxembourg: EU Publications Office.

Euronews (2020). Ελλάδα - Covid-19: Τα 10 μέτρα στήριξης εργαζόμενων και επιχειρήσεων [Greece – Covid-19: the 10 measures supporting workers and firms]. *Euronews*, 5/11/2020, https://gr.euronews.com/2020/11/05/staikouras-dieurinete-to-paketo-stirixis

European Commission (2007). Communication. Towards common principles of flexicurity: More and better jobs through flexibility and security, http://eur-lex.europa.eu/LexUriServ/LexUriServ.do?uri=COM:2007:0359:FIN:EN:PDF

European Council (2020). COVID-19: Council adopts a recommendation to coordinate measures affecting free movement, 13/10/2020, https://www.consilium.europa.eu/en/press/press-releases/2020/10/13/covid-19-council-adopts-a-recommendation-to-coordinate-measures-affecting-free-movement/#

Ewing, K. (2019). The changing workplace revisited. In E. Tucker & J. Fudge (Eds.), *The class politics of law: Essays inspired by Harry Glasbeek* (pp. 74–95). Nova Scotia: Fernwood Publishing.

Fairwork (2020). *The Gig Economy and Covid-19*, Fairwork Report on Platform Policies.

Felstead, A., & Jewson, N. (Eds.), (1999). *Global trends in flexible labour*. London: Macmillan Press.

Fernandez, E. (2017). Pedals en peu de Guerra. *Mes economia*, 30/6/2017, http://www.meseconomia.cat/pedals-peu-guerra/

Fernandez, M., & Delgado, C. (2014). High Court strikes down Coca-Cola's decision to lay off 821 workers in Spain. *El Pais*, 14/6/2014, https://english.elpais.com/elpais/2014/06/13/inenglish/1402672349_633731.html

Fernandez Rodriguez, C. J., Ibanez Rojo, R., & Martinez Lucio, M. (2021 forthcoming) Spain. In J. Waddington, T. Müller & K. Vandaele (Eds.), *Trade unions in the European Union, Vol. III*. Brussels: ETUI.

Fernandez Rodriguez, C. J., Ibanez Rojo, R., & Martinez Lucio, M. (2019). Spain: challenges to legitimacy and representation in a context of fragmentation and neoliberal reform. In T. Müller, K. Vandaele & J. Waddington (Eds.), *Collective bargaining in Europe: Towards an endgame, Vol. III* (pp. 563–582). Brussels: ETUI.

Fernandez Rodriguez, C. J., Ibanez Rojo, R., & Martinez Lucio, M. (2016). Austerity and collective bargaining in Spain: The political and dysfunctional nature of neoliberal deregulation. *European Journal of Industrial Relations*, *22*(3), 267–280.

Fernandez Rodriguez, C. J., & Martinez Lucio, M. (2013). Narratives, myths and prejudice in understanding employment systems: The case of rigidities, dismissals and flexibility in Spain. *Economic and Industrial Democracy*, *34*(2), 313–336.

Ferreiro, J., Gálvez, C., & González, A (2016). Financialisation and the economic crisis in Spain. In E. Hein, D. Detzer & N. Dodig (Eds.), *Financialisation and the financial and economic crises: Country studies*. Cheltenham: Edward Elgar.

Fine, B. (1998). *Labour market theory: A constructive reassessment*. London: Routledge.

Fine, B., & Saad Filho, A. (2017). Thirteen things you need to know about neoliberalism. *Critical Sociology*, *43*(4–5), 685–706.

Fishman, R. M. (1990). *Working class organization and the return to democracy in Spain*. New York: Cornell University Press.
Flesher Fominaya, C. (2017). European anti-austerity and pro-democracy protests in the wake of the global financial crisis. *Social Movement Studies*, *16*(1), 1–20.
Flesher Fominaya, C. (2020). *Democracy Reloaded: Inside Spain's Political Laboratory from 15-M to PODEMOS*. Oxford: Oxford University Press.
Foskolos, Y. (2020). Εργασιακό νομοσχέδιο: Αλλάζουν όλα σε ωράρια, υπερωρίες, άδειες, απεργίες, τηλεργασία [Labour bill: everything changes in working time, overtime, time off, strikes, telework]. *Ethnos*, 29/10/2020, https://www.ethnos.gr/oikonomia/130621_ergasiako-nomoshedio-allazoyn-ola-se-oraria-yperories-adeies-apergies-tilergasia
Foti, A. (2004). Precarity and N/European identity: an interview with Alex Foti (Chainworkers). *Mute*, *2*(0), https://www.metamute.org/editorial/articles/precarity-and-neuropean-identity-interview-alex-foti-chainworkers
Foti, A. (2017). The precariat for itself. In E. Armano, A. Bove & A. Murgia (Eds.), *Mapping precariousness, labour insecurity and uncertain livelihoods*. London: Routledge.
Fotinatos-Ventouratos, R., & Cooper, C. L. (2015). *The economic crisis and occupational stress*. Cheltenham: Edward Elgar.
Franzosi, R. (2006) [1995]. *The puzzle of strikes: Class and state strategies in postwar Italy*. New York: Cambridge University Press.
Frassanito network (2005). Precarious, precariazation, precariat?, http://precariousunderstanding.blogsome.com/2007/01/05precarious-precarization-precariat/
Frazer, N. (2011). Marketization, social protection, emancipation: Toward a neo-polanyian conception of capitalist crisis. In C. Calhoun & G. Derluguian (Eds.), *Business as usual: The roots of the global financial meltdown* (pp. 137–158). New York: New York University Press.
Frege, C. (2007). *Employment research and state traditions: A comparative history of Britain, Germany and the United States*. New York: Oxford University Press.
Fumagalli, A. (2005). Bioeconomics, labour flexibility and cognitive work: Why not basic income. In G. Standing (Ed.), *Promoting income security as a right: Europe and North America*. London: Anthem Press.
Gallie, D., White, M., Yuan, C., & Tomlinson, M. (1998). *Restructuring the employment relationship*. New York: Oxford University Press.
Gallo, P., & Gene-Badia, J. (2013). Cuts drive health system reform in Spain. *Health Policy*, *113*, 1–7.
Gerbaudo, P. (2017). The indignant citizen: Anti-austerity movements in southern Europe and the anti-oligarchic reclaiming of citizenship. *Social Movement Studies*, *16*(1), 36–50.
Gialis, S., & Tsampra, M. (2015). The diverse regional patterns of atypical employment in Greece: Production restructuring, re/deregulation and flexixurity under crisis. *Geoforum*, *62*, 175–187.
Giannakopoulos, N., & Laliotis, I. (2019). Firm level adjustments before and during the crisis: Evidence from the 2011 industrial relations reform. In H. Voskeritsian, P. Kapotas & C. Niforou (Eds.), *Greek employment*

*relations in crisis: Problems, challenges and prospects* (pp. 83–102). London: Routledge.

Gill, J., McCaffrey, D., & Cavallone, E. (2020). Frugal four take on France and Germany as coronavirus recovery plan divides EU. *Euronews*, 27/5/2020, https://www.euronews.com/2020/05/26/frugal-four-take-on-france-and-germany-as-coronavirus-recovery-plan-divides-eu

Gill, J., & Chadwick, L. (2020). EU summit: Leaders reach landmark €1.82 trillion COVID-19 recovery deal and budget. *Euronews*, 21/7/2020, https://www.euronews.com/2020/07/21/eu-summit-deadlock-see-talks-stretch-into-sunday

Ginès-Fabrellas, A (2019). The rise of precarious work in Spain: the effects of the increase in labour market flexibility. In J. Kenner, I. Florczak & M. Otto (Eds.), *Precarious work: The challenge for labour law in Europe* (pp. 75–98). Cheltenham: Edward Elgar.

Giokas, A. (2020). Υπόθεση «σκοιλ ελικικου»: Το παρασκήνιο πίσω από το φιάσκο της τηλεκατάρτισης [The "skoil elikikou" case: the background behind the fiasco of tele-training]. *Ethnos* 26/4/2020, https://www.ethnos.gr/politiki/102098_ypothesi-skoil-elikikoy-paraskinio-piso-apo-fiasko-tis-tilekatartisis

Goetschy, J., & Jobert, A. (2004). Employment relations in France. In G. Bamber, R. Lansbury, & N. Wailes (Eds.), *International and comparative employment relations*. London: Sage Publications.

Gumbrell-McCormick, R., & Hyman, R. (2013). *Trade unions in Western Europe: Hard times, hard choices*. Oxford: Oxford University Press.

Gutiérrez, R. (2014). Welfare performance in Southern Europe: Employment crisis and poverty risk. *South European Society and Politics*, *19*(3), 371–392.

Gramsci, A. (1972). *Selections from the Prison Notebooks*. London: Lawrence and Wishart.

Greer, I. (2016). Welfare reform, precarity and the re-commodification of labour. *Work, Employment and Society*, *30*(1), 162–173.

Hall, S. (2005) [1982]. The rediscovery of "ideology": Return of the repressed in media studies. In M. Gurevitch, T. Bennett, J. Curran & J. Woollacott (Eds.), *Culture, society and the media* (pp. 52–86). London: Routledge.

Hall, S., Critcher, C., Jefferson, T., Clarke J., & Roberts B. (1978). *Policing the Crisis: Mugging, the state, and law and order*. London: Macmillan Press.

Hall, S. (2017) [2011]. *The neoliberal revolution, in selected political writings*. Durham: Duke University Press.

Hall P. A., & Soskice D. (2001). *Varieties of Capitalism: The institutional foundation of comparative advantages*. Oxford: Oxford University Press.

Hall, P. A., & Thelen, K. (2009). Institutional change in varieties of capitalism. *Socio-Economic Review*, 7, 7–34.

Hamann, K. (2011). *The politics of industrial relations: Labor unions in Spain*. London: Routledge.

Hamann, K., & Martinez Lucio, M. (2007). Trade union revitalisation in Spain. In C. Phelan (Ed.), *Trade union revitalisation: Trends and prospects in 34 countries*. Bern – Switzerland: Peter Lang.

Hardt, M., & Negri, A. (2000). *Empire*. Cambridge: Harvard University Press.

Harman, C. (2010) [2009]. *Zombie capitalism: Global capitalism and the relevance of Marx*. Chicago: Heymarket Books.

Harvey, D. (1989). *The condition of postmodernity*. Oxford: Blackwell.
Hayes, G. (2017). Regimes of austerity. *Social Movement Studies*, *16*(1), 21–35.
Heisenberg, D., & Richmond, A. (2002). Supranational institution building in the European Union: A comparison of the European Court of Justice and the European Central Bank. *Journal of European Public Policy*, *9*(2), 201–218.
Heery, E., & Kelly, J. (1994). Professional, participative and managerial unionism: an interpretation of change in trade unions. *Work, Employment and Society*, *8*(1), 1–22.
Herman, E., & Chomsky, N. (1988). *Manufacturing consent: The political economy of the mass media*. New York: Pantheon Books.
Heyes, J. (2011). Flexicurity, employment protection and the job crisis. *Work, Employment and Society*, *25*(4), 642–657.
Hochschild, A. (2003) [1983]. *The Managed Heart: Commercialization of Human Feeling*. California: University of California Press.
Hope, K. (2019). People's anger over 2018 wildfires weighs on Greece elections. *Financial Times*, 6/7/2019, https://www.ft.com/content/02ddec34-9e66-11e9-b8ce-8b459ed04726
Howell, C. (2005). *Trade unions and the state: The construction of industrial relations institutions in Britain 1890–2000*. New Jersey: Princeton University Press.
Howell, C. (2016). Regulating class in the neoliberal era: the role of the state in the restructuring of work and employment relations. *Work, Employment and Society*, *30*(4), 573–579.
Hyman, R. (1989). *The political economy of industrial relations: Theory and practice in a cold climate*. London: Macmillan.
Hyman, R. (2001). *Understanding European trade unionism: Between market, class and society*. London: Sage.
Hyman, R. (2015). Austeritarianism in Europe: What options for resistance? In D. Natali & B. Vanhercke (Eds.), *Social policy in the European Union: State of play 2015 Sixteenth annual report*. Brussels: ETUI.
Hyman, R., & Gumbrell-McCormick, R. (2010). Trade unions, politics and parties: Is a new configuration possible? *European Review of Labour and Research*, *16*(3), 315–331.
Hyman, R., & Gumbrell-McCormick, R. (2017). Resisting labour market insecurity: Old and new actors, rivals or allies? *Journal of Industrial Relations*, *59*(4), 538–561.
Ibsen, C. L., & Tapia, M. (2017). Trade union revitalisation: Where are we now? Where to next? *Journal of Industrial Relations*, *59*(2), 170–191.
ILO (2020). Protecting migrant workers during the COVID-19 pandemic. Policy Brief, April 2020, https://www.ilo.org/global/topics/labour-migration/publications/WCMS_743268/lang--en/index.htm
IMF (2020). World Economic Outlook Update, June 2020, https://www.imf.org/en/Publications/WEO/Issues/2020/06/24/WEOUpdateJune2020
INEK-PEO (2014). Έκθεση για την οικονομία και την απασχόληση, [Report on economy and employment], http://www.inek.org.cy/index.php.
INEK-PEO (2018). Έκθεση για την οικονομία και την απασχόληση, [Report on economy and employment], http://www.inek.org.cy/index.php.

INEK-PEO (2019). Έκθεση για την οικονομία και την απασχόληση, [Report on economy and employment], http://www.inek.org.cy/index.php.

Ioakimoglou, E., & Soumeli, E. (2008). Οι Μισθοί στην Κύπρο: Προσδιοριστικοί Παράγοντες και Μισθολογικές Ανισότητες *[Wages in Cyprus: Determining factors and wage inequalities]*. Nicosia: INEK-PEO.

Ioannou, C. (2019). Collective bargaining decentralization and wage adjustment for internal devaluation. In H. Voskeritsian, P. Kapotas & C. Niforou (Eds.), *Greek employment relations in crisis: Problems, challenges and prospects* (pp. 31–58). London: Routledge.

Ioannou, G. (2015). Labor force fragmentation in contemporary Cyprus. *WorkingUSA: The Journal of Labor and Society*, *18*(4), 595–612.

Ioannou, G. (2016a). Employment in crisis: Cyprus and the extension of precarity. In C. Schierup & M. Bak Jørgensen (Eds.), *Politics of Precarity: Migrant conditions, struggles and experiences* (pp. 138–159). Leiden/Boston: Brill/Haymarket.

Ioannou, G. (2016b). The connection between trade unions and political parties in Cyprus. In G. Charalambous & C. Christophorou (Eds.), *Party-society relations in the Republic of Cyprus* (pp. 110–128). London: Routledge.

Ioannou, G. (2020a). *The normalization of Cyprus' partition among Greek Cypriots: Political economy and political culture in a divided society*. Basingstoke: Palgrave Macmillan.

Ioannou, G. (2020b). The communicative power of trade unionism: labour law, political opportunity structure and social movement strategy. *Industrielle Beziehungen/ German Journal of Industrial Relations*, *27*(3), 286–309.

Ioannou G. (2020c). Authoritarianism masking incompetence? The case of the Republic of Cyprus. *Open Democracy*, 7th April 2020, https://www.opendemocracy.net/en/can-europe-make-it/authoritarianism-masking-incompetence-case-republic-cyprus/.

Ioannou, G., & Sonan, S. (2017). Trade unions and politics in Cyprus: An historical comparative analysis across the dividing line. *Mediterranean Politics*, *22*(4), 484–503.

Ioannou, G., & Sonan, S. (2019). Cyprus: A divided island – state with diverging collective bargaining patterns, weakened yet still standing. In T. Müller, K. Vandaele & J. Waddington (Eds.), *Collective bargaining in Europe: Towards an endgame* (pp. 109–129). Brussels: ETUI.

Ioannou, G., & Sonan, S. (2021 forthcoming) Cyprus: A divided society with trade unions on a slow retreat. In J. Waddington, T. Müller, & K. Vandaele (eds.), *Trade unions in the European Union. Vol. I*, Brussels: ETUI.

Ioannou, G., & Sonan, S. (2016). Youth unemployment in Cyprus: An examination of the "lost generation". *Friedrich Ebert Stiftung Study*.

Ioannou, G., & Charalambous, G. (2016). The Left and the crisis in Cyprus. In L. March & L. Keith (Eds.), *The radical Left and the crisis*. London: Rowman & Littlefield, pp. 273–288.

Ioannou, G., & Charalambous, G. (2017). The social and political impact of the Cyprus economic crisis: 2010–2017. *Friedrich Ebert Stiftung Study*.

Ioannou, G., & Charalambous, G. (2020). West European trade unions and the people: From the golden era to the times of austerity. In G. Charalambous &

G. Ioannou (Eds.), *Left Radicalism and Populism in Europe* (pp. 204–222). London: Routledge.
Jessop, B. (2012). Narratives of crisis and crisis response: Perspectives from North and South 'Narratives of crisis and crisis response: perspectives from North and South'. In P. Utting, S. Razavi & R. V. Buchholz (Eds.), *The global crisis and transformative change* (pp. 23–42). Basingstoke: Palgrave Macmillan.
Jessop, B. (2013). Recovered imaginaries, imagined recoveries: A cultural political economy of crisis construals and crisis-management in the North Atlantic Financial Crisis. In M. Benner (Ed.), *Beyond the Global Economic Crisis: Economics and Politics for a Post-Crisis Settlement* (pp. 234–254). Cheltenham: Edward Elgar.
Jódar, P., Vidal, S., & Alós, R. (2011). British union activism in an inclusive system of industrial relations: Evidence from a Spanish case study. *British Journal of Industrial Relations*, *49*(S1), 158–180.
Joris, W., d' Haenens, L., & Van Gorp, B. (2014). The euro crisis in metaphors and frames: Focus on the press in the low countries. *European Journal of Communication*, *29*(5), 608–617.
Kalleberg, A. L. (2011). *Good jobs, bad jobs: The rise of polarised and precarious employment systems in the United States, 1970 to 2000s*. New York: Russel Sage Foundation.
Kalosinatos, P. (2019). Industrial relations. Cyprus: Developments in working life 2018, annual review of working life 2018, National Contribution. *Eurofound*, https://www.eurofound.europa.eu/publications/report/2019/annual-review-of-working-life-2018#tab-03
Kapsalis, A. (2018). The development of Greek migration policy and the invention of "para-legality" in labour relations of immigrants. *Κοινωνική Πολιτική*, *9*, 67–87.
Karakioulafi, C., & Spyridakis, M. (2017). Εισαγωγή [Introduction]. In C. Karakioulafi & M. Spyridakis (Eds.), *Κοινωνία, ανεργία και κοινωνική αναπαραγωγή [Society, unemployment and social reproduction]* (pp. 9–48). Athens: Gutenberg.
Karakioulafi, C. (2018). Οι εργασιακές σχέσεις στη δίνη της νέας οικονομικής διακυβέρνησης της Ευρωπαϊκής Ένωσης [Labour relations in the whirlpool of the "new economic governance of the European Union"] In S. Tombazos & N. Serdedakis (Eds.), *Όψεις της ελληνικής κρίσης [Faces of the Greek Crisis]*. Athens: Gutenberg.
Karakioulafi, C. (2019). Unions and labour solidarity: Pending between Inclusiveness and Exclusiveness – the case of Greek Trade Unions. In M. Christodoulou & M. Spyridakis (Eds.), *Emotions, temporalities and working-class identities in the 21stCentury* (pp. 125–150). New York: Nova Science Publishers.
Karamesini, M. (2012). Greece: women's difficult road to economic independence. In A. Bugra and Y. Ozkan (Eds.), *Trajectories of female employment in the Mediterranean* (pp. 65–90). Basingstoke: Palgrave Macmillan.
Katsaroumpas, I. (2018). De-constitutionalising collective labour rights: the case of Greece. *Industrial Law Journal*, *47*(4), 465–503.
Katsaroumpas, I. & Koukiadaki, A. (2019). Greece: 'contesting' collective bargaining. In T. Müller, K. Vandaele & J. Waddington (Eds.), *Collective bargaining in Europe: Towards an endgame* (pp. 267–293). Brussels: ETUI.

Keating, D. (2020). EU Unveils Plan To Reopen Tourism This Summer. *Forbes*, 13/5/2020, https://www.forbes.com/sites/davekeating/2020/05/13/eu-unveils-plan-to-reopen-tourism-this-summer/

Keeley G. (2020). Spain sees historic rise in unemployment as nearly 900,000 lose jobs since coronavirus lockdown. *The Independent*, 2/4/2020, https://www.independent.co.uk/news/world/europe/spain-coronavirus-lockdown-unemployment-job-loss-update-a9442146.html

Keller, B. (2004). Employment relations in Germany. In Greg Bamber, Russell Lansbury & Nick Wailes (Eds.), *International and Comparative Employment Relations*. London: Sage Publications.

Kelly, J. (1998). *Rethinking industrial relations: Mobilisation, collectivism and long waves*. London: Routledge.

Kioupkiolis, A., & Katsambekis, G. (2020). New left populism contesting and taking power: the cases of SYRIZA and PODEMOS. In G. Charalambous & G. Ioannou (Eds.), *Left radicalism and populism in Europe* (pp. 129–155). London: Routledge.

Köhler, H.D. (2018). Industrial relations in Spain – strong conflicts, weak actors and fragmented institutions. *Employee Relations*, *40*(4), 725–743.

Köhler, H. D., & Calleja Jiménez J. P. (2012). Transformations in Spanish trade union membership. *Industrial Relations Journal*, *43*(3), 281–292.

Köhler, H. D., & Calleja Jiménez J. P. (2017). Spain: A peripheral economy and a vulnerable trade union movement. In S. Lehndorff, H., Dribbush & S. Thorsten (Eds.), *Rough waters European trade unions in a time of crisis* (pp. 61–81). Brussels: ETUI.

Köhler, H. D., & Calleja Jiménez J. P. (2018). Social movements and trade union revitalization in Spain [Soziale Bewegungen und gewerkschaftliche Erneuerung in Spanien]. *Industrielle Beziehungen*, *25*(2), 147–165.

Kotronaki, L. (2018). Από το δρόμο στο κοινοβούλιο: οι τοπογραφίες της διαμαρτυρίας και ο ΣΥΡΙΖΑ στα χρόνια της κρίσης [From the street to parliament: topography of protest and SYRIZA in the crisis years]. In S. Tombazos & N. Serdedakis (Eds.), *Όψεις της ελληνικής κρίσης [Faces of the Greek Crisis]*. Athens: Gutenberg.

Koukiadaki, A. (2019). Συλλογικές συμβάσεις, κοινωνικός διάλογος και ανισότητες στην περιφέρεια της Ευρώπης [Collective agreements, social dialogue and inequalities in the periphery of Europe]. In M. Karamesini (Ed.), *Ανισότητες, νεοφιλελευθερισμός και ευρωπαϊκή ενοποίηση [Inequalities, neoliberalism and European unification]*. Athens: Nisos and Poulantzas Institute.

Koukiadaki, A., & Kokkinou C. (2017). Το πρεκαριάτο την περίοδο της κρίσης και η εδραίωση της εργασιακής επισφάλειας: η περίπτωση μελέτης της 'ενοικίασης εργαζομένων' [The precariat in the crisis period and the consolidation of labour precarity: the case study of rented employees]. In C. Karakioulafi & M. Spyridakis (Eds.), *Κοινωνία, ανεργία και κοινωνική αναπαραγωγή [Society, unemployment and social reproduction]* (pp. 327–348). Athens, Gutenberg.

Koukiadaki, A., & Kokkinou C. (2016). The Greek system of collective bargaining in (the) crisis. In A. Koukiadaki, I. Tavora & M. Martinez-Lucio (Eds.), *Joint regulation and labour market policy in Europe during the crisis* (pp. 135–203). Brussels: ETUI.

Koukiadis, I. (2017). *Ατομικό και συλλογικό εργατικό δίκαιο επιτομή [Individual and collective labour law: abridgement]*, (6th ed.). Athens: Sakkoula.

Kousis, M., & Paschou, M. (2017). Alternative form of resilience: A typology of approaches for the study of citizen collective responses in hard economic times. *PArtecipazione e COnflitto*, *10*(1), 136–168.

Koutsampelas, C. (2016). The Cypriot GMI scheme and comparisons with other European countries. *Cyprus Economic Policy Review*, *10*(1), 3–26.

Kouzis, Y. (2001). Εργασιακές Σχέσεις και Ευρωπαϊκή Ενοποίηση *[Labour relations and European integration]*. Athens: INE-GSEE.

Kouzis, Y. (2007). Τα χαρακτηριστικά του ελληνικού συνδικαλιστικού κινήματος: Αποκλίσεις και συγκλίσεις με τον ευρωπαϊκό χώρο *[The characteristics of the Greek trade union movement: divergences and convergences with the European space]*. Athens: Gutenberg.

Kouzis, Y. (2013). Οι εργασιακές σχέσεις στην Ευρώπη και στην Ελλάδα *[Labour relations in Europe and Greece]*. *Annual Report 2013*, n. 11, Observatory of Social, Economic Developments. Athens: INE-GSEE.

Kouzis, Y. (2014). Η εργασία στη δίνη της οικονομικής κρίσης και των μνημονίων [Labour in the whirlpool of economic crisis and memoranda]. In Zambarloukou, S. and Kousis M. (eds), *Κοινωνικές πτυχές της κρίσης στην Ελλάδα* [*Social Aspects of the Crisis in Greece*] (pp. 231–246). Athens: Pedio Publisher.

Kouzis, Y. (2018). Το νέο εργασιακό τοπίο με αφορμή την κρίση [The new labour landscape after the crisis]. In Y., Kouzis, and K., Demoulas (eds.), *«Κρίση και κοινωνική πολιτική: Αδιέξοδα και λύσεις», [Crisis and social policy: dead ends and solutions]* (pp. 121–136). Athens, Topos.

Kouzis, Y. (2020). Η εργασία και η παγίωση της νέας "κανονικότητας" [Labour and the consolidation of the new normal]. In C. Laskos & D. Papadatos-Anagnostopoulos (Eds.), *SYRIZA in government, the Left? [Ο ΣΥΡΙΖΑ στην κυβέρνηση, η Αριστερά;]*. Athens: Topos.

Kouzis, Y., & Kapsalis, A. (2020). Οι εργασιακές σχέσεις στο πλαίσιο του Τρίτου Μνημονίου. Τα επίμαχα πεδία της διαπραγμάτευσης με τους δανειστές και το ευρωπαϊκό περιβάλλον *[Labour relations in the context of the third Memorandum. The contested fields of negotiation with the lenders and the European environment]*. Athens: INE-GSEE.

Kovras, I., & Pagliari, S. (2020). Crisis and Punishment? Explaining Politicians' Appetite for Retribution in Post-Crisis Europe. *Comparative Politics*, Online First, https://www.ingentaconnect.com/content/cuny/cp/pre-prints/content-jcpo_53405;jsessionid=auu5bfcr9p6a8.x-ic-live-01

Kretsos, L. (2014). Youth policy in austerity Europe: The case of Greece, *International Journal of Adolescence and Youth*, *19*(S1), 35–47.

Kretsos, L. (2011). Grassroots unionism in the context of economic crisis in Greece. *Labor History*, *52*(3), 265–286.

Kriesi, H. (2006). Political context and opportunity. In D. A. Snow, S. A. Soule & H. Kriesi (Eds.), *The blackwell companion to social movements* (pp. 67–90). Oxford: Blackwell.

Labrianidis, L., & Pratsinakis, M. (2017). Crisis Brain drain: short-term pain/long term gain? In D. Tziovas (Ed.), *Greece in crisis: The cultural politics of austerity* (pp. 87–106). London: I.B. Tauris.

Ladi, S., & Graziano, P. R. (2014). Fast forward Europeanisation: welfare state reform in the light of the Eurozone crisis. In R. Coman, T. Kostera &

L. Tomini (Eds.), *Europeanisation and European integration: from incremental to structural change*. Cham: Palgrave Macmillan.

Laeven, L. (2020). COVID-19 and the effects of social distancing on the economy. *VoxEU* 31/8/2020, https://voxeu.org/article/covid-19-and-effects-social-distancing-economy

Lallement, M. (2011). Europe and the economic crisis: Forms of labour market adjustment and varieties of capitalism. *Work Employment Society*, *25*(4), 627–641.

Las Heras, J., & Ribera-Almandoz, O. (2017). When corporatism fails: Trade union strategies and grassroots resistance to the Spanish economic crisis. *Journal of Labor and Society*, *20*, 449–466.

Las Heras, J. (2018). Unions as "managers of precariousness": The entrenchment of micro-corporatism in the Spanish automotive industry and its drawbacks. *Employee relations*, *40*(6), 1054–1071

Las Heras, J., & Rodriguez, L. (2020). Striking to renew: Basque unions' organizing strategies and use of the strike-fund, *British Journal of Industrial Relations*, OnlineFirst, https://onlinelibrary.wiley.com/doi/10.1111/bjir.12582

Lehndorff, S., Dribbush, H., & Thorsten, S. (2017). European trade unions in a time of crises – an overview. In S. Lehndorff, H. Dribbush & S.,Thorsten (Eds.), *Rough waters European trade unions in a time of crisis* (pp. 7–35). Brussels: ETUI.

León, M., & Pavolini, E. (2014). 'Social Investment' or Back to 'Familism': The impact of the economic crisis on family and care policies in Italy and Spain. *South European Society and Politics*, *19*(3), 353–369.

Leonardi, S. (2017). Trade unions and collective bargaining in Italy during the crisis. In S. Lehndorff, H. Dribbush & S. Thorsten (Eds.), *Rough waters European trade unions in a time of crisis* (pp. 83–107). Brussels: ETUI.

Lewchuk, W., Clarke, M., & de Wolff, A. (2008). Working without Commitments: Precarious Employment and Health. *Work, Employment and Society*, *22*(3), 387–406.

Lewis-Beck, M. S., & Costa Lobo, M. (2017). The economic vote: Ordinary vs. extraordinary times. In K. Arzheimer, J. Evans & M. S. Lewis-Beck (Eds.), *The Sage handbook of electoral behavior vols. 1–2*. London: SAGE Publications.

Liapi, M. (2016). The effects of the economic crisis on gender pay gap: A comparative analytical report between Cyprus, Greece, and Portugal (2008-2014) *Centre for Research on Women's issues DIOTIMA*.

Livanos, I., & Pouliakas, K. (2019). The rise of involuntary non-standard employment in Greece during the great economic depression. In H. Voskeritsian, P. Kapotas & C. Niforou (Eds.), *Greek employment relations in crisis: Problems, challenges and prospects* (pp. 31–58). London: Routledge.

Livitsanos, G. (2020). Εργασιακά: Ένα νομοσχέδιο που περνάει μόνον με … lockdown [Employment: a bill that passes only with … lock-down]. *News 24-7*, 30/10/2020, https://www.news247.gr/politiki/ergasiaka-ena-nomoschedio-poy-pernaei-monon-me-lockdown.9034417.html

Lopez-Andreu, M. (2020a). Breaking fragmentation through mobilization: The development of a collective identity during movistar's contractors' and technicians' strike in Spain *Work, Employment and Society*, *34*(4), 661–677.

Lopez-Andreu, M. (2020b). Employment Institutions under liberalization pressures: Analysing the effects of regulatory change on collective bargaining in Spain. *British Journal of Industrial Relations*, *57*(2), 328–349.

Lucas, R. (2004). *Employment relations in the hospitality and tourism industries*. London: Routledge.

Lukacs, G. (1968) [1922]. *History and class consciousness*. London: The Merlin Press.

Mair, P. (2007). Political opposition and the European Union. *Government and Opposition*, *42*(1), 1–17.

Markantonatou, M., & Kennedy, G. (2019). Enduring austerity: Memoranda politics and its impact on labour in Greece. In S. Schmalz & B. Sommer (Eds.), *Confronting crisis and precariousness: Organized labour and social unrest in the European Union* (pp. 111–128). London: Rowman and Littlefield.

Marx, K. (1976) [1867]. *Capital, Vol. 1*. London: Penguin.

Marx, K. (1978) [1885]. *Capital, Vol. 2*. London: Penguin.

Marx, K. (1981) [1894]. *Capital, Vol. 3*. London: Penguin.

Meardi, G. (2014). Employment Relations under External Pressure: Italian and Spanish Reforms during the Great Recession. In M. Hauptmeier & M. Vidal (Eds.), *The comparative political economy of work and employment relations*. Cham: Palgrave.

Meardi, G., Donaghey, J., & Dean, D. (2016). The strange non-retreat of the state: Implications for the sociology of work. *Work, Employment and Society*, *30*(4), 559–572.

Meyer, D. (2020). COVID-19 resurgence sets back Europe's economic recovery hopes. *Fortune*, 5/11/2020, https://fortune.com/2020/11/05/covid-19-resurgence-sets-back-european-economic-recovery-hopes/

Mitropoulos, A. (2006). Precari-Us? *Mute*, *1*(29), https://www.metamute.org/editorial/articles/precari-us

Molina, O. (2014). Beyond de-centralization: The erosion of collective bargaining in Spain during the Great Recession. *Stato e Mercato*, *102*, 371–396.

Molina, O., & Barranco, O. (2016). Trade union strategies to enhance strike effectiveness in Italy and Spain. *Transfer*, *22*(3), 383–399.

Moreno, L. (2014). Spain's catch up with the EU core: The implausible quest of a flying pig? In C. Balkir, H. T. Bolukbasi & E. Ertugal's (Eds.), *Europeanisation of public policy in Southern Europe*. London: Routledge.

Morlino, L., & Raniolo, F. (2017). *The impact of the economic crisis on south European democracies*. London: Palgrave Macmillan.

Moschonas, G. (2002). *In the Name of Social Democracy, The Great Transformation: 1945 to the Present*. London: Verso.

Müller, T., Vandaele, K., & Waddington, J. (2019). Conclusion: towards an endgame. In T. Müller, K. Vandaele & J. Waddington (Eds.), *Collective bargaining in Europe: Towards an endgame, Vol. III* (pp. 625–668). Brussels: ETUI.

Müller, T., Rainone, S., & Vandaele, K. (2020). Fair minimum wages and collective bargaining: A key to recovery. In ETUI and ETUC (Eds.), *Benchmarking Working Europe 2020*. Brussels: ETUI.

Murcia Today (2020). ERTE temporary redundancy schemes and how they affect businesses and the workforce, 17/3/2020, https://murciatoday.com/erte-temporary-redundancy-schemes-and-how-they-affect-businesses-and-the-workforce_1358281-a.html

Mylonas, Y. (2014). Crisis, austerity, and opposition in mainstream media discourses in Greece. *Critical Discourse Studies*, *11*(3), 305–321.

Mylonas, Y., & Kombatsiaris, P. (2013). "Cultural" interpretations of the "Greek debt-crisis": Faces of neoliberal discourse in the Greek public space. In G. Pleios (Ed.), *The crisis and the mass media* (pp. 387–420). Athens: Papazisi. [in Greek].

Narotzky, S. (2017). 'Η πρόκληση της κοινωνικής αναπαραγωγής σε περιόδους κρίσης οι εντάσεις μεταξύ γενεών στην Ισπανία' [The challenge of social reproduction in crisis periods: the tensions between generations in Spain]. In C. Karakioulafi & M. Spyridakis (Eds.), *Κοινωνία, ανεργία και κοινωνική αναπαραγωγή [Society, unemployment and social reproduction]* (pp. 139–175). Athens: Gutenberg.

Neilson, B., & Rossiter, N. (2008). Precarity as a political concept, or, Fordism as exception. *Theory, Culture, Society*, *25*(7–8), 51–72.

Negri, A. (1988). Archeology and project: the mass worker and the social worker. *Revolution Retrieved: Selected Writings on Marx, Keynes, the Capitalist Crisis and New Social Subjects, 1967–1983*. London: Red Notes.

Npress (2020). Πανό έξω από το Μαξίμου από εργαζομένους στην εστίαση – Προσαγωγές από την αστυνομία [Banner outside Maximou by food provision workers – arrests by the police]. *Npress.com*, 16/12/2020, https://www.npress.gr/greece/pano-exo-apo-to-maximoy-apo-ergazomeno/

Nowak, T. (2018). The turbulent life of the Working Time Directive. *Maastricht Journal of European and Comparative Law*, *25*(1), 118–129.

Offe, C. (1985). *Disorganised Capitalism*. New York: Polity Press.

Oxfam (2013). *The true cost of austerity and inequality: Spain Case Study*. Oxfam.

Paleologos, N. (2006). Labour and trade unions in the 21st Century. *[Εργασία και Συνδικάτα στον 21ο αιώνα*]. Athens: INE-GSEE.

Papadopoulos, O., & Lyddon, D. (2020). Deregulation and institutional conversion in the Greek hotel industry: an employment relations model in transition. *Industrial Relations Journal*, *51*(1–2), 92–109.

Papadopoulos, T., & Roumpakis, A. (2018). Rattling Europe's ordoliberal 'iron cage': the contestation of austerity in Southern Europe. *Critical Social Policy*, *38*(3), 505–526.

Panayiotopoulos, N., & Schultheis, F. (2015). Η οικονομία της αθλιότητας. [*The economy of misery: Greece 2010–2015*]. Athens: Alexandreia.

Panayiotopoulos, P. (2005). The globalisation of care: Filipina domestic workers and care for the elderly in Cyprus. *Capital and Class*, *29*(2), 99–134.

Panayiotou, A. (2013). Οι Τράπεζες, τα ΜΜΕ και οι Προσπάθειες Συγκάλυψης, Μετατόπισης και Λογοκρισίας των Σκανδάλων [The Banks, the Mass media and the Effort of Covering the Scandals], http://koinonioloyika.blogspot.com/2013/01/

Papanikolopoulos, D., Katsoridas, D., Kolias, G., & Dermani, V. (2018). Το απεργιακό φαινόμενο στην Ελλάδα: καταγραφή των απεργιών κατά την περίοδο 2011–2017 [The strike phenomenon in Greece: registering the strikes in the period 2011–2017]. Athens: INE-GSEE.

Pancyprian Federation of Labour (PEO). (2016). Ανακοίνωση Γενικού Συμβουλίου ΠΕΟ [Announcement of PEO General Council], 28 November 2016.

Pancyprian Federation of Labour (PEO). (2017). Έκθεση Δράσης για το 27° Συνέδριο [Action Report 27th Conference].

Pancyprian Federation of Labour (PEO). (2019). Ανακοίνωση Γενικού Συμβουλίου ΠΕΟ [Announcement of PEO General Council], 31 October 2019.

Parreñas, R. S. (2001). *Servants of globalization: Migration and domestic work*, (1st ed.) Stanford: Stanford University Press.

Pavlou, V. (2016). Migrant domestic workers, vulnerability and the law: immigration and employment laws in Cyprus and Spain. *Investigaciones Feministas*, 7(1), 149–168.

Pavolini, E., León, M., Guillénc, A. M., & Ascolid U. (2015). From austerity to permanent strain? The EU and welfare state reform in Italy and Spain. *Comparative European Politics*, *13*(1), 56–76.

Peel, M. and Khan, M. (2020). Frugal four' fight to protect EU budget rebates. *Financial Times*, 18/08/2020, https://www.ft.com/content/55f6796e-4a9f-43b2-8d94-da0804d1f83b

Pegasiou, A. (2013). The Cypriot economic collapse: More than a conventional South European failure. *Mediterranean Politics*, *18*(3), 333–551.

Petrou, P., & Vandoros, S. (2018). Health care reforms in Cyprus 2013-2017: Does the crisis mark the end of the health sector as we know it? *Health Policy*, *122*, 75–80.

Perez, S. A., & Matsaganis, M. (2018). The political economy of austerity in Southern Europe. *New Political Economy*, *23*(2), 192–207.

Perez de Guzman, S., Roca, B., & Diaz-Parra, I. (2016). Political exchange, crisis of representation and trade union strategies in a time of austerity: Trade unions and 15M in Spain. *Transfer*, *22*(4), 461–474.

Persianis, M. (2015). Bleak recovery and signs of hope. *Friedrich Ebert Stiftung Study*.

Petmezidou, M. (2018). Τα ευρωπαϊκά κοινωνικά κράτη μετά τη μεγάλη ύφεση [European welfare states after the great depression]. In K. Demoulas & Y. Kouzis (Eds.), *«Κρίση και κοινωνική πολιτική: Αδιέξοδα και λύσεις», [Crisis and social policy: dead ends and solutions]* (pp. 21–43). Athens: Topos.

Pfau-Effinger, B. (2009). Varieties of undeclared work in European societies. *British Journal of Industrial Relations*, *47*(1), 79–99.

Piore, M., & Sabel, C. (1984). *The second industrial divide*. New York: Basic Books.

Pilavaki, A. (2020). Οι Έμφυλες Επιπτώσεις της Πανδημίας *[The gendered consequences of the pandemic]* Hypatia Foundation Promoting Equality, https://www.hypatia.org.cy/

Pleios, G. (2013). The mass media vis a vis the crisis: intense adoption of the logic of the elite. In G. Pleios (Ed.), *The crisis and the mass media* (pp. 87–134). Athens: Papazisi.

Polanyi, K. (1944). *The great transformation*. New York: Rinehart and Company.

Prassl, J. (2018). *Humans as a service: The promise and perils of work in the gig economy*. Oxford: Oxford University Press.

Pulignano, V. (2017). Precarious work, regime of competition, and the case of Europe. In V. Pulignano, A. L. Kalleberg & S.P. Vallas (Eds.), *Precarious work (Research in the Sociology of Work, Vol. 31)* (pp. 33–60). Emerald Publishing Limited.

Purcel, K. (2000). Gendered employment insecurity?. In E. Heery & J. Salmon (Eds.), *The insecure workforce*. London: Routledge.

Rakopoulos, T. (2021). Η Δημοκρατία της ιδιοκτησίας (ή όταν η ιθαγένεια πωλείται): Χρυσά διαβατήρια και πολιτική κοινότητα στην Κύπρο, [The republic of property or when citizenship is for sale: Golden passports and political community in Cyprus] Synchrona Themata, 150.

Rethymiotaki, E., Kapardzani, C., & Flyntzanis, I. (2017). Φωνές από τα κάτω: το δίκαιο στον λόγο των κοιωνικών κινημάτων στην Ελλάδα της οικονομικής κρίσης [Voices from below: justice in the discourse of social movements in economic crisis Greece] In C. Konstantopoulou (Ed.), *Αφηγήσεις της κρίσης: μύθοι και πραγματικότητες της σύγχρονης κοινωνίας [Narratives of Crisis: Myth and realities of modern society]*. Athens: Papazisi, pp 269–308.

Reuters (2019). Amazon workers strike in Spain ahead of Three Kings gift-giving. *Reuters* 3/1/2019, https://uk.reuters.com/article/us-amazon-com-strike-spain/amazon-workers-strike-in-spain-ahead-of-three-kings-gift-giving-idUKKCN1OX16P

Rigby, M., & García Calavia, M. A. (2018). Institutional resources as a source of trade union power in Southern Europe. *European Journal of Industrial Relations*, *24*(2), 129 –143.

Ritzer, G. (2004) [1996]. *The MacDonaldisation of society*. Thousand Oaks, CA: Pine Forge Press.

Rubery, J., & Grimshaw, D. (2003). *The organisation of employment: An international perspective*. New York: Palgrave Macmillan.

Rubery, J. (2006). Segmentation theory thirty years on. University of Manchester: European Work and Employment Research Centre, http://www.docstoc.com/docs/34413508/Segmentation-theory-thirty-years-on

Rüdig, W., & Karyotis, G. (2013). Beyond the usual suspects? New participants in anti-austerity protests in Greece. *Mobilization: An International Quarterly*, *18*(3), 313–330.

Saad Filho, A. (2010). Crisis in neoliberalism or crisis of neoliberalism? In L. Panitch, G. Albo & V. Chibber (Eds.), *Socialist register* (pp. 242–259). London: Merlin Press.

Sakellaropoulos, S. (2014). *Κρίση και κοινωνική διαστρωμάτωση στην Ελλάδα του 21ουαιώνα [Crisis and social stratification in 21stCentury Greece]*. Athens: Topos.

Salido, O., & Moreno, L. (2012). Female employment and welfare development in Spain. In A. Bugra & Y. Ozkan (Eds.), *Trajectories of female employment in the Mediterranean* (pp. 91–113). Basingstoke: Palgrave Macmillan.

Sánchez Nicolás, E. (2020). Spain takes 'giant step' on guaranteed minimum income. EU Observer 29/5/2020, https://euobserver.com/coronavirus/148517

Sánchez Mosquera, M. (2018). Trade unionism and social pacts in Spain in comparative perspective. *European Journal of Industrial Relations*, *24*(1), 23–38.

Sapelli, G. (1995). *Southern Europe since 1945: Tradition and modernity in Portugal, Spain, Italy, Greece and Turkey*. London: Longman.

Schmitt, J., & Mitukiewicz, A. (2012). Politics matter: changes in unionisation rates in rich countries, 1960–2010. *Industrial Relations Journal*, *43*(3), 260–280.

Schierup, C. U. (2007). Bloody subcontracting in the network society: migration and post Fordist restructuring across the European Union. In E. Berggren, B. Likic-Brboric, G. Toksöz & N. Trimikliniotis (Eds.), *Irregular migration, informal labour and community: A Challenge for Europe*. Maastricht: Shaker Publishing.

Serdedakis, N. (2018). Η διαμαρτυρία στην Ελλάδα της κρίσης [Protest in crisis Greece]. In N. Serdedakis & S. Tombazos (Eds.), *Όψεις της ελληνικής κρίσης [Faces of the Greek crisis]*. Athens: Gutenberg.

Sennet, R. (1998). *The corrosion of character*. New York: Norton.

Seferiades, S. (2017). Το κόκκινο νήμα μιας δεκαετίας. Αναλύσεις και κείμενα στα χρόνια της κρίσης *[The red thread of a decade: analyses and texts in the crisis years]*. Athens: Topos.

Seferiades, S. (2018). Κόμματα και κινήματα χωρίς την πολιτική; Το μοντέλο του κόμματος καρτέλ υπό το φως της εμπειρίας του ΣΥΡΙΖΑ [Parties and movements without politics? the model of the cartel; party in the light of the SYRIZA experience]. In N. Serdedakis & S. Tombazos (Eds.), *Όψεις της ελληνικής κρίσης [Faces of the Greek crisis]*. Athens: Gutenberg.

Serrano, M. R. (2014). Between accommodation and transformation: The two logics of union renewal. *European Journal of Industrial Relations*, *20*(3), 219–235.

Seymour, R. (2014). *Against austerity*. London: Pluto Press.

Siani-Davies, P. (2017). *Crisis in Greece*. London: Hurst.

Siefkes, M. (2010). Power in society, economy, and mentality: Towards a semiotic theory of power. *Semiotica*, *181*(1/4), 225–261.

Silver, B. J. (2003). *Forces of labor: Workers' movements and globalization since 1870*. Cambridge: Cambridge University Press.

Silver, B. J., & Arrighi, J. (2011). The end of the long twentieth Century. In C. Calhoun & G. Derluguian (Eds.), *Business as usual: The roots of the global financial meltdown* (pp. 53–68). New York: New York University Press.

Simms, M., & Charlwood, A. (2010). Trade unions: Power and influence in a changed context' In T. Colling & M. Terry (Eds.), *Industrial relations: Theory and practice*. West Sussex: Wiley.

Sisson, K. (1987). *The management of collective bargaining: An international comparison*. Oxford: Basil Blackwell.

Slavnic, Z. (2007). Informalisation of the economy and the recommodification of labour. In E. Berggren, B. Likic-Brboric, G. Toksöz & N. Trimikliniotis (Eds.), *Irregular migration, informal labour and community: A challenge for Europe*. Maastricht: Shaker Publishing.

Sotirakopoulos, N., & Ntalaka, O. (2016). From the streets and the occupied squares to the central political field: the narratives of the ani-austerity camp. In R. Figueiras & P. Do Espirito Santo (Eds.), *Beyond the internet: unplugging the anti-austerity protest wave*. London: Routlegde.

Sotirakopoulos, N., & Sotiropoulos G. (2013). 'Direct democracy now!': The Greek indignados and the present cycle of struggles. *Current Sociology*, *61*(4), 443–456.

Soumeli, E. (2014). Cyprus: Changes to wage-setting mechanisms in the context of the crisis and the EU's New Economic Governance regime. Online at: http://www.eurofound.europa.eu/eiro/studies/tn1402049s/cy1402049q.htm.

Spyridakis, M. (2018). *Homo precarius: εμπειρίες ευαλωτότητας στην κρίση [experience of vulnerability in the crisis]*. Athens: Pedio.

Standing, G. (1999). *Global labour flexibility: Seeking distributive justice*. London: Macmillan Press.

Standing, G. (2011). *Precariat: The New Dangerous Class*. London and New York: Bloomsbury Academic.

Stavrakakis, Y., & Katsambekis, G. (2014). Left-wing populism in the European Periphery: The case of SYRIZA'. *Journal of Political Ideologies*, *19*(2), 119–142.

Stephanou, C. (2011). The banking system in Cyprus: Time to rethink the business model?. *Cyprus Economic Policy Review*, *5*(2), 123–130.

Stockwatch (2020a). Διάταγμα για κατώτατο μισθό σε επαγγέλματα ξενοδοχειακής βιομηχανίας [Statutory minimum wage by decree for hospitality occupations]. *Stockwatch*, 8/1/2020, https://www.stockwatch.com.cy/el/article/toyrismos/diatagma-gia-katotato-mistho-se-epaggelmata-xenodoheiakis-viomihanias

Stockwatch (2020b). Μπουμ 315% στην μακροχρόνια ανεργία [315% boom in long-term unemployment]. *Stockwatch*, 7/12/2020, https://www.stockwatch.com.cy/el/article/ergasiaka/mpoym-315-stin-makrohronia-anergia?utm_source=facebook&utm_medium=07-12-20-sw1&fbclid=IwAR3GPcIsEkZ6D5jtVF7BIgQ4vu4Yd6blv5eYeA9XBCjr1JzNs1bbPUODFm0

Streeck, W. (2010). *E Pluribus Unum? Varieties and Commonalities of Capitalism*, MPIfG Discussion Paper 10/12. Cologne: Max Planck Institute for the Study of Societies.

Streeck, W. (2014). *Buying time: The delayed crisis of democratic capitalism*. London: Verso.

Streeck, W. (2019). Progressive regression: Metamorphoses of European Social Policy. *New Left Review*, *118*, 117–139.

Streeck, W. (2020a). State-building by stealth?, Letters from Europe. *El Salto*, 20/5/2020, https://wolfgangstreeck.com/carta-desde-europa/

Streeck, W. (2020b). It's the state debt all over again, Letters from Europe. *El Salto*, 19/7/2020, https://wolfgangstreeck.com/carta-desde-europa/

Streeck, W. (2020c). Italian futurism, or European castles in the air, Letters from Europe. *El Salto*, 18/10/2020, https://wolfgangstreeck.com/carta-desde-europa/

Sumonja, M. (2019). The Habermas-Streeck debate revisited: Syriza and the illusions of the left-Europeanism. *Capital and Class*, *43*(3), 437–458.

Supiot, A. (2013). Towards a European policy on work. In N. Countouris & M. Freedland (Eds.), *Resocialising Europe in a time of crisis*. Cambridge: Cambridge University Press.

Surubaru, C. (2020). Europe to the rescue? EU funds and the COVID-19 crisis – who gets what, how and why. *Maastricht University blog*, https://www.maastrichtuniversity.nl/blog/2020/05/europe-rescue-eu-funds-and-covid-19-crisis-%E2%80%93-who-gets-what-how-and-why-0

Tarrow, S. (1994). *Power in Movement.* Cambridge: Cambridge University Press.
Taylor, S., & Tyler, M. (2000). Emotional labour and sexual difference in the airline industry. *Work, Employment and Society*, *14*(1), 77–95.
Taylor, G., Mathers, A., & Upchurch, M. (2011). Beyond the chains that bind: the political crisis of unions in Western Europe. *Labor History*, *52*(3), 287–305.
Teperoglou, E. Freire, A. Andreadis, I., & Leite Viegas, J. M. (2014). Elites' and voters' attitudes towards austerity policies and their consequences in Greece and Portugal. *South European Society and Politics*, *19*(4), 457–476.
The Local (2015). Spanish workers celebrate victory over Coca-Cola factory closure, 25/10/2015, https://www.thelocal.es/20151025/spanish-workers-celebrate-victory-over-coca-cola
Thelen, K. (2014). *Varieties of liberalization and the new politics of social solidarity.* Cambridge: Cambridge University Press.
Thelen, K. (2018). Regulating uber: The politics of the platform economy in europe and the United States. *Perspectives on Politics*, *16*(4), 938–953.
Theodoropoulou, S. (2015). National social and labour market policy reforms in the shadow of EU bailout conditionality: The cases of Greece and Portugal. *Comparative European Politics*, *13*, 29–55.
Theodoropoulou, S. (2016). Severe pain, very little gain: internal devaluation and rising unemployment in Greece. In M. Myant, S. Theodoropoulou & A. Piasna (Eds.), *Unemployment, internal devaluation and labour market deregulation in Europe*. Brussels: ETUI.
Theodoropoulou, S. (2020). Economic developments and policies: Is this time different? In ETUI and ETUC (Eds.), Benchmarking Working Europe 2020. Brussels: ETUI.
Theodossopoulos, D. (2014). The ambivalence of anti-austerity indignation in Greece: Resistance, hegemony and complicity. *History and Anthropology*, *25*(4), 488–506.
Therborn, G. (2013). *The killing fields of inequality*. Cambridge: Polity Press.
Thompson, E. P. (1991) [1963]. *The making of the English Working Class.* London: Penguin.
Thompson, E. P. (1971). The moral economy of the English crowd in the 18th century, *Past & Present*, *50*, 76–136.
Tombazos, S. (2018). Οι δυο όψεις της ελληνικής οικονομίας [The two faces of the Greek economy] In N. Serdedakis & S. Tombazos (Eds.), *Όψεις της ελληνικής κρίσης [Faces of the Greek crisis]*. Athens: Gutenberg.
Tombazos, S. (2019). *Global crisis and reproduction of capital.* Cham: Palgrave Macmillan.
Toyer, J., & Gonzalez, A. (2012). Spain unveils new austerity under European pressure. Reuters, 11/7/2012, https://www.reuters.com/article/us-spain-economy-cuts/spain-unveils-new-austerity-under-european-pressure-idUSBRE86A0CP20120711
Triantafyllidou, A., & Gropas, R. (2014). "Voting With Their Feet": Highly skilled emigrants from Southern Europe. *American Behavioral Scientist*, *58*(12), 1614–1633.

Trimikliniotis, N. (2004). *Ανεργία, Υποαπασχόληση και Ετεροαπασχόληση: Μια Έρευνα για την Εργασιακή Αβεβαιότητα και Ανασφάλεια των Νέων στην Κύπρο, [Unemployment, underemployment and irregular employment: a research on labour uncertainty and insecurity of the youth in Cyprus]*. Nicosia: INEK-PEO.

Trimikliniotis, N. (2009). The use and abuse of undeclared/unprotected labour: Migration, Europeanisation and the role of trade unions. In A. Neergard (Ed.), *European perspectives on exclusion and subordination: The Political economy of migration*. Maastricht: Shaker Publishing.

Trimikliniotis, N. (2016). New forms of employment in Cyprus. In R. Blanpain & F. Hendricks (Eds.), *New forms of employment in Europe*. Alphen aan den Rijn: Wolters Kluwer.

Trimikliniotis, N., & Demetriou, C. (2011). Labour integration of migrant workers in Cyprus: a critical appraisal. In M. Pajnic & G. Campani (Eds.), *Precarious migrant labour across Europe*. Ljubljana: Mirovni Institut.

Tronti, M. (1976) [1965]. 'The strategy of refusal' [*Workers and Capital*, Einaudi, Turin]. In *The labour process and class strategies*, Conference of Socialist Economists, Pamphlet No.1.

Tsianos, V., Stephenson, N., & Papadopoulos, D. (2008). *Escape routes, control and subversion in the 21stcentury*. London: Pluto Press.

Tsitsiou, Z. (2020). *The social constitution of Europe in the national courts: the case of Cyprus*, PhD thesis, University of Glasgow.

Turner, T., & D' Art, D. (2012). Public perceptions of trade unions in countries of the European Union: A causal analysis. *Labor Studies Journal*, *37*(1), 33–55.

Umney, C. (2018). *Class matters: Inequality and exploitation in 21st century Britain*. London: Pluto Press.

UNWTO (2020). International tourist numbers down 65% in first half of 2020 UNWTO reports, https://www.unwto.org/news/international-tourist-numbers-down-65-in-first-half-of-2020-unwto-reports

Upchurch, M., & Mathers A. (2011). Neoliberal globalisation and trade unionism: Toward radical political unionism?. *Critical Sociology*, *38*(2), 265–280.

Upchurch, M., Taylor, G., & Mathers A. (2009). The crisis of 'social democratic' unionism: the 'opening up' of civil society and the prospects for union renewal in the United Kingdom, France, and Germany. *Labor Studies Journal*, *34*(4), 519–542.

Valero, J. (2020). Commission proposes unprecedented suspension of EU's fiscal rules. *Euractic.com*, 20/3/2020, https://www.euractiv.com/section/economy-jobs/news/commission-proposes-unprecedented-suspension-of-eus-fiscal-rules/

Vallas, S. (1999). Rethinking post Fordism: The meaning of workplace flexibility. *Sociological Theory*, *17*(1), 68–101.

Vallas, S. (2018). The puzzle of precarity: Structure, strategies, and worker solidarity. In V. Doellgast, N. Lillie & V. Pulignano (Eds.), *Reconstructing solidarity: Labour unions, precarious work, and the politics of institutional change in Europe*. Oxford: Oxford University Press.

Vallas, S., & C. Prener. (2012). Dualism, job polarization, and the social construction of precarious work. *Work and Occupations*, *39*(4), 331–353.

Van der Meer, (2000) Spain. In J. Visser & B. Ebbinghaus (Eds.), *Trade unions in Western Europe since 1945*. London: Palgrave Macmillan.
Van Vossole, J. (2016). Framing PIGS: Patterns of racism and neocolonialism in the Euro crisis. *Patterns of Prejudice*, *50*(1), 1–20.
Verney, S., & Bosco, A. (2013). Living parallel lives: Italy and Greece in an age of austerity. *South European Society and Politics*, *18*(4), 397–426.
Viebrock, E., & Klasen J. (2009). Flexicurity and welfare reform: A review. *Socio-Economic Review*, *7*, 305–331.
Visser J. (2000). Italy. In J. Visser and B. Ebbinghaus (Eds.), *Trade unions in Western Europe since 1945*. London: Palgrave Macmillan.
Visser, J., & Ebbinghaus, B. (Eds.) (2000). *Trade unions in Western Europe since 1945*. London: Palgrave Macmillan.
Visser, J. (2019). Trade unions in the balance. ILO ACTRAV working paper, ILO.
Vogiatzoglou, M. (2017). Re-paving the path to hell: Greek trade unions amid crisis and austerity. In S. Lehndorff, H. Dribbush & S. Thorsten (Eds.), *Rough waters European trade unions in a time of crisis* (pp. 109–125). Brussels: ETUI.
Vogiatzoglou, M. (2018). Labour resistance: From steel works to rank and file unions [Εργατικές αντιστάσεις: από την χαλυβουργία στα σωματεία βάσης]. In S. Tombazos & N. Serdedakis (Eds.), *Όψεις της ελληνικής κρίσης [Faces of the Greek Crisis]* (pp. 350–373). Athens: Gutenberg.
Voskeritsian, H., & Kornelakis, A. (2019). Power, institutional change and the transformation of Greek employment relations. In H. Voskeritsian, P. Kapotas & C. Niforou (Eds.), *Greek employment relations in crisis: problems, challenges and prospects* (pp. 14–30). London: Routledge.
Waddington, J., Müller, T., & Vandaele, K. (2019). Setting the scene: Collective bargaining under neoliberalism. In T. Müller & K. Vandaele J. Waddington (Eds.) (2019). *Collective Bargaining in Europe: towards an endgame* (pp. 1–32). Brussels: ETUI.
Walby, S. (2015). *Crisis*. Cambridge: Polity Press.
Walker, M. (2020). Europe Imposes New Covid-19 Restrictions as Second Wave Accelerates. *The Wall Street Journal*, 25/10/2020, https://www.wsj.com/articles/european-countries-announce-new-covid-19-restrictions-record-infections-11603638712
Wallerstein, I. (2011). Dynamics of (Unresolved) Global Crisis. In C. Calhoun & G. Derluguian (Eds.), *Business as usual: The roots of the global financial meltdown* (pp. 69–88). New York: New York University Press.
Wallusch, J., & Wozniak-Jechorek (2015). United in diversity: Consequence for common labour market policy in the times of crisis. In S. Fadda & P. Tridico (Eds.), *The economic crisis in social and institutional context: Theories, policies and exit strategies* (pp. 178–199). London: Routledge.
Wills, J. (2009). Subcontracted employment and its challenge to Labor. *Labor Studies Journal*, *34*(4), 441–460.
Williams, C. C., & Lapeyre, F. (2020). Dependent self-employment and newer forms of informal employment: Trends, challenges and policy responses in the EU. In I. Islam & F. Lapeyre (Eds.), *Transition to Formality and Structural Transformation Challenges and Policy options*. Geneva: ILO.

Wilthagen, T. (1998). Flexicurity: a new paradigm for labour market policy reform?. "Social integration by transitional labour markets" project. Berlin: Wissenschafszentrum Berlin für Sozialforschung (WZB).

Wilthagen, T., & Tross, F. (2004). The concept of 'flexicurity': a new approach to regulating employment and labour markets. *Transfer, European Review of Labour and Research*, *10*(2), 166–186.

Worth, O. (2020). Corbyn, Sanders and the contestation of neoliberal hegemony. In G. Charalambous & G. Ioannou (Eds.), *Left Radicalism and Populism in Europe* (pp. 89–107). London: Routledge.

Wood, A. (2020). *Despotism on demand: How power operates in a flexible workplace*. New York: Cornel University Press.

Wright, E. O. (2000). Working class power, capital-class interests, and class compromise. *American Journal of Sociology*, *105*(4), 957–1002.

Yannakourou, S., & Tsimpoukis, S. (2016). 'Flexiblility without Security and Deconstruction of Collective Bargaining: The New Paradigm of Labor Law in Greece' (2013–2014). *Comparative Labor Law and Policy Journal*, *35*(3), 331–370.

Yannakourou S. (2016). *Κυπριακό Εργατικό Δίκαιο [Cyprus Labour Law]*. Athens: Nomiki Vivliothiki.

Young, B. (2015). The battle of ideas in the Eurozone crisis management. In S. Fadda & P. Tridico (Eds.), *The economic crisis in social and institutional context: Theories, policies and exit strategies* (pp. 78–90). London: Routledge.

Zambarloukou, S. (2014). 'Κοινωνικός διάλογος και συλλογικές συμβάσεις πριν και μετά τη κρίση' [Social dialogue and collective agreements before and after the crisis]. In S. Zambarloukou & M. Kousis (2014) (Eds.), *Κοινωνικές πτυχές της κρίσης στην Ελλάδα [Social Aspects of the Crisis in Greece]* (pp 247–272). Athens: Pedio Publisher.

# Index

For Product Safety Concerns and Information please contact our EU representative GPSR@taylorandfrancis.com
Taylor & Francis Verlag GmbH, Kaufingerstraße 24, 80331 München, Germany

www.ingramcontent.com/pod-product-compliance
Ingram Content Group UK Ltd.
Pitfield, Milton Keynes, MK11 3LW, UK
UKHW022353190926
475702UK00015B/2270
* 9 7 8 1 0 3 2 0 3 9 6 3 3 *